Also by Colin Fletcher

The Complete Walker III (1984)

The Man from the Cave (1981)

The New Complete Walker (1974)

The Winds of Mara (1973)

The Man Who Walked Through Time (1968)

The Complete Walker (1968)

The Thousand-Mile Summer (1964)

The Secret Worlds of Colin Fletcher

The Secret Worlds of COLIN FLETCHER

Illustrations by Tom Lacey

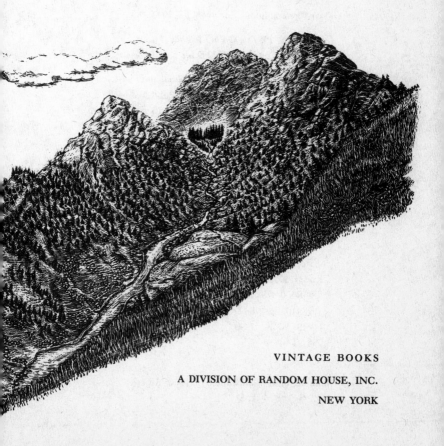

VINTAGE BOOKS

A DIVISION OF RANDOM HOUSE, INC.

NEW YORK

FIRST VINTAGE BOOKS EDITION, JUNE 1990

Copyright © 1989 by Colin Fletcher
Illustrations Copyright © 1989 by Tom Lacey

Library of Congress Cataloging-in-Publication Data
Fletcher, Colin.
　　The secret worlds of Colin Fletcher / illustrations
by Tom Lacey.
　　　　p.　　cm.
　　Reprint. Originally published: 1st ed. New York :
Knopf, 1989.
　　ISBN 0-679-72554-7
　　1. Hiking.　I. Title.
GV199.5.F54　1990
796.5′1—dc20　　　　　　　　　　　　　　　　89-40551
　　　　　　　　　　　　　　　　　　　　　　　　CIP

Manufactured in the United States of America
10　9　8　7　6　5　4　3　2　1

Learn of the green world what can be thy place.

—EZRA POUND

Contents

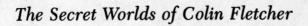

The Secret Worlds of Colin Fletcher

1 Into the Forest

At the bend in the road I pulled over and parked tight against the fence. I got out and began to walk around the back of the car, eyes reaching for the two worlds, and at that moment the sun came easing up over the valley's rim.

Warmth and vivid light flooded the scene spread out before me. Earthy spring smells welled up from wet grass.

I took another step forward and stood beside the fence, already partway excluded and included; stood there looking out over the view that had become so familiar yet always remained fresh.

Many years before, the first time I drove this road on my way to the forest that lay at its end, the view was what had made me brake to an abrupt stop. I am no longer sure whether I sensed, even as I braked, the two worlds that faced each other across the green and plunging space beyond the rickety barbed-wire fence; but I know I saw them as soon as I got out of the car. Down at the foot of the valley lay the flatlands and the houses. At its head, framed between steep slopes, rose the billowing green folds of the forest.

After that first day I took to stopping at the bend in the road each time I drove up to walk into that forest. I would pull in beside the fence and stand for a few moments looking out over the steep side valley. Down the years, this pause became a minor but valued personal tradition: a sign that I had begun to break free from the flatlands and the houses and their world all wrapped in schedules and money and other tinsels; a signal that I had already moved across some invisible line, halfway to the forest; had moved a decisive step closer to a world in which the things that ruled would once more be the creak of pack harness and the rhythmic brush of boots through damp leaves and a glimpse of a squirrel leaping high and free, treetop to treetop—a world in which I would know that the hours and days ahead lay safely cradled in no one else's hands but my own.

In time, the side valley itself had become part of my ritual pause at the bend in the road. The bend overlooks the valley's most beautiful part. Beyond tree-green depths my eye meets pale, smooth, steeply sloping grassland, all curves and delight. Wedges of dark woodland confront and dramatize. Between them, bands of warm brown sandstone change texture with every visit but always cry out—dawn or dusk, rain or sun, spring or fall—to have my hand brushed across their smooth surfaces. The sandstone is pierced here and there, like Swiss cheese, with the mouths of small caves, and I think it is these black and mysterious openings that give the valley its primordial overtones. Far off to my right, out beyond the flatlands and houses, gleams a sliver of the ocean that has been called "the eye of the world."

Mostly, the side valley plunges too precipitously to interest flatland housebuilders, but directly opposite the bend, halfway up the far slope, hangs a meadow, and I have heard rumors. So perhaps I also stop at the bend in the road to make sure the valley is still all right, still safe. That spring morning, when I turned away from the fence at last and got back into the car, I knew that all was well.

An hour later I had parked at road's end, swung the pack up onto my back and was walking along the jeep track that led toward the forest.

I walked easily, taking my time. The pack held three days' food and all the necessary equipment, but on this trip, even more than most, the number of days consumed would, like the number of miles covered, be irrelevant.

The jeep track crossed a meadow. All around me, again, grass and scented air spoke of spring—of youth and the future and surging hope. At its center, the meadow cradled a small pond. Although the pond was artificial, time had muffled its man-echoes, and the meadow's soft greenness helped mute the lingering noise of the outside, flatland world; helped nourish my unfolding sense of solitude, of inclusion.

Beyond the meadow, the jeep track crossed a small creek, tunneled into an oak grove. Off to the right, a deer snorted alarm. I glimpsed its white rump flouncing away up a steep, brushy slope. From the place it vanished, a stone came tumbling down, bounced high, hit the creek's bedrock with a crash. Then silence returned to the little grove. But I knew that I had not yet really broken free. There was more to it, too, than the grove's being on private property and my still having a mile to go before I reached the boundary of the national forest. When I first knew this grove, ten years earlier, only a foot trail had threaded through it. Then the jeeps had gone in, for firewood. Had gone in almost every year. Gone in roughshod. No live trees had been cut, but the glade had lost its natural harmonies and now, for all its convalescing greenness, it was a place of blunt stumps and the gougings of jeep wheels and dragged logs.

At the far end of the grove the track ended and the foot trail began—faint and indecisive, small and beautiful, just right for its job. Not many people were lucky enough to know the property owner sufficiently well to get permission to cross his land, and the few footprints I ever saw on the trail suggested that I used it more than anyone else.

The trail angled up a slope. Off to my left, a woodpecker plodded away at its work, erratically yet steadily, like a metronome with the queasies. The slope steepened and the trail spiraled around the bole of a madrone. The tree's red-brown roots, splayed and curving, formed a cascade of six steps, like the rungs of a turret staircase. I climbed slowly, deliberately, one foot and then the other, up the rungs' sinuous and almost sexual curves. I took my time, savoring it, because this little natural staircase had, like the bend in the road, become a private signal. On every trip, as I stepped clear of its last rung, I knew that the unheard noise of the flatlands would soon, if I allowed it to happen, be drowned out by the silence of the forest.

Above the madrone-root staircase the trail leveled off. But I did not, as sometimes happened at this point, shift into a higher gear. What mattered was where my mind went, not my body.

Now, I do not mean that I had come up into the forest that day for any very discernible reason. In fact, I would have been hard put to it to say just why I was there. At a guess, an impasse in a certain private matter had triggered my final decision to make the trip; but my frustration was not something you could call "the reason." I think I simply felt that the time had come. I had been away too long. And when I had been away too long the world began to look out of kilter; or to put it another way, as a friend of mine once did, I "turned into a surly Welsh bastard." So over the years this had become the natural thing for me to do from time to time, as the occasion demanded: take a walk up and out into the forest that was, in large part, my reason for living where I now did. In a sense, I suppose, you could say that I had come to need such trips in much the same way as other people occasionally need coffee or booze or affairs or fixes that generate different kinds of trips. Anyway, as I walked without haste along the level stretch of trail above the natural madrone-root staircase I knew that, even though I might not understand just why I was there, it once again felt right and natural to be back, and I rejoiced that I had come.

The trail angled up again, more steeply this time. I slackened the pack's harness adjustments just a touch, up at each collarbone. The pack eased away from my body, very slightly, so that although I had, without thinking about it, leaned forward in response to the slope, the pack continued to ride upright. That way, the load remained on my hips, not shoulders, but the harness still kept the pack moving in unison with my body's rhythmic sway.

The trail humped over a crest, cut down into a new watershed. I retightened the pack harness. Underfoot, my boots skirled through damp leaves with the rhythm that pulses at the core of walking: the essential, unchanging rhythm that, once achieved, carries your body almost effortlessly over the miles; the rhythm that also lubricates your mind.

At some stage of every day's walking, or almost every day's walking, there comes a moment when your cerebral synapses seem to click into gear. For a few minutes or half an hour or perhaps even for the rest of the day, you fire on all cylinders. You soar, embrace the universe, see everything, solve the insoluble at a glance—you operate, that is, the way you wish you always did.*

* Please do not imagine that I'm talking only of walking with a pack on

That morning as I walked on down into the bowl of the second watershed my mind remained tethered, leadenly unsoaring. And I chafed at the constriction. I do not want to suggest that I was traveling Scholar-Gypsylike, waiting for the spark from heaven to fall; you could probably say, though, that for some reason I was vaguely expecting an elevated, or at least clarified, mode of mind to click in fairly early that day—and that I just about as vaguely resented its failure to do so.

The trail skirted a leaning sycamore tree under which I sometimes camped. Beyond the sycamore it crossed a creek and began to climb again. I strode on, then reminded myself there was no hurry, that three days of freedom lay ahead. I slackened the pace.

A side creek tumbled across the trail. My feet moved almost automatically to the right places on the familiar boulders. A covey of quail scuttered off into underbrush. A squirrel complained, high in his treetops, at my unwarranted intrusion. Yes, it was good to be back. I found myself relishing familiar yet changing landmarks: the trailside spring that in a dry year might never break but that now, with the forest's springs all prodigally sprung, was a rivulet tumbling over moss-rich stones; the two halves of the big sycamore that had fallen across the trail five or six winters before and which I had sawed through two summers later; the thimbleberry thicket in which I had once surprised a magnificent buck standing shoulder-deep among the big, fleshy leaves. I walked on, beginning to hear the silence and the new rhythms, beginning to forget the clock. But when I came to a little clearing with a side creek running through it and

---

your back. You can graduate to soaring—almost as easily, in fact—during an unladen day walk. If you need reassurance on that score, turn to Chapter 4. Better still, though, just hang in here until you reach Chapter 4.

checked my watch and found that an hour had passed since I left the car and that it was therefore time for a rest, my mind still remained anchored, ordinary.

Ten minutes, and I was on my way again. I walked for another hour, content but still unsoaring, before I came to a certain fallen log that lay beside the trail. I paused beside the log, then stepped over it onto the start of a little cutoff trail that I had begun building almost a year earlier. At the time I had had only efficiency in mind: the cutoff would eliminate an unnecessary loop and two creek crossings. But because I wanted to avoid luring people onto my trail before it was complete I had left its entrance blocked and camouflaged by the fallen log: anyone using the main trail would almost certainly continue along it, unaware of the entrance to the bypass.

Before long I discovered that my embryo detour had created a safe and secret little world, a sort of *sanctum sanctorum* within the forest.

Even on the main trail there was little risk of meeting anyone. I discovered, though, that when I paused or rested or lunched or even camped at any point along the cutoff I knew, about as near as you can ever know, that I would not be disturbed. Now at last, the work on the cut-off trail was almost complete; but as I stepped over the fallen log I knew I would be tempted to leave it in place, camouflaging the turnoff, preserving my sanctuary.

Halfway along the cutoff, in another little grassy clearing with convenient side-creek plumbing, I halted, unbuckled the pack, slipped it off my shoulders and let it slide down onto the short, still-damp grass. I loosened the pack flap, lifted the black plastic groundsheet from its place on top of everything else, partly unfolded it, spread it on the grass beside the pack and sat down on it.

Sunlight streamed into the little clearing. Rich smells

rose from damp earth and leaves, damp underbrush, damp tree roots. Around the edges of the clearing, brambles and poison oak crowded close, but overhead all was space and light. A pair of jays, scrawning at each other, planed blue and raucous across the bright window, from greenery to dappled greenery. Beside me, the creek rejoiced. I felt my shoulders relax.

I took pots and stove and the big white plastic bag of food out of the pack and put them beside me, on the groundsheet. I removed the funny little metal yo-yo of a stove from its nylon bag, assembled it into something that looked rather more like a stove, sucked its inlet needle for a moment so as to coat it with saliva, then slid the rubber orifice of the fuel cartridge over it. I would not have trusted this particular kind of stove under hostile conditions, but had brought it because I knew the weather would almost certainly hold fair and because the stove was easy to light and clean to use. I put the stove down beside the groundsheet, lit it, heated some soup, poured the first cupful into my metal cup. I took my time over eating lunch, over everything.

When I had finished, I leaned back against the pack and let myself doze off. When I opened my eyes again the sun still shone and the creek still sang and the treetops still spread dappled green and the air still hung rich with sweet spring scents. I sat there for a while, leaning against the pack, barely half awake. Then I relit the stove and brewed tea. But when I had drunk the tea and the juices were stirring in me again, I went on leaning, sitting. Somehow I was not yet ready to move on, beyond my *sanctum sanctorum*. So I went on sitting. The sun eased its slow way across my open window.

At last I stood up, pulled from its scabbard the machete strapped to the side of the pack and walked a few yards on up my trail. The final stretch of the cutoff, before it rejoined the main trail, still needed work. On my last trip, several months earlier, I had reconnoitered an alignment up a gentle slope and had marked it but had barely begun to clear a practical route through the low brush. Fifteen or twenty minutes, I figured, would finish the job.

I came to the end of the section of trail that I had already cleared, and began swinging my machete.

An hour later I was still at work. There had been more left to be done than I remembered; but I also found, as always seemed to happen, that once I started work I did not want to stop. When I had cleared a way through to the junction with the main trail, I turned back and began to tidy up the new route. It is curiously rewarding work, trail-making, especially if you have the right basic, Neanderthal cast of mind.

When I had finished tidying things up, all the way back to the clearing and side creek, I moved on beyond them. I went to the foot of a certain tree and unwrapped a hoe and mattock from the big black plastic bag in which I had protected and hidden them, last time in. Then I worked my way happily back along the whole cutoff, smoothing out rough places and making surer footholds—but always keeping the trail small and beautiful, so that it did not really wound the forest.

All afternoon I sweated away. When I quit at last the cutoff was essentially finished. But I did not walk back and remove the camouflaging log from the turnoff. I think I told myself that things were not yet quite ready for other people to use it.

When I got back to my pack in its side-creek clearing, I brewed yet more tea. But my mind remained in its ordinary, humdrum mode. At last I stowed the lunchtime gear away, stood up and swung the pack up onto my back.

Once I had moved out beyond my cutoff, back onto the main trail, and begun to walk on up the valley of the second watershed, everything was fine, after all. The late afternoon sun had already sunk behind the western rim of the narrowing valley and ahead the forest sloped dark and quiet. The trees grew taller now, the underbrush less dense. Except for the faint trail, there was no sign that man existed. I walked on and up, at ease.

It began not with a flood but a trickle; hardly more than a seep, really. An idea formed in my head. I paused on the trail and pulled a little red notebook out of the "pocket office" on the yoke of my pack harness and jotted the idea down. Then I slid the notebook back into the office and walked on. A couple of hundred yards, and another idea. Another pause, another notation. Soon, a third. And then, as I walked on once more to the soft rhythm of my footsteps, the floodgates opened. I saw, almost in a single instant, the thrust of a letter that would breach the impasse in the private matter that had, in a superficial sense, triggered this trip. The letter would be long, and difficult to write, but I felt sure it would solve the problem that had loomed.

I walked steadily on, stepping over and around familiar obstacles, hardly noticing them, just letting thoughts flow out. Details emerged, coagulated, solidified. There were too many of them now, too much complexity, for mere notation. Besides, the thrust of the letter was something I would not forget. I kept going. Before long, though, the information swirled so dense in my mind that I could no longer be sure I would remember it all, and in the middle of a thimbleberry thicket, at a point where the trail recrossed the creek, I halted and slipped the pack off and opened it and took out the groundsheet and the few sheets of paper I always carry in my pack. I sat down on the partly unfolded groundsheet, beneath the canopy of big, fleshy thimbleberry leaves, and began to draft the letter.

I must have scribbled for a long time, for at a moment

when the flow slackened I became aware that the light had almost gone. I looked around. There had barely been room to sit down, in among the thin, gangly stalks of the thimble-berry bushes. It was certainly not a place I would normally choose to camp. One evening the previous summer, though, I had reached this same thicket feeling very tired, just as the light failed, and because I knew there would be no more sur-face water until I crossed the next crest, I had decided to camp there. I had had to trample a coffin-size space in the thimbleberries, in the one place that was more or less flat enough for a bed. I had not enjoyed doing so: I like to leave campsites with little or no trace of my intrusions. But now, peering through the thimbleberry stalks, I saw that they had already overgrown my sleeping place so effectively that there was virtually no sign of it. Within minutes I had once again cleared a space, fully unfolded the groundsheet, rolled out pad and sleeping bag on it and begun to cook dinner. Almost immediately after dinner I fell asleep.

In the morning, after my first caffeine-fix of tea, I reread the letter and found it good. I tidied it a bit, put it away. And then, rather to my surprise, I sat on, there among the thim-bleberry stalks. When I camped at that place the previous summer I had arrived too late at night and left too early and hurriedly next morning to appreciate it; but now, wrapped in the soft green light that filtered down through the leaf can-opy, and in no kind of hurry, I found myself smiling around at the dense, dark, mysterious undergrowth pressing in from every side; at the fleshy leaves that crowded overhead, al-most meshing, like airborne lily pads; and, through rare and limited spaces between them, at small and fractured samples of the world beyond. Somehow, it was a new and almost ex-citing way of seeing the forest. It is often like that, I find, when you are forced to use what seems to be a poor campsite, hardly even a viable halting place. You lack the view or spaciousness or consonances or whatever it is that you tend to favor when you have the luxury of choice; but you gain a fresh, untidy view of the country, so that your understanding of its complexities takes an unexpected step forward.

By midmorning, for all the attractions of the place, I was ready to move on. And although I think I harbored, just for a moment, the hint of a thought that the spark from heaven had apparently fallen and my "reason" for coming up into the forest had therefore been annulled, I recognized at once that this was nonsense. I had no idea of what remained to be done, but it was still there all right, waiting. And as soon as I considered the matter I knew what I would do. What I would do, that is, on the basic, physical level.

I would go on up for a couple of hours, into the third watershed, and would camp on a certain little knoll that stands capped by a half-ring of madrones. The first time I camped on that knoll, years before, I had stayed two days and finished reading *Zen and the Art of Motorcycle Maintenance*, and ever since then it had been one of my favorite retreats. It sat well back from the trail, too, and I had never found any sign of another human's having been there. It would make, as it always did, a perfect place to sit and think—though "think" might not be the right word for what I suspected I still wanted to do.

I restowed everything into my pack, rearranged the thimbleberry stalks as best I could and heaved the pack up onto my back.

At first the trail twisted along close by the creek, past familiar landmarks: the steep, crumbling slope with the urn-shaped boulder that I had to skirt with care; the chopped-off limbs of the fallen alder that I had found blocking the trail when I came down at night, years before, after a big storm, and had had to hack my way past with the ax that I had fortunately been carrying for trail work, up near the crest. I walked on, at peace. Familiarity can breed content. I crossed a small, grassy clearing. I always remembered this clearing, now, the way I had seen it two winters earlier: an oblong of smooth snow bisected by a line of tracks so sharp and vivid that I could almost see golden-brown fur flexing on the mountain lion's haunches as it padded silently from shadow back into shadow.

The trail swung away from the creek, circumnavigated a granite outcrop, rejoined the creek. I paused to watch a dull orange salamander, down beside my left boot, salaclamber up a dead-leaf slope. Soon, a chipmunk quizzed me from a log, all stripes and sinew and twitches, then hightailed away into dark fern caverns. The trail swung away from the creek again, cut steeply upward. The valley closed in tighter, steeper, rougher, rockier. But all around me, except for the creek's faint music and my boots' steady rhythm, there was only silence.

I crossed over into the third watershed, walked on down, came to the little knoll capped by its half-ring of madrones.

The trees enclosed a flat, open space covered with a delicate yellow and brown carpet of fallen leaves, so I did not have to disturb anything before I spread out my groundsheet; did not even have to bend any grass. Soon I was leaning back against my pack, looking around at the velvety, moss-covered madrone boles. The last sunlight beamed low through a gap in the nearby trees. I slid down, full-length, onto my sleeping bag and lay there looking up into the quivering, sunlit, emerald-green canopy of madrone leaves. The sunlight snuffed out. The leaves assumed a quieter resonance. I continued to lie there, gazing up into them. When I woke from a doze, the light had almost gone.

I stood up, grabbed my canteens, scrambled down to the creek that skirted the knoll, filled the canteens, climbed back up to camp.

When I had put the canteens down by the orange sleeping bag I stood there for a moment and then, for no particular reason, walked six or seven paces and stood beside a low granite boulder. The last light was fading now, but I could just see, on the flat top of the boulder, two sets of dark droppings. A coyote or fox or bobcat or mountain lion had dropped them to mark its territorial boundary, and as I stood there I wished, briefly, that I knew which species produced precisely such droppings. Then I stepped up onto the boulder, carefully avoiding my neighbor's signposts, and found myself standing there in the dying light, looking up at the faint line of the valley's rim, far above. Just standing there. Doing nothing but look, really—except that from time to time I half heard two owls question-and-answering each other across the valley. I began to wish, rather vaguely, that I could tell what kind of owls they were; then unwished. That really didn't seem to matter much, either, and I went back to just standing there. The line of the valley's rim, far above, dimmed toward extinction. The closer shadows—the pale shadows and dark shadows and pitch-black shadows—were melding, too. Occasionally the owls rehooted; otherwise there was only the quiet lap of silence. I went on standing. Just standing and half listening.

At last I became aware that my bare legs were growing cold. And slowly there eased into me, like a tide easing up an estuary, the knowledge that I must have spent twenty or thirty minutes standing there on the boulder. Or perhaps forty. I realized, now I came to consider the matter, that I did not really know what I had been thinking about—did not really know what I could have been said to have been doing, just standing there and looking up at the diminishing rim or peering deep into the blackness of the forest, and half listening to the owls or to the lappings of the silence.

I stepped down from the boulder and walked back to my

sleeping bag. I had precious little idea, really, of what those twenty or thirty minutes had been all about. In themselves, they hardly constituted anything you could call an event. I knew, though, that they had been good minutes. Very good minutes. They lay, perhaps, at the core of the trip. Come to think of it, serene caesuras of that kind—unplanned, concordant pauses—often seemed to lie at the heart of a good trip.

This was the way, in fact, that things nearly always turned out. I mostly came up into the forest—or even went up for a week into higher mountains, or out into the desert—without quite knowing what I wanted and without focused plans about what I'd do. More often than not I did nothing. Nothing you could easily tell someone else about, anyway—because, by flatland standards, nothing had really happened. Yet by the end of the trip, whether it lasted a day or a week, I was almost always ready to go back home. And often eager to do so.

I sat down on my sleeping bag and cooked dinner, there in the darkness and the silence, with the shadowy madrone trunks mysterious and reassuring all around me, their leaves black against dark sky. Soon after dinner I fell asleep. In the morning, after breakfast, I stowed everything back into my pack and came down off the knoll and began the long, slow walk back toward the flatlands—toward that other and better-known world to which I also belonged.

2 Beyond the Divide

The little Forest Service ranger station nestled among trees, a hundred yards from the end of the road. Late afternoon shadows had reached out around it, softening the heat. I parked outside and went in.

The ranger was young, redheaded, new to the job, still eager. "Wish I was coming with you," he said as he filled out my fire permit. "Haven't had a chance to get over into the main valley yet, but they say it's a beautiful place."

"So I hear."

"Be doing some fishing?"

"Maybe. I'll take a rod along, anyway. Little five-piecer. Fits into my pack."

"How far d'you aim to go?"

"Oh, over the divide and down into the valley, for sure—

but . . . well, it really doesn't matter much. Guess I'll go as far as the spirit moves me. Right now, I just feel I want to get the hell out."

"I know what you mean," said the ranger. He handed over the permit. "Yes, I'd have to say you look as if you could do with a spell out there."

We chatted some more and arranged that because I was going alone he would special-watchdog for me. I would stay overnight in the nearby campground, then get an early start next morning. If I didn't check out with the ranger by nightfall seven days later, he would know I was in trouble and would institute a search.

An hour later I was standing at the tailgate of my station wagon making a final check of the gear in my pack when a man came out of the Winnebago that was the only other vehicle in the campground. He walked over and stood looking at my outspread gear.

"You don't take a little TV set, or even a radio?"

"No."

"What d'you do then, out there for a whole week?"

"Oh, there's always plenty to do. Never seems to be enough time."

"But what do you *do*? Just hike like crazy?"

"Well, some trips I do a lot of walking, sure. Every day, morning and afternoon. But sometimes I just . . . do a lot of sitting around."

The man shook his head. He stood there for a few minutes, watching, then turned on his heel, walked back to his fortress and went inside and shut the door. I was left wondering why I had once again failed to come up with a coherent let alone satisfactory answer to a recurring question.

Next morning I began the long, steep climb toward the crest that lay between roadhead and the valley.

The night at roadhead had partway acclimatized me to the

elevation, but I found myself struggling. Hour after hour I labored upward under a heavy load and hot summer sun, following a trail that wound through trees and then across open granite. But even as I labored, one sector of my mind remained content: a day's hard sweating, it said to the rest of me, would help slough off the human world; would begin to work me into the week.

All day, though, I kept meeting echoes.

In the course of the morning I passed no less than seven people, in parties of two and three, coming down the trail. Mostly we exchanged only monosyllables, but one markedly comely damsel wore shorts bearing the printed message: "Dangerous curves ahead!" The shorts fitted her perfectly. At noon I lunched beside a rockbound lake, and had barely finished eating when a dozen college-age kids, paired males and females, erupted onto the far shore, a hundred yards away. They promptly stripped off and dived into the lake, then stood around in shallow water, talking and flirting. Fifteen minutes passed before one of the girls noticed me and the show ended.

In late afternoon, thunderclouds assembled, coalesced. The air cooled. By the time I camped at sunset beside a smaller and starker lake, innocent of skinny-dippers, the clouds were dispersing and shafts of sunlight struck vivid on granite cliffs. A double rainbow arched over castellated peaks. The silence of high places reigned. As I set up camp beside the gnarled and curlicue trunk of a juniper tree, it seemed as if I had finally left the human world behind; but next morning, as I labored on up the last steep stretch below the crest, I found I still needed to sweat something out.

The view from the 10,000-foot pass, though magnificent, was not quite what I had expected. All I could see, clearly, was a long, sloping land of rocky spurs and side canyons. The valley itself lay hidden, several miles away, almost a vertical mile below. I could make out the line of its axis but little else.*

I rested briefly at the pass, relishing the vista and nibbling goodies. Then I began the long descent. Soon, I struck away from the trail and started to detour around a string of lakes. I think I broke away from the trail to celebrate having crossed the divide, thereby cutting off the outer world and finally freeing myself; but I had barely reached the first lake and was following a faint game trail and a train of thought that I had been trying to board for a long time when a young couple with a small black dog materialized from a stand of trees. They seemed a pleasant enough pair. But they somehow succeeded in achieving an effect that takes some doing when you have only two human bodies and a dog at your command: they crowded around me.

"Isn't it wonderful up here, away from everybody?" gushed the man.

"So peaceful," said his mate. "Why, only yesterday

---

* *Warning!* Do not be misled by any topographical information I give. It will not necessarily help you identify our valley. For I have messed around with just enough of the facts to throw any would-be sleuth off the track—as I have already messed around with such facts earlier in this book. I suppose I should also warn you that I am not above dragging plain red herrings across any page.

I have practiced these obfuscations and deceits—and will continue to practice them, without notice or apology—because I am fearful that beautiful places I cherish may be violated by what I write. Part of such places' beauty often lies in their relative freedom from people. And publicity publicizes. You could say, I guess, that Heisenberg's Uncertainty Principle applies: if I describe a place, some people will be encouraged to go there and, simply by going, will alter it. Besides, this book is meant to draw maps of the mind. If you are reading primarily in order to discover good places to go walking, I suggest you stop right now and go out and turn the book in and try to get your money back.

Well, all right, if you insist, I will in this one case relent sufficiently to feed you a generous clue: the valley we are heading for lies west of the Mississippi.

we were still on the main trail, over on the other side of that ridge, and we met fourteen people inside of two hours. *Fourteen!*"

I held my peace.

"Yes, that was just too much of a crowd for us," said the man. "So we struck away from the trail."

"And now it's wonderful, being out here on our own. We're camped beside the lake, you know. You're the first person we've seen all day."

I began to ease on down the game trail. My companions took up escort positions.

"Yes, it's so much better over here," the man said to the back of my head. "I mean, that's what you come up into the mountains for, isn't it? Getting away from people."

His mate, who had stationed herself in front of me, with the dog, halted and pointed off to the right. "Our camp's just down there. Wouldn't you like to come and have a cup o' coffee with us?"

I declined, tried to edge forward.

"But it's just beautiful down there. So quiet."

I managed to step around her and get moving again. I set a stiff pace.

They kept up gamely, close behind, still chattering in tandem. I suppose I grunted a response from time to time. The dog remained mercifully silent.

We must have progressed like that for a couple of hundred yards. It began to feel like a scene from a bad movie. At last I stopped and turned and fixed the man with what I hoped was only a semi-steely gaze. "Look, I really have to agree with you that the reason we come up into the mountains is to get away from people. I certainly do. And at the moment I simply want to be alone."

Both of them looked disappointed, almost shocked. I rather think the dog's tail went between its legs. Just for a moment, I regretted having been so blunt. "Sorry," I said. "I hope you'll understand."

But they gave no obvious sign that they did, and there was nothing left for me to do except turn and walk on down the game trail.

As I walked, I kept telling myself it was ridiculous to let the incident disturb me. They were no doubt perfectly nice people, just a little rattled by the unaccustomed condition of being alone. Rattled and unaware of it. Unaware, that is, of the gulf that yawns between loneliness and solitude—those two internal states that both arise from the physical condition of being alone, yet stand poles apart. The fact remained, though, that the train of thought that had been steaming up just before I met them had long since left the station, and in its place surged an unruly mob. For at least half an hour I kept striding fiercely on—around the string of lakes, then over a low ridge and back onto the man-made trail.

The lonely young couple turned out to be the last of the echoes, though, and before long the walking and the mountains began to work their therapy.

The trail lipped over into the head of a long side canyon and began to wind down it, following the line of a tiny creek, threading a tortuous route among huge granite boulders that littered the canyon's floor. Many of the boulders lay at odd angles, like a giant's forgotten playthings. Some of their flanks had been glaciated smooth as glass, others roughed and greened by lichen.

The creek gained stature, began to support more greenery, even small meadows. When I took my hourly rest in one of the meadows I watched a surprisingly trusting gopher come clear out of his hole, scythe down a plant that must have been all of three feet distant, return to his hole with the harvest stored in puffed cheeks, then close the hole from inside—apparently by bunting up with his rear end some soil he had just excavated, head down, a few inches below the entrance. Long before afternoon eased over into evening I had begun to merge with the country.

I was far down the side canyon, with the peaks standing well behind me and the day dying, when the trail for the first time cut away from the creek and began to angle up the flank of a rocky spur. I halted and stood looking down the canyon's deep glaciated U; stood there deliberating.

The topo map offered conflicting evidence about my options. It showed that the trail would curve around the crest of the spur before dropping down into the main valley; and this apparent rejection of the side canyon as a route made me suspect that at some stage it became impassable. When I checked the part of the map that represented what was clearly the crucial stretch—the point at which the side canyon fell steeply away into the main valley—tightly packed contours seemed at first to confirm my suspicions. But the more closely I examined the contours, the more hopeful I became that there might be a way through. Other things came into it, too. With the sun now only a glowing memory behind jagged peaks, I would soon have to camp, and from where I stood the lower part of the side canyon—tumbling creek and attendant strip of green cradled between steep granite walls—looked very inviting. Neither map nor eye showed a man-made trail. That in itself promised well. And a quarter of a mile ahead I could see a little meadow with a rocky outcrop on one flank, and trees protecting it. The creek bent around the outcrop's buttresses like a moat around a castle.

I did not stand there on the trail for very long, debating. I suppose there was never much doubt, really; and before long I hitched the pack a notch higher on my hips, stepped off the trail and began to walk down toward the meadow.

I think it was in that moment, as I broke free from the man-made trail, with almost two days of walking tucked safely under my hip belt and five more stretching out ahead, that I finally moved from one world into another.

I walked at first through open brush, following my instincts, then a game trail. As I walked I kept glancing ahead. The meadow had slipped from view, but the moated-castle outcrop still jutted up like a beacon. For the second straight afternoon, dark thunderclouds had failed to reach a climax, and now, as they dispersed northward, they reflected the last of the sun's glow onto the castle's granite walls. I found myself smiling. It is not every day that you walk toward a place you have never been before and feel that you are coming home.

The open brush gave way to scattered conifers, then aspen groves. The game trail cut confidently through them. From time to time I could still glimpse the castle outcrop, up ahead.

I walked on, taking my time, savoring the taper of the day.

By the time I reached the edge of the meadow the light was seeping away, but the castle outcrop, even with its reflected illumination gone, still invited. On its lower flanks I found, sure enough, a perfect campsite: a small, level, grass-carpeted ledge, just far enough from the creek to avoid any danger of my polluting it but close enough for easy water supply and for music.

The view from my little ledge embraced meadow, canyon, sawtooth peaks. Everything except a lingering glow behind the peaks had subsided now to a study in subdued greens and grays. The scene cried out, in its quiet way, to be contemplated; but after the long day's walking there were other, more insistent demands.

I slipped the aluminum-framed pack off my back and stood it upright near one end of the green-carpeted ledge and propped it there with my bamboo staff jammed at an angle against a convenient rock wall. I opened the pack, took out the black plastic groundsheet and spread it on the grass in front of the pack. Next, because the air had suddenly chilled, I put on my down jacket and an Orlon balaclava. Then I rolled out the foam pad on the groundsheet, spread the sleeping bag on the pad, and unpacked and deposited the kitchen—food bag, pots and pans, stove—on the right side of the groundsheet, near its head.*

Next, I took a white plastic tarpaulin out of the pack and stood with it in my hand, pondering. The afternoon thunderclouds had vanished now, off to the north, and it seemed unlikely they would return during the night. Besides, the view from the ledge, still softening toward night, was not one you could in decency block out with plastic. I set the tarp down beside the groundsheet, on the opposite side from the

---

* Note that this trip took place some years ago, before many western bears lost their fear of backpacking humans and thereby became such a perishing nuisance, such a potential danger, that you could no longer dine or breakfast at ease in your sleeping bag because even a hint of food smell on the bag was said—no doubt correctly—to encourage night-prowling bears who might investigate and possibly dine on you.

In most bearish places you nowadays have to cook at some distance from your tent or sleeping bag and afterward hang your pack, containing all the food and most other gear too, high in a tree. You have to go to considerable engineering pains to outwit educated bears who have always known how to climb trees and now know perfectly well that most backpacks contain excellent entrees and that not all backpackers have honed their gear-hanging techniques into unfailingly bearproof modes.

Some people seem to find the bear-defeating process—which starts with choosing a campsite that has the right kind of tree—rather good fun; part of the "woodsy" game. Others just accept it. Frankly, I find the whole thing a goddam hassle that has gone a long way toward ruining, in bear-infested places, the relaxed pleasures of backpacking—which for me include being able to camp almost anywhere that is flat enough and being able to sit up cozily in my sleeping bag, night and then morning, while I eat and contemplate the universe.

That evening I camped on the ledge at the foot of my moated castle, though, the whole modern bear fandango lay mercifully concealed in the mists of the future.

kitchen, where it would be ready for pulling over the bag if my weather forecasting turned out to have been lousy, and also for use as a dew-defying shroud for any other gear, including boots, that would find a night-place on that side of the bed. Then I took all three quart-size plastic water canteens out of the pack and walked down to the creek.

I was filling the last canteen when I heard, somewhere downstream, a splash that might have been a big trout or an otter or a muskrat or possibly a beaver—or could even, I suppose, have been dismissed as imagination had it not, almost at once, come again. I peered into the shadows. Nothing—except the deep U of the canyon framing a moonlit blueness that I knew was the space above the valley.

I walked back to camp and put the canteens down beside the groundsheet—one in the kitchen, two on the opposite side—and unzippered the sleeping bag halfway and sat down on it. I leaned back against the pack and took off first one boot and then the other, removed my socks and slid both legs into the sleeping bag. I rezippered the bag far enough for it to snug tight against the down jacket so that bag and jacket together formed an uninterrupted shell around my body. Then I paused, relishing the cozy assurance of warmth.

The moon, hanging above my left shoulder, was vanquishing the rearguard daylight. The meadow, and the lines of the canyon, had begun to regain definition. A different, moon-blued definition. High above, the outline of the peaks was fading. I sat looking at it all for a moment; then I reached back and took the flashlight from a side pocket of the pack and slipped its attached loop of nylon cord around my neck.

All at once I felt tired, uninterested in cooking. I knew, though, that the one thing guaranteed to re-motivate me was a shot of fast-acting calories. So I reached back into another side pocket of the pack, took out a plastic bag of candies, unwrapped two, slipped them into my mouth and began to set up the kitchen. Within minutes I had the stove unpacked and standing ready, one pot half full of water, and a foil package of "chili con carne" lying beside it, top torn open. Two more minutes and I had the stove roaring and the pot standing on it, and I could lean back once more against the soft, half-empty pack bag.

The stars were out now. The peaks had become little more than a broad and jagged saw of blackness, blacker than the sky only because it was devoid of stars. A night breeze already flowed down the canyon, cool on my face. I pulled the jacket hood over my head. The roar of the stove built an igloo of sound around me.

The pot on the stove muttered. I switched on the flashlight and saw, sure enough, steam rising from around the pot lid. With bandanna-wrapped fingers I removed the lid, poured the chili mix into the water, stirred, turned the stove to low, slipped an asbestos-lined wire gauze—the kind you used at school with Bunsen burners—between it and the pot, and sat back again while dinner simmered.

The stove only whispered now. Far up the canyon, a coyote yowled. Then, behind the stove's whisper, there was only silence, filling the canyon, cold and solid. I sat watching moonlight rout the last of the day. Soon, it filled the canyon, blue and solid, in tandem with the silence.

I checked my watch. Ten minutes. I lifted the lid from the pot and ladled a first serving of chili into the metal cup. In the flashlight beam it steamed, brown and appetizing. It tasted almost elegant, and I sat there and ate it, spoonful by spoonful, looking out over sleeping bag and meadow and cold blue canyon but no longer seeing very much. By the time I had finished the fourth and last cupful of chili and had scraped most of the goo from the pot and poured a little water into it to aid final cleaning in the morning, I was barely awake enough to eat my ordained piece of meal-ending chocolate. I think I was still eating it—oblivious, now, of the view—when I fell asleep. When I came half-awake again I was still sitting up, leaning against the pack, and my watch reported that two hours had passed. I slid down into the sleeping bag, pulled it loosely around me, and once more slept.

In the morning, before breakfast, two fawns stood beside the creek, ears alert, bodies silhouetted in the first sunlight against lush green grass. And after breakfast, as I sat considering how soon to move on, a coyote emerged from the trees on the far side of the meadow and trotted out into the open, legs tripping doglike and dainty among the tussocks. It quartered twice across the middle of the meadow, then began to move, nose to ground, into the breeze that had just begun to ease gently up the canyon. I reached out, very slowly, lifted my binoculars from the boot in which they had spent the night, and focused on the hunting coyote. Almost at once, it pounced, like a kitten on a ball of wool, on some unseen target. Clearly, the coyote had missed its prey. For it stood there looking down—no doubt into a gopher hole—its body as eloquent of frustration as a golfer's after a missed two-foot putt. But a few minutes later I watched it, after another pounce, fling back its head, readjust a small, dark, struggling shape held in its teeth, chomp a couple of times, swallow, then resume its breakfasteering. Twice more in the next five minutes it pounced and missed. Just after the second miss it moved out of sight behind a rock wall of my little ledge that angled down, six feet beyond the kitchen. I slid out of bed and very slowly, on hands and knees, eased toward the wall. I reached it, peered over. Off to my right, a chipmunk chirped alarm. Out in the meadow, the coyote swung its head toward me, froze for a moment—and then was racing away across the open grass—legs no longer dainty but frantic, digging turf. Within seconds the streaking brown body had vanished into dark trees.

Half an hour later I struck camp and walked on down toward the space, hanging blue at the canyon's mouth, that I knew was the valley.

Almost at once, the country mutated. The canyon began to slope more steeply, the creek to tumble more boisterously. The meadows grew smaller and less frequent, the conifer stands between them, taller and more stately. The granite boulders studding the canyon floor crowded closer.

Above all, though, there were the flowers. A quartet of crimson columbines—five trumpets per player—extemporized in sun-filled silence to a captive bracken audience. Beside a rotting juniper log, a saprophytic snow plant spiked up through dead leaves, scarlet buds bunched tight around its core like a string of small, rather tattered pomegranates. I walked on down among the tumbled boulders. In a natural granite courtyard beside the creek, nodding tiger lilies curved up and gracefully over, each flower with its yellow, brown-spotted petals peeling back on themselves into delicate yet startling orbs; each orb with its ring of six flattened-miniature-taco stamens dangling like wind chimes. Against a lush mossy backdrop, a galaxy of shooting stars—chocolate-brown cones, yellow tail bands, pale pink plumes—hung suspended in plunging stationary orbit.

I had just passed the shooting stars when I stepped onto a granite ledge and found myself looking out over the valley.

A lot depends, of course, on the mood you are in when you first see a place. But I am sure that even without the flowers' Elysian prelude I would have halted in surprise on that open granite ledge. The valley was deeper and more dramatic than I had expected. It was, to an extent the topo map had somehow not prepared me for, a canyon rather than a valley—almost in the same way that Yosemite is a canyon, though it too is always called "Valley." But the plunging granite side walls did no more than frame the picture. Tall, elegant conifers clothed the valley floor in a dense green mat. Shadows cast by the trees' spired summits gave the mat depth and texture. Wedges of deeper shadow, from spurs on the valley's rim, drew sharper, communal contrasts. And down the center of the valley, furrowing its mat, meandered a river that was a chain of white rapids, mottled brown shallows and blue-green pools.

Yet the elements of the scene were not its core. Even in that first moment there was something else about the valley —the morning light, perhaps, or my flower-decked mood— that invited; that left me slightly breathless. I had been afraid, I think, that the weeks of anticipating the trip might have created an expectancy barrier. Standing on that granite ledge, I knew I need not have worried.

I stayed on the ledge only long enough to savor through binoculars the close-woven richness of green-tree mat and beckoning river; but while I stood there a military jet cut down the valley's cleavage, so low that it kept vanishing below my line of sight. The jet tore the quiet air, bouncing crass thunder off the plunging rock walls. By rights, I should have cursed its pilot—for breaking sensible flying regulations, for disturbing my peace. Yet, just as had happened once before, years earlier, in a similar situation, I found myself instead admiring his competence and thrust and lawlessness; found myself acknowledging the vivid way he represented us restless, driving humans. I stood listening until the plane's last echoes died away, then brought my mind back to practical matters.

Below the ledge, a jumble of rocks slanted steeply away. It was far from clear whether I would be able to find a route down. I scrambled off one end of the ledge and began the descent.

At first I had to thread my way through a chaos of huge granite boulders. But between them plunged precipitous,

loose gravel slopes, and I slipped and slid down these runways, scaled route-blocking boulders big as cottages, then returned to gravel. Ten minutes, and the worst seemed over.
Trees began, in among the boulders: junipers with their
warm, twist-pattern trunks; firs with soft, green-tipped pa-
goda branches; then huge, stately ponderosa pines. It was hot
now, even in the shade, and the air grew heavy with the
sweet toffee smell of pine sap.

At last the gravel runways began to flatten out and the
trees to grow closer together, so that you could call the place
a forest. Soon I was walking on almost level ground across a
cushioning carpet of pine needles, and the pines rose huge
and silent and there was almost no undergrowth, just the
towering trees. It was big, dignified country. Before long I
could hear the river.

I found a flawless campsite a hundred feet from the river,
near a side creek that was just a healthy trickle, really, but
had a natural log dam that broadened it out into a miniature
pool, two feet across, with a walkway down into it and a triangular stone exquisitely placed in a moss-bank setting. I
rolled out my groundsheet and pad under a big ponderosa
pine. A squirrel rasped up a neighboring tree, then peered
at me around one side of it and complained. When I had set
up camp and brewed a pot of tea I found myself just sitting
there, leaning against my pack, suddenly content, after all
the hard walking, to do nothing.

And that was almost all I did for the rest of the day: just
sat and looked around. In the due course of time, though, I
began—as nearly always happens when you stay for a while
in one place—to notice details that at first had melded into
the backdrop. Mind you, I saw nothing that could be called
even remotely exciting. I watched cobwebs drift by on silent
journeys that were invisible, too, except in slanting beams of
sunlight. I watched the labored flights of clapper-rattle grass-

hoppers that clappered on the way down and not, as you would expect, when taking off and gaining height. I watched a little brown bundle of a bird land on a twig, seven feet away, and sit there, body pulsating, beady eye casing me, until I reached for the camera; and as it departed I resolved for the hundredth time in ten years to get myself a bird book and at least learn to identify the most common species. I watched an ant carry a small catkin head, six times bulkier than itself, for a vast distance over an obstacle course of pine needles and then across the cleared space that was my kitchen; carry it, presumably, toward some goal—yet pass on the way, every few inches, catkins that to me looked identical to the one that formed its prodigious burden. I watched the obvious frustration of a mosquito that settled on my shirt sleeve: smelling warm flesh below, it kept boring down with its slender proboscis but never managed to drill quite deep enough to strike blood. Once, I watched a bat, looking rather lost in bright sunlight, stutter an erratic course downriver. And all the time, sitting there at my ease, I half-heard the tinkle of the little side creek and, as the afternoon wore on, the brush of wind across treetops.

Once, in midafternoon, I got up and walked to the riverbank and sat on a tree that beavers had felled. The tree's tip lay out in the main current and its whole trunk pulsated. I sat there, feeling the river's ceaseless life, gazing without real thought at a patch of willows that grew on an island—or rather, on what would earlier in the year be an island but was now surrounded by an open expanse of dry pebbles that you would be able to walk over, even at dusk, without fear of treading on a concealed rattlesnake. I got up and strolled out onto the smooth, water-rounded pebbles. On one of them lay the mottled brown husk of a helgramite, split neatly down its center. The split was so clean, so eloquent, that I could almost see the new, transformed insect emerging, unfurling its wings, then flying up and away into the new, surprising element of air. I walked out onto the tip of the willow patch. Upstream, below a rapid, there was a long, gentle run—not quite a pool but not a shallow either—in which the water had just the right movement and just the right depth of color. At that hour, with the sun beating down, there was no sign of fish. Somehow, anyway, it was not yet time to fish. I walked back to camp and brewed more tea.

By the time I had finished drinking it the afternoon clouds were building their black threat, and I stretched my white plastic tarpaulin out between the trunk of the big pine tree and a pair of nearby saplings. I rigged the tarp high, so that although it would protect me from a thunderstorm there was still plenty of space under its eaves for me to look out at the forest. With the sun cut off and a grayness lying heavy, nothing much seemed to be happening there. But a spider undertook a long diagonal trip across the tarp and I lay watching its progress. All I could see through the white plastic, except for a blurred suggestion of the body, was the circular pattern of its outspread legs at the points they touched the tarp. Watching the moving pattern, it occurred to me that this was what an insect-eating fish, such as a trout, must see when a fly or spider came floating down the river, out in the broad expanse of mirrorlike reflecting surface that would fill all its view except for a small window above its head. Within that window the trout's angle of sight was wide enough for light to be refracted through the water instead of reflected, and through the window the trout could look out into the non-watery world and sometimes detect, near the window's edge, bulky two-legged animals waving thin poles to and fro; animals that the trout knew, from instinct or experience, were not to be trusted in any damned way. When the current carried an insect downstream into the circular window, the trout could see the whole insect instead of just the pattern of leg-prints previously visible on the water's mirror surface; and the fish could therefore make a final decision about whether it should rise in the water and engulf the morsel. Lying under my white plastic tarp, I watched the spider complete its journey, vanish. It was a long time, I realized, since I had thought like a trout, the way I used to as a kid—and as a man ostensibly much older than a kid. It was a long time since I had fished, even. Sudden sunlight transformed the white plastic into a glaring expanse. I stuck my head outside. The thunderclouds had slid away, frustrated, and the sun was reclaiming the day. I took down my tarp and went back to watching the forest.

I suppose I did not really spend all that first day watching the forest. I do not think I opened the paperback I had brought, and I cannot remember anything else I did—nothing I can put a finger on, I mean—so I'm tempted to say that I sat there under my pine tree, thinking. But "thinking" is the wrong word, really. What you do at such times, I find, is not proper thinking. Even what we normally call "thinking" is not an easy process to pin down. Perhaps Robert Musil came close when he wrote, "It is not the case that we reflect on things. Rather, things think themselves out within us." Sitting under a tree when you are pleasantly tired and giving yourself up to the forest is certainly a very passive business. Still, thoughts trip by. And at some point that afternoon, as I sat there contentedly under my big ponderosa pine, doing what would to anyone else have looked like nothing—and would probably have looked like it to me, had I considered the matter—I for some reason found myself remembering the Winnebago man in the campground, three days earlier, and the way I had once again failed to come up with a satisfactory answer to his central question; and all at once there popped up into my mind, apparently unbidden, a memory that had lain unpopped for more than thirty years.

Back when I was ten or eleven there was a boy at my school in England who lived on a farm and who, when asked what he had done on a free day or weekend or long vacation, always produced the same answer. His response became so predictable that we little embryo terrorists would on every possible occasion ask him, "John, what did you do this weekend?"—or whatever the period had been. Then we would wait in delicious expectation. And John always produced. Without fail, he would give his slow smile and say, "Oh, just mucked about." Sitting there under my pine tree, I found myself understanding, thirty years late, the rightness and richness of his response.

The hours passed and I sat and mucked statically about. First, I think, I began to itemize the wealth of detail. A pale blur on a rotting tree trunk focused into the orange remnants of a pine cone, half dismantled and left lying there in the dining room of the squirrel that had chided me when I arrived but was now accepting enough, or at least resigned enough, to sit out on a branch and just watch me before flouncing off on a safari to quieter parts. When I looked out across the hidden river I found myself not just seeing tangled forest canopy but zeroing in for some reason on a particularly tall ponderosa pine; found myself appreciating the way its ruler-straight trunk thrust up orange against the pale gray of the valley's granite wall, and the way big green cones bent its branches in delicate downcurves, like a loaded Christmas tree's; found myself delighted by the way sunlight kept bouncing off the cones' resin so that the tree sometimes glistened as if dusted with Christmas frosting. Back closer to my couch, around the boles of mature pines, dried-out cones lay thick, as if big, rough, circular tarpaulins had been spread there. Closer still, the ants still scurried, busier than beavers. Offstage, the ceaseless river whispered. And always there were the trees, in all their slow chapters: slender saplings; thrusting midlifers; towering, triumphant giants; snags, gaunt and stark as skeletons; then rotting, moss-shrouded windfalls. I sat on, idly watching, details often fading back into the whole, so that I was aware only of a glorious richness, prodigality, wantonness.

The day faded toward extinction. But I did not light a fire. I like to watch night fall, then become a part of the shadowed darkness, and a fire, for all its cheer, cuts you off. Soon, bats were flitting silent against pale sky. Then the moon rose. My eyes and mind wandered among blue shadows, then up to and along the great waves of gray that were the valley's limits.

In the morning, at first eye-open, there was a deer standing barely twenty paces away, so camouflaged by a fir sapling that I could see only the black-tipped white tail and, through slowly raised binoculars, a single big eye, unblinking but somehow full of fearfulness. For a long moment we examined each other. Then there was only the sapling.

Before breakfast, I went fishing.

Out in the "civilized" world, the human population can be divided, with no more than routine oversimplification, into three groups: those who regard all fishing as a cruel and near-criminal aberration (and who commonly climb to their elevated opinions from a firm base of ignorance); those who "sport-fish" merely to catch fish (and who may indeed treat fish with cruel and near-criminal disregard); and those who understand that the catching of fish is largely a means to an end and that the essence of fishing is a close-to-innocent pleasure that can border on, even lap over into, sheer artistry. These graduates are often—though by no means exclusively—people who fly-fish for trout.

It was barely seven o'clock when I walked eagerly down to the river. The sun had not yet cleared the valley's rim, and along the riverbank the air was cold, going on bloody cold. But because I knew I would have to wade a little in order to fish the run above the willow-patch island I wore shorts, and leather moccasins on bare feet. I had my heavy down jacket on, though, with its hood pulled tight. I walked across the isthmus of water-rounded pebbles that joined the island to the bank, looked for and failed to find the split-open helgramite husk, came to the foot of the run, hesitated, took off the moccasins, stuffed them into the fishing satchel slung around my neck, hesitated again, then waded out into the river.

The water felt bitterly cold. My feet slipped and slithered on smooth, slime-coated pebbles. I waded carefully out until the willow patch was far enough behind my right shoulder to give me room to cast. The water barely reached my knees but my feet were already almost numb. From its little holding ring just above the rod's cork handle, I unhooked the artificial fly—a dainty confection of fur and feather, with the feather wound spirally around the hook so that its fibers stood out like the legs of a real fly or spider. Then I began false-casting: flexing the rod to and fro so that the stiff, heavy line extended forward, then backward. With my left hand I kept stripping more and more line off the reel so that its airborne part, reaching out in a constantly mobile curl, grew steadily longer. At first I kept turning my head to watch the line flow backward on its smooth and beautiful path. I watched mainly to make sure that at its full extension, when it hung for an instant, green and almost straight against the shadows of the far bank, the fly at the end of the gut leader did not snag the willow patch. But I also watched because it was a long time since I had fished, and watching the line helps you regain your timing—a delicate response to the rhythm of the cast that is transmitted to your fingers down the slender and supple rod. When the line was long enough, I let one forward cast follow through to completion. The line curled out upstream, over the edge of the run. At its full extent, the pale fly hung poised for an instant, a foot above the water. Then it landed, delicate as thistledown, and began floating with the current, back toward me. With my left hand I kept pulling in line, so that if a fish rose and engulfed the fly there would be little or no slack line between us and I could tighten before he sensed that there was something wrong. Like the casting and many other things, this keeping in touch with the fly by constant retrieving of the line was something I still did almost automatically, the way I had done it as a kid during those long, glorious days when such arts were the only things that mattered. Were sometimes the only things that existed.

The first three or four casts, no fish rose. Then one splashed untidily at the fly. Automatically, I tightened. I knew at once that it was a small fish, but because of my long abstinence there was still a mild thrill when the fish fought against the pressure and the rod came alive in my hand. I reeled in and held the little rainbow trout, barely six inches long, on the surface of the water, close beside my left knee. It lay there on its side, momentarily exhausted. It was so young that there were still vertical black parr marks at intervals along the gleaming, rainbow-hued flanks. I tucked the rod into my right armpit, reached down with my left hand, grasped the fish gently but firmly, still in the water, and with my right forefinger and thumb pressed back and down on the hook so that the barb disengaged and I could slip the fly free. I opened the palm of my hand partway so that the fish, though no longer captive, was held upright in normal swimming position. For a long moment it stayed there, unmoving. Then with a flick of its tail it darted forward, streaked out into the run and vanished. Because it had not been exposed to air or to a dry, slime-removing hand, it would suffer no harm. In bright sunlight, when I could see everything that happened, I had once watched a small trout that I had just caught and released, in just this way, rise almost immediately to the same fly floated down over the same place.

A little farther up the run, the tip of a dark nose broke the surface and annexed an invisible insect. I eased forward a couple of steps—and discovered that my feet were now so numb that it was all I could do to keep my balance. The fish rose a second time. I reforgot my feet and recast upstream. The fly landed dead on target, four or five feet above the place the fish had risen, and began to float down with the current. As I retrieved line with my left hand I found myself imagining the trout, poised in its feeding place, watching the mirrorlike surface that stretched away upstream; watching a circular, outspread pattern that was the imprint of the hackle tips at the points they touched the water; watching the pattern move swiftly down toward the window above its head, where it would be able to see the whole body of the expected fly or spider. Up in my reality, above the surface, I watched intently as the pale and barely visible blur of feather hackle swept on downstream. I kept imagining that it had moved into the trout's window and that the fish was at that moment making its decision to eat or not to eat. For long, ticking seconds, the fly kept floating down with the current; and then, when I felt sure it had passed beyond the trout's window, the dark nose broke the surface again and the pale blur that was my fly had vanished. I flicked my wrist back, felt the fish, solid. Then line was cutting out across the run at an angle and then the fish was cartwheeling through the air, a bar of glorious, glistening silver; and then the pressure of the rod was too much for it and it was coming back toward me, still struggling but already halfway defeated. Within a minute I had it lying quietly at the surface, close beside my knee. It was ten or eleven inches long: perfect eating size. I tucked the rod under my arm again, reached down and grasped the fish firmly in my left hand, lifted it clear of the water, put my right thumb in its mouth, ball upward, laid my right forefinger along the top of the head, and jerked the thumb smartly backward. I felt the neck break. The fish, already dead, quivered, then lay still. For a long moment I let it lie there in my open palm while I admired the glistening spotted scales and still-shimmering rainbow tints. Then I took a plastic bag out of the satchel slung around my neck, slid the fish into the bag, slipped the bag into the satchel.

In the next twenty minutes I caught two more pan-size rainbows. And then, at the very head of the run, on the same pale dry fly, I hooked a bigger fish that careened almost to the far side of the river before I brought it back and eventually landed it by stumbling to the bank and coaxing the now exhausted and almost immobile fish into water so shallow that it could no longer swim freely and I could grasp it with reasonable safety and quickly break its neck. It was only then that I realized I could barely feel my feet. I also realized for the first time that the sun had cleared the far rim of the valley. I took stock. Four fish were plenty for the morning, for food as well as fun. I sat down on the smooth, dry pebbles, rubbed my benumbed feet halfway dry and slid them into the moccasins. And all at once, there on the open pebbles, it was warm. I took off the down jacket, began cleaning the trout. By the time I came to the last one I had taken off my shirt and the sun was beating hot on my bare shoulders.

Afterward, when I looked back at the week as a whole, it almost seemed as if nothing much happened after I caught those first trout: the rest of the week gave an impression of tapering off in anticlimax. At the time, though, it did not feel like that at all. Very much the reverse. Yet while the fishing on that fourth morning was in no sense a climax it turned out, I guess, to be the last "new" thing I did all week. Perhaps that is the point: afterward, I did nothing different from what I had already done. Just more of the same. Let there be no doubt, though—for three more days the valley continued to hold me content in the palm of its cupped hand.

After a trout breakfast on that fourth morning, I toyed with the idea of striking camp and exploring upriver. But after giving the matter some thought—that is, by letting the possibility swirl around my head for a while and then pulling it out and remeasuring it—I decided that the week was not going to evolve into one of my hard-walking treks. The first two and a half days had taken care of all that. So I did not strike camp for another twenty-four hours.

Some of that time I sat and read, or simply went on looking around at the forest. Two or three times, I took local strolls. On one of them I met a rattlesnake, but he lay out in the middle of an open patch of pine needles and was therefore almost as visible and unthreatening as he would have been on smooth pebbles. He rattled at me, anyway, when I was still a dozen paces away, so I did not even suffer the kind of scare you get from almost treading on one. During that same stroll I talked briefly to a couple of people camped half a mile downstream, under a rocky overhang. They were pleasant folks, out on their first weeklong trip, and reveling in the experience. Later, a packtrain passed close to my camp, heading upriver on the main trail, and I exchanged a few words with the man on the last of the seven or eight horses. He was relaxed and amiable, up there under his big hat. Yes, he said, the valley was just the same for several miles downstream. Just as beautiful.

That evening I fished again—for dinner and next morning's breakfast. I also fished for other things, of course. And although I had within half an hour caught four trout big enough to complement two meals, I went on fishing—under a new rubric: If I caught more fish I would release them.

As it turned out, I went on fishing far too long—just the way I always did as a kid, and as a young man too—and eventually, although my timing had now improved, I snagged the fly in a branch that I had not seen in the fading light. I could not reach the branch (even though I wore boots this time, and did not wade, because I was exploring some distance upstream), and I had to break the leader. To tie on a new fly I had to hold the hook's tiny eye up against the palest sector of sky, and even then I could barely see either it or the end of the fine gut leader. As I fought the familiar reluctance of the gut to be threaded through the eye I was vaguely conscious of the dark tips of conifers, high against the sky, just as I had often been with other trees, other skies, in many other places—almost, it seemed, in other lives. Then the fly was safely knotted on at last and I was casting up into the gloaming, into a calm pool, and guessing, most of the time, just where my fly might be floating. On one cast I saw the ripples of a widening circle, up on the flat surface of the pool, roughly where the fly could have been, and almost instinctively I raised the rod. Just for a moment there was a weight on the line—a more solid weight, it seemed to me, than any other of the day's fish had generated. Then the weight had gone and the line was slack and I was left trying to decide if the fish had really been so much bigger than all the rest or whether I should attribute the impression to a vivid imagination. Somehow, by now, it did not matter very much, and I went on casting up into the paleness that was the pool. Soon it was too dark even for that, even for me, and I fumbled the flashlight out of my satchel and turned and walked home to camp.

Next morning, after an early breakfast, I stowed everything into my pack and walked downstream along the main trail. It was good to feel the weight of the pack on my hips again, and the smooth surface of the bamboo staff in my right hand; good to feel the rhythmic stride I fell into, almost without thinking. The sun beat down on my bare shoulders. It was not yet hot, though—only warm and comforting.

The valley floor kept opening up into broad, lush meadows. Each of these meadows, too, cried out in its own way to be contemplated, but I kept walking. Now, somehow suddenly, I had only two days left.

That day, I walked barely five miles. At the far end of the biggest and lushest meadow, I paused. The map showed that half a mile ahead the trail struck away from the valley floor; and there was another thing, too. I could see that less than a mile downstream the steep granite walls began to flatten out. Beyond that point, the valley would be a different place. So I cut away from the trail, toward the river, and found a good campsite on the meadow's edge, a hundred feet short of the river, in an aspen grove.

Most of that day I just sat in camp with the meadow spread golden-green before me and aspens whispering at my elbow and the pale blue sky overhead slowly filling with clouds. Up in another world, jets kept painting white contrails across that sky. Fortunately, contrails rarely seem to intrude on my solitude. They are too remote, too unreal. Some people, I know, feel differently—though an honest fellow backpacker once admitted, "Well, maybe I just mean that they wreck my photography."

In late afternoon I went fishing again. I caught nothing big enough to eat—perhaps because the fish, too, were disturbed by the way the day's clouds, spreading down the valley from invisible peaks, had a new, determined look. Soon, little flurries of spinning wind began to push across the meadow, printing whirligig patterns in the tall grass, then erasing them. The clouds built thicker, blacker. The gloom deepened. At last, a few drops of rain fell, cold and heavy. When the storm exploded I was safely back under my little white tarp, which I had tied to neighboring aspen trunks. I sat listening with pleasure to the way the tarp prattled under the lashing rain and heaved in response to the swaying aspens. By nightfall the thunderstorm had blown itself out, and I took the tarp down and dined by freshly laundered starlight.

Next morning, with the whole world washed clean and shining, I went for a walk along the river, watched trout rising, then came back to my aspen trees. I sat there, leaning against my pack, for half an hour. But by then I knew I could procrastinate no longer. Around noon, I struck camp. Twenty minutes later I began climbing the steep side trail that slanted toward the divide.

I did not say goodbye to the valley. In midafternoon I became aware, too late, that I had crossed a shallow rise that cut me off from it. From its floor, anyway. All I could see was the upper part of the now familiar granite wall. Somehow it did not matter too much. I knew, now, that I would be coming back.

That night I camped in high country again, among granite slabs and boulders, beside a dead juniper tree with its curlicue bark bleached palest orange. By midafternoon next day I was climbing toward the pass that would take me back, over the divide, into the little valley in which the ranger station stood.

The pass was lower than the one I had crossed on the second day, and softer. As I approached it, a deer wandered over the skyline, skirted a snowbank, then sauntered down through a sloping bed of blue lupines that was bigger than the statutory football field. I reached the crest. The air buzzed with bees beelining to and from the lupines. All around, sunlit space rested on a maze of peaks that sawtoothed away into immense, hazy distances. Below, the ranger-station valley lay green and inviting. The whole scene fitted together. Everything fitted together now. There was none of the gaping meaninglessness that had hung so heavy on me, seven days earlier.

I started down the slope, into the little valley. Another

hour, and I could see the ranger station tucked in among its trees. Just before five o'clock I climbed up the steps onto the wooden veranda, slipped the pack off my back and went in through the screen door.

The young redheaded ranger looked up from his desk, glanced at his watch, smiled. "I was beginning to wonder," he said. "Had a good time?"

"Great."

"Do some fishing?"

"Sure."

"Any luck?"

"Oh, all I needed—and more."

"Good," said the ranger. He got up and moved toward the counter. "What else did you get to do?"

"Well, you know how it is, I walked and fished and . . ." I hesitated. "Oh, I just mucked about."

The ranger nodded. "I know what you mean," he said. He reached the counter, shook my hand, ran his eye over me. "Well, one thing's for sure. Whatever you did out there, it's done you a whole lot of good."

3 Along the Colorado

The desert can be a wonderful place for walking. It offers the earth at its most naked and honest (alpine country, though often as naked, somehow presents a different face). Virgin desert, unviolated by man, is at once simple and complex, strong yet vulnerable. Although sometimes dusty, it is supremely clean. It is also the sovereign place of silence.

You should understand, though, that in order to enjoy desert walking—perhaps even to survive it—you must pay sharpish attention to two elements: heat and water. The best way to deal with heat is to sidestep it by selecting sane times of year and sapient times of day. The water problem remains. Mostly, in fact, it dominates. But once in a while, given luck and sagacity, you can liquidate it by co-opting a river—and although you may then find that your little journey turns out rather differently from dry-desert walking, the results can be halcyon.

I walked out of the small, dog-day town in the coolness of a spring morning. Almost at once I crossed a silent railroad track and heard half-forgotten echoes. Then I had climbed a levee and stood looking down at the Colorado.

The river, for all its own echoes, was not the river I remembered; was not the river I had followed for two hundred miles, ten years earlier, at the start of a summer-long walk. That river had been almost the Colorado of legend—"too thick to drink, too thin to plow." It could have been what T. S. Eliot had in mind:

> I do not know much about gods; but I think that the river
> Is a strong brown god—sullen, untamed and intractable.

But the river below me now flowed clear and blue, serene and welcoming. It also seemed narrower, or at least less vast, than I remembered. I stood there on the levee and pondered this mildly disturbing mismatch. In the end I decided that although the Colorado might now indeed be objectively rather smaller—because of new dams that had bled off its silt and sullenness—the change probably lay mostly in me. When you go back, to almost anywhere, things tend to look smaller. If you revisit childhood haunts the shrinkage is often ludicrous, but even within adult spans it can be disconcerting.

When I had assimilated the Colorado's new color and size I walked on, upriver. Thick, heavy clouds imposed an undesertlike oppressiveness, and I walked slowly; but within half an hour I had broken free from the last tatters of the town.

I was not yet out in desert, though. Not real desert.

Another thing I had forgotten about this lower Colorado country was the way man kept clawing at it, speculatively—scraping and destroying yet rarely substituting anything of value. I skirted a square of stony, recently bulldozed soil. In the center of this flattened, pulverized, naked space, a pile of brush burned bleakly. I could see no people, but nearby stood two dusty pickups, doors open, CB radios blaring, raucous and static-filled. I walked on, back into the richness of barren desert: green creosote bushes and mildly comic cactus gardens; sudden brilliant flower beds; athletic lizards, fleeing from my boots; gentle slopes and gullies all interlaced with subtle meanings. Then I came to another "improved" square. Its surface had begun to heal but the land still stretched flat and meaningless. In the center of the square stood a single wooden shack, ugly, uninhabited, already eloquent of disuse.

I joined a dirt road that ran along the top of the levee, followed it for an hour, then scrambled down the levee's flank and found a lunch site in the strip of greenery, rarely more than ten feet wide, that lined the river.

The little alcove in the greenery was the sort of lunch place I had often chosen ten years earlier; but until I slipped my pack off and propped it up as usual with the bamboo staff so that I could sit down and lean back against it, I had forgotten just how such lunches had been. In that first instant of leaning back, though, it was almost as if a ten-year screen had been whisked away. I sat in the same skimpy, filtered band of shade, with the world out beyond it hot and glaring, in spite of the clouds, and the river lapping at my feet. There were the same smells, too—those most burry of memories: an indefinable blend of alkaline river and damp sandy soil and the bark or leaves—or, most likely, the pollen—of arrowweed and salt cedar. Sitting there in the alcove, I remembered it all, as a coherent, interweaving whole. There was one big difference, though. Ten years earlier I had been a

stranger to the desert, and anything but an experienced backpacker. Now, I felt secure in my knowledge and expertise.
So I could walk and lunch and camp and all the rest with relaxed confidence. In itself, of course, that was good. It left me
free to reach out for other things. But I could not help understanding at the same time that experience had blunted,
as it almost always does, the edge of expectation, even of
sensation; had blunted but not, I was relieved to find,
banished.

I rested, there in riverside shade, through the heat of the
day. The clouds mollified the sun, and I could if necessary
have kept walking without discomfort; but I had spent the
night before on a bus, being freighted from home to the town
in which I started walking, and I kept dozing off. The logistics
imposed by the terrain ahead and the amount of food in my
pack meant that I did not have time to squander. Still, the
pressures were not yet urgent. Besides, at the start of a trip
I often need to put finishing touches to the furnishings of the
house on my back, and that first afternoon beside the river,
between dozes, I checked all gear, reorganized food and sili-
coned my leather moccasins. I did not spend much time, as
I often do, studying maps and daydreaming ahead, for I had
vigilantly eschewed the USGS topo maps that I almost always
carry in unknown country and instead had brought a single
four-by-nine-inch section cut from a large-scale road map.
This backpackingly uninformative diagram told me nothing
about the lie of the land: other than the river's general
course, it showed little but the boundaries of a small Indian
reservation and a huge Recreation Area, and the only three
roads that cut into the river in the next hundred or so miles.
These three roads led to a dam and to two boat marinas,
spaced about twenty straight-line miles apart. I was still un-
decided about whether to end the trip at the second marina;
if I felt like it, I might replenish supplies there—as I would

certainly have to at the first marina—and walk on to a large lake, another twenty miles upriver.

I carried only my rudimentary map because, to keep the trip from being dull and truly pedestrian, I needed the challenge of uncertainty. For I knew that during the ten days or two weeks I expected to be walking I would traverse no real mountains, no deep and desiccated troughs, only rolling river plain and perhaps the fringes of some low desert hills. Now, I do not normally select such undramatic country for my walks. But a fortnight before, standing in my shower, I had generated one of those ridiculous, brilliant ideas that, if properly nourished, can go a long way toward making life bearable.

Ten years earlier I had walked the length of California— and at the start of that trip the Colorado had for two hundred miles been my lifeline. Five years later I had walked the length of the Grand Canyon of the Colorado. And as I stood there in the shower, with warm, projected water massaging body and mind, one half of the mind chewed at the unpalatable fact that I was for no apparent reason suffering from one of my periodic bouts of general dissatisfaction and ennui; meanwhile, the other half of the mind ruminated on the recent tenth anniversary of the start of the California walk and kept recalling with immense pleasure and satisfaction, as highlights of my life, both that walk and the one through Grand Canyon, not very far upriver of the California walk's first stretch. And all at once, standing there in the shower, I made a simple connection—and a decision. I decided that in the course of the next one hundred and fifty years, unless graver matters intruded, I would complete, in a series of short trips taken when troughs in my life bellowed for them, a walk the entire length of the Colorado River.

Two weeks later, and almost exactly ten years since I walked out of the small, dog-day town that marked the end of the Colorado reach of my California walk, I got off a Greyhound bus in that town and crossed the familiar railroad track and began to walk upriver. The town had seemed the obvious place to start my new project. But choosing it meant that I would face few physical obstacles, or even any radically new type of terrain: the country above the town clearly echoed that immediately below it. So I had brought only my small and uninformative fragment of road map. Having to route-find by guesswork and experience would at least pose some measure of challenge.

That first lunchtime beside the river I did not leave my shady alcove until the cool of evening. Even then, I walked for only an hour, still following the dirt road that ran along the top of the levee. Around me, as before, stretched man-struck desert.

I camped at dusk beside a stub of an old side road. While I was eating dinner under the bright red poncho I had rigged as a tarpaulin because of threatening clouds, a police car came slowly up the dirt road and stopped twenty paces away. Its spotlight flicked on, impaled me. I waved. The spotlight went out. The patrol car moved on. A pall of dust drifted over me, then drifted on, out over the river.

Soon, the clouds decanted a few drops of rain. As I fell asleep they were pattering harmlessly, pleasantly, on my poncho-tarp. I woke at five o'clock to find the dawn sky stretching pale and clear, washed clean, and the air cool, going on cold. While I was eating breakfast the sun came up over Arizona, warm and comforting. By the time I struck camp it was hinting at heat.

I had walked for barely half an hour when I came to a boundary between two worlds—between the worlds delineated back home, from a certain bend in the road, by flatlands and forest.

On top of the levee, the dirt road had tapered away into

a stony track. Then, without warning, the track ended and the levee too, and I was looking down onto a slough that reached back four or five hundred yards. At this low-water state of the river, the place was a meadow-slough, really: around its margins ran a swath of grassland, but its upper end cradled a small circular lake, connected to the river by a narrow channel. In the lake stood five white herons, tall and elegant and statue-still. Below me, in the channel, shoals of fish tumbled, backs breaking the water's calm surface. Beyond, in a fringe of lush green trees, birds bustled and chattered. The only sign of man's hand was a line of stepping-stones across the narrowest part of the channel. Even they were incomplete, reassuringly inefficient. Nowhere could I see a harsh, straight line. Everything was soft and curving, natural.

I was still standing where I had stopped, reveling in this peaceful little world that had opened out below me, swabbing away the one that lay behind, when a coyote emerged from tree shadows beyond the channel. It walked forward to a point just below the stepping-stones, put its head down and drank. From its muzzle, rings spread outward across the mirrorlike channel.

When the coyote had finished drinking it trotted a few paces, to above the stepping-stones, and began to eat something. All at once it looked up, directly at me. For a moment it stood still. Then it had turned and almost instantly vanished, back into the shadows that underlay the trees. From behind the trees, a big black hawklike bird with a red head flapped out and away. Up in the lake, the herons took wing. They, too, circled away from me, angled upriver.

I moved slowly forward and eased, as quietly as possible, down the steep end slope of the levee. The fish continued to tumble. I came to the foot of the levee and stepped out onto the swath of meadowland—and at that moment memory tilted and I was relishing yet another forgotten delight. When you step from open, glaring desert into one of those small green enclaves with which the desert sometimes surprises you, the light—and more than the light—can be transformed, as if by the flick of a switch. Only rarely do you walk into a true oasis. But you experience almost as vivid a change when you walk into any patch of rich desert greenery. Water, of course, creates all these enclaves. The water may be invisible, underground. It may be a tiny surface trickle, or a sizable creek. Or it can be a major river, like the Colorado, that supports, in all but its most rock-stark reaches, a soft and shade-giving strip of such shrubbery as arrowweed or salt cedar.

The drama of the switch you experience, from one cosmos into another, no doubt stems from two sources. First there is the diamond-cut clarity of most unpolluted desert air. The potential for exquisite brilliance is always there. Out in the open, glare sometimes stuns this potential, that is all. The second source of drama is sheer contrast. Your eye, shuttered against the glare, embraces a sudden soft green luxury; your mind—also often battened down against the glare, though you hardly know it—relaxes and rejoices.

I had many times walked into small green desert enclaves—oases or other watered places—and rejoiced and rested. Almost always, while resting, I could look beyond the limits of my retreat and catch glimpses, or at least hints, of the glaring outside world. Such reminders, though they enrich by sheer contrast, in another sense detract from the luxuriousness: your green cocoon remains incomplete. But when I reached the foot of the levee and stepped out onto flat emerald-green meadowland, I found myself cut off. Down in that sunken place, the man- and sun-struck outside world had been erased.

I walked a few yards over lush, damp grass. All around

me, water and grass and trees and sky, everything I could see—even the shadows—seemed to glow, almost luminously. It was very quiet: just a faint tree rustle and a half-whisper of water sliding past the stepping-stones.

Normally, when I am walking with any intent of putting miles behind me, I halt every hour, almost metronomically, and rest for ten minutes. When I came to the slough I had been walking for barely half an hour; but although I do not think I moved down into it with any firm plan in mind, I found that after standing in the open for a few moments, thinking how sad it was that I had frightened all wildlife away, I began to look for a shady resting place that would conceal me. For this sunken slough was clearly the kind of place that, even innocent of events, makes my kind of walking worthwhile, and I must have decided on the spot that it would be criminal, or at least plain stupid, not to pause and savor it. Within minutes, anyway, I had slipped my pack off and was tucked in under a bush that grew on a low mound, just above the stepping-stones, almost at the water's edge. The whole wide slough lay spread out before me.

I loosened my bootlaces, leaned back against the pack. And I stayed there in my "blind," or within a few yards of it, for two full hours.

It is once again going to be difficult, I think, to convey the sum of the very simple events that held me there—content, and often much more than content—for that span of time.

At first I suppose there were only the luminous light and the rustling, tinkling quietness and the fish. The fish, I could now see, were carp—an Oriental species, introduced into the lower Colorado in the 1890's, that had spread upstream for hundreds of miles. The carps' dark, curving, dorsal-finned backs kept breaking the surface of the channel's shallowest reach, just below the stepping-stones, a dozen paces from my hiding place. The backs broadcast slow, concentric ripples.

Occasionally, as the breeze fluctuated, I detected a faint fishy smell; but it seemed a paltry price to pay for Eden.

Perhaps ten minutes passed before another animal appeared: a single heron (unless the "herons" had been egrets) that mounted an apparent reconnaissance to determine if the intrusion were over. The bird obviously detected my "concealed" presence, for it quickly swerved away over the river and vanished.

Six feet to my left, at the water's edge, a flicker of movement: a sparrow-size bird feeding on flotsam. I watched it much more closely than I would have done a few months earlier. As I jotted down salient features in my notebook—yellow bill and legs, gray underbelly, speckled back, top of head white with two thick black bars—I found myself regretting, not for the first time since walking out from the town, that I had failed to buy a bird book before leaving home.*

The small black-and-white-headed sparrow took off across the slough. As I watched it go, my eye was caught by a big, black, hawklike, redheaded bird—the one that had flapped away when I arrived, or an indistinguishable other. It planed in over the lake, landed at the water's edge, a hundred yards away, and stood looking toward me. Through binoculars I

* Events in my glacially slow-moving bird-book field had recently taken a quantum lurch forward.

I had revisited East Africa, where I once lived, and my eyes had been opened to its astonishingly rich birdlife. I had bought a local bird book—and discovered that birdwatching was not just a matter of collecting species but a fascinating game that made you "see." Within days I was a full-fledged convert, always eager to try out the new plumage by reaching for my bird book. Before long I had determined, finally and resolutely, that I would, once home, buy an identification book of the birds of the western United States. In the weeks since my return I had several times teetered on the brink of going out and actually doing something about this resolve, but my formidable powers of procrastination had always succeeded in fending off the deed.

Now, sitting in my blind, I cursed those powers, and re-resolved.

could see that the redness of its head derived not from feathers but from bare red skin. The whole of the neck lacked feathers, in fact. I found myself remembering how, back in Kenya, while watching a vulture insert almost its entire neck through the anus of a dead zebra in order to get at its intestines (apparently because the hide was too tough for other ingress), I had realized that a neck devoid of feathers must be of considerable survival value to a scavenger, such as a vulture: feathers on its neck would collect blood and other liquids, and would quickly mat and become useless or worse. I think I was just deciding that the "hawk" was therefore almost certainly a vulture of some kind—and the more I tasted this brilliant diagnosis and considered the bird's general resemblance to African vultures, the more plausible it seemed—when the corner of my eye detected a hint of motion. It came from the shade of the trees that lined the far side of the channel.

I shifted attention. A coyote. It was trotting unconcernedly up from the direction of the main river, following the shade line under the trees. Color and markings and general persona suggested that it was the animal I had scared away. It came level with the stepping-stones, still in shadow, hesitated, then moved out over sunlit grass toward the place it had been eating something when it looked up and saw me silhouetted on the levee. It reached the water's edge, barely twenty paces from my blind, put its muzzle down, picked up the remains of a half-eaten carp that had been hidden in the grass, turned, walked back into shadow, vanished.

It must have been a considerable time later, I suppose, that another coyote, smaller and leaner, with a dark mark on one shoulder, came strolling up from the river. It approached through a strip of arrowweed, sometimes half concealed, sometimes invisible. It was momentarily out of my sight when I heard the sounds of a scuffle. Next instant, both coyotes erupted from the arrowweed onto open grass, a hundred yards from me. At first I assumed they were fighting. But it soon became clear that the larger animal, a female, was being propositioned by the smaller male, and was merely rejecting his advances. For all at once the skirmishing stopped and she was standing her ground and baring her teeth and curling her lips back and looking pretty damned discouraging, and he was standing quietly beside her, looking hardly at all discouraged, just resignedly patient. The pair stood there for a moment, almost motionless. Then they turned, trotted back together into shadow and once again vanished. I swung my binoculars back to where the hawk-vulture had been standing. It too had vanished.

About this time I moved out from my blind to confirm the identity of an object I had detected, through binoculars, lying in long, partly submerged grass bordering the channel. It turned out, sure enough, to be another half-eaten carp. Nearby I found several other remains. Some were mere skeletons that could have been chewed clean by coyotes. Other corpses lay with bodies untouched but heads pecked apart. One lacked only its gut. This mortuary, I now realized, generated the fish smell. Yet somehow the sickly stench did not convey a sense of death. Standing there in sunlight beside the calm, slow-moving shallows, I could see only a pivotal place where shoals of a species that ensured its continuance by sheer numbers would from time to time be terrified by sudden murderous attacks from an uncomprehended world; but a place that to other species—coyotes and vultures, for example—was a bountiful dining room. I saw, that is, only a sunlit scene of natural, healthy, productive recycling.

I had moved back into my shady hiding place when the coyotes reappeared. They came running and sliding down a low bluff that was half hidden by the line of trees, then trotted into open meadow, farther up the slough, and began walking toward me. By this time I had my camera ready. The two animals moved side by side toward the stepping-stones. I centered them in the viewfinder, pressed the shutter release. In that quiet place, the click almost reverberated. The coyotes stopped, looked toward me. Then they came on again. I took several more shots. The coyotes ignored the shutter clicks. They had almost reached the stepping-stones when, from somewhere out beyond the boundaries of the slough, in a world that I had forgotten, there came the bang of a car door being slammed. The coyotes turned, ran back into the trees, vanished yet again.

This time, they did not reappear.

Now that I have written down the insignificant events that I remember taking place while I sat in my hiding place in the slough (and notebook and photographs support memory in suggesting that what I say happened is essentially the sum total of everything that could be said to have "happened" during those two quiet hours), it occurs to me that there must have been longer pauses than I realized between events. True, pauses often lie at the heart of great music. But perhaps that is reaching for justification. At least some of the pauses that punctuated my two-hour sojourn in the slough were commonplace, utilitarian, mundane. I brewed my statutory tea, of course. And I scribbled some notes. But for much of those two hours, when nothing was "happening," I must indeed have just leaned back against my pack and enjoyed the place. Enjoyed, that is, the ongoing luminous light and the rustling, tinkling quietness and the fish that still kept breaking the calm surface of the channel with their dorsal fins and dark, curving backs.

I must, though, have spent at least a few minutes of those two hours in the slough studying my map. For at some point it occurred to me why the crass, engineering world behind me had suddenly ended. The map suggested—but was too rudimentary to confirm beyond all shadow of doubt—that the slough marked the southern boundary of a small Indian reservation. And when I had repacked my gear and swung the pack onto my shoulders and crossed the stepping-stones—which turned out to be not too blightingly inefficient after all—and had climbed the low bluff beyond the trees and was standing there looking back, with the probable reservation boundary drawn vivid across the forefront of my mind, I found I could see not only the emerald-green countersunk slough and the flat, man-struck plain beyond, with the straight line of the levee guarding its scattered and pitiful little buildings like the battlement it was; I could also see, beyond all that, just what we efficient, engineering, empire-building white men have done to the Colorado, to the desert, to the West, to the world.

When I left the slough and began to walk northward along natural, unleveed riverbank—across soil that, though still dry and stony, had been given meaning by its integrated humps and hollows and gullies, and had been softened into pleasance by flowers and shrubs and trees—I hoped I would be traveling for several days through such unspoiled desert. But after a few miles—around about the place the map suggested that I had reached the end of the Indian reservation —the riverine softness ended. Another levee began.

Behind it, man had so far touched the land only inter-mittently. At times I walked through stretches of uncankered landscape. But the desert, as I have said, is simple and frank and vulnerable, and even when man touches it lightly, with no intent of "improving" that particular place, he soils, cor-rupts, sometimes crucifies. Wheel marks persist for years, bulldozer tracks for decades, a narrow dirt road for centuries. And much of the country that lay between the slough and a dam twenty-odd miles upriver had been unsightlied by creeping roads and power poles and a scattering of cranky buildings.

On the third morning, soon after passing through a gate in a fence that was adorned with an odd pair of signs—one proclaiming the start of a national recreation area, the other warning "U.S. Property, No Trespassing"—I came to the dam.

The dam itself stood stark and stern, all concrete and metal and straight-line engineering. It had a certain cold beauty as it sat there, blocking the river, but it was the beauty of Wall Street on a Sunday, when you walk among its huge, deserted cathedrals to Mammon.

Above the dam, of course, the river ceased to be a river.

A natural river melds with the land it flows through. That is hardly surprising. The river has created the land. So its margins fit. Earth and water mate, merge, coalesce. Everything connects. All is harmony.

A man-made lake, such as builds behind a dam, lies awkward on the land. Except at highest water, its shoreline is scar tissue: a rim of dead and naked soil that the water's fluctuations have sterilized against both aquatic and terrestrial plant life. A discerning eye will also see that this ugly margin fights the land's natural contours. Earth and water now challenge, clash, grapple. Nothing fits. Nothing connects. All is discord.

Not everyone, of course, looks at the world through discerning eyes, and artificial lakes tend to be very popular with humans. They can indeed be superficially attractive, if temporary, artifacts. They provide—above and beyond their apparent and heavily touted short-term economic benefits—fishing and boating and easily accessible picnicking and camping. It must be admitted, too, that the unnatural tension between land and water can generate unusual and interesting scenery.

When I walked out into the country above the dam, my

tourist and photographic eyes delighted in a panorama of peninsulas and reefs and islands the lake had created when it pushed back into the stark, rocky upthrustings that I had expected to be hills but were incontrovertibly mountains. (These mountains, forming natural abutments on both sides of the river, were the reason the dam had been built at that point.) But my walking eye, taking in the same scene, knew all too well what those peninsulas and reefs and islands meant: the artificial relationship between land and water would modify the rhythm of my days.

I find that on almost any desert walk the days assume a certain basic rhythm. Except in cool or cold weather, I tend to sidestep the heat by waking early, walking from around sunrise until the temperature has climbed too high or my energy fallen too low, then taking a long rest through the heat of the day at some place there is shade and preferably water; in the cool of evening I travel again for an hour or two and then, as darkness falls, camp at almost any flat and convenient place.

Above the dam, the landscape imposed an overtone on this rhythm.

You can walk along most rivers—except in their deepest and starkest canyons—with reasonable ease: the river, as I have said, has smoothed your route. A natural lakeshore often provides easy going, too. But you can rarely find a practical route along the shore of a river that has been dammed into a lake. And when I came to the dam and looked ahead I saw at once, and remembered from similar situations ten years earlier, that the peninsulas and reefs and the fjordlike lagoons between them—created when the rising lake backed up into dry canyons—would keep forcing me inland. Even when it was possible to walk along the shoreline, its deep indentations would saddle me with a ridiculously serpentine route. So in order to travel in a reasonably direct line—or at least in one that was not too tortuous and time-wasting—I would often have to cut away from the lake and strike northward through the mountains, returning to the lake only when I needed water or when the shoreline looked as if it offered a promising route. Even beyond the mountains, I guessed, the shoreline's indentations, though less severe, would impose the same pattern on my days.

That is exactly what happened.

For the rest of the trip I spent most of my walking hours away from the lake, cutting across the grain of the land. (Even after I had moved beyond the mountains—with their spine, you will remember, running at right angles to the river, and therefore to my route—and was out in flatter country, all the drainage, and therefore the canyons and gullies, ran down toward the river, and therefore still at right angles to my path.) There were times, especially when heading back toward water, when I could take straightforward if foot-sucking routes along sandy washes; but mostly I weaved through a maze of minor gullies and low saddles, trying to hold a northerly bearing while making use of the best route the terrain seemed to offer. Because I lacked the topo maps that I normally carry in such country, it was an interesting exercise.

During the four rhythmic days that it took me to walk from the dam to the first boat marina, the map-free route-finding probably amplified the tension that is always there when you walk for pleasure—the tension between, on the one hand, getting from A to B and, on the other, seeing what lies in between. In the kind of walking we are talking about, the getting is only a motivational excuse; the seeing—really seeing—is what matters. And although the surface of my mind was at least intermittently occupied during those days by a whole spectrum of ongoing decisions, big through minuscule, about just where to head next—toward which distant saddle, along which low ridge, around or across this minor gully—I was at a deeper and more satisfying level constantly aware of the unfolding landscape.

When I first walked out beyond the dam into the mountains and left the man-world behind at last, I felt as if I had cast off a heavy cloak of restrictions; had escaped into freedom; had moved out into a place of new possibilities; into a realm given new edge by hints of danger.

The newness and the danger hints were both muted, of course. The country was new in the parochial sense that I had never visited those particular mountains before, but I had walked through many similar ones, so the newness was different from the newness of ten years earlier, at the start of my summer-long walk, when I walked out above my first Colorado dam into my first desert mountains. The difference was the difference between being a practiced city visitor in yet another new city and being a country boy in your very first. The dangers were different, too. Or, rather, the sense of danger. Ten years earlier, I had been edgily conscious that if anything went wrong as I walked alone through those first mountains, I would be in deep trouble. But since then I had, as I say, walked through many such mountains, and nothing serious had ever gone wrong. So I did not really believe that anything would go wrong this time. And although the remoteness and somber aspect of these new mountains added an edge to the walking, I was able to give myself up from the start to the fresh yet familiar virgin desert.

I found, at once, things I had almost forgotten. They had in a sense been there all the time, ever since I walked away from the town, but they had been screened off, muted, submerged by human overlay. Now they all came flooding back. The cleanness and openness, which I always, somehow, forget. The apparent barrenness and actual richness. The way the landscape seems at first to consist of nothing but rock and stony soil. The way even rock and soil often mutate. The way you at last comprehend, when you move in close, their own rich natural overlay.

From the dam, the mountains had looked drably gray. But once I moved out into them I discovered that their rock and soil were brown rather than gray—the old, mottled, burned brown that you sometimes find, or used to, on chocolate bars bought in hot climates. Soon I began to see beyond individual ridge and canyon, specific gully and basin.

Virgin desert, though concrete to the point of brutality, often resembles an abstract painting. Your eye follows flowing patterns: angled rock slab answering angled slab; soft gray slopes repeating, almost endlessly, into vast distances; close by, chocolate-brown hump echoing pitted, chocolate-brown hump; and always—because in the desert the earth's story is laid bare—swirls and convergences and subtle shifts of hue that signal dry watercourses, enormous, big and minute. Above the dam, I began to see these patterns, and to detect—connecting them, and much else too—an overriding and deeply satisfying unity.

Once I had walked out into the mountains I also heard, at last, the silence.

In deep desert, the silence is nearly always there, enfolding you. I am not talking, of course, about simple lack of sound, mere zero decibels. The silence I mean is something positive, something that lies almost physically over the land. Yet you are not often aware of it, except last thing at night or at first awakening. Then, though—and sometimes when you are merely resting briefly, or even walking—you hear its full, resonant richness and understand its value. You understand its value most clearly, and longingly, when it has almost gone—when you have just moved back to the fringes of the hubbub that emanates from the insistent animal, the noisy animal. It is then that you hear, clearly, a long way off, a sort of echo of the silence.

It was among all these concordances that I moved when I walked through the mountains above the dam; walked across the earth at its most naked and honest, rolling and jaggling away before me, mile after desiccated mile. It was not hot, back there in the desiccation—not hot, that is, in the way desert can be hot. Even in midafternoon my thermometer rarely registered over 80 degrees in the shade. Not that there was much shade, of course, except—as happened occasionally during those four rhythmic days I spent walking between the dam and the first marina—when clouds built up and covered the sun. Once or twice, the clouds even threatened rain. Then, an undesertlike mugginess hung over the mountains and, later, the plain. So it was always good, sun or cloud, to come back down, when the time was right, to the lakeshore. Often, when I got there, I stripped off such clothes as I was wearing and dived into the cool water. Afterward, it was almost luxurious to lean back against my pack in the shady alcove I always managed to find, in among the shoreline greenery.

Mostly, I took my long midday rests beside the lake—because it assured me of both drinking water and shade. The lake was essentially full, and therefore almost free from the ugly rim of barren soil that often afflicts man-made lakes, so I could spend the midday hours resting among curving branches of arrowweed or salt cedar, with waves lapping gently just beyond my feet.

I often night-camped beside the lake, too. I remember one camp, at the end of a sandbar that wind-driven waves had built across the entrance to a shallow wash, creating a small and separate wedge-shaped lake on its landward side. The evening was very calm, and the water fitted against both sides of the sandbar like glass, and when I had finished dinner and there was no longer the scrape of spoon against pot, let alone a roaring stove, silence lay over everything, soft and seductive. The day had already slipped through sunset, the desert's magic entr'acte, and now hung suspended, waiting for its curtain call. I sat there enveloped by those rich twilight hints that can blur your sense of time, and found myself looking out across the lake toward the faint black line that was the Arizona shore and wondering what would happen when, in due course, the dam crumbled and its lake subsided, then vanished. Would the vegetation in the once submerged river valley eventually return to its former state? Or would there be changes? And if men still walked the earth—or if our intellect-dominated twig of evolution had not burned itself out, and a post-man organism still thought along the lines we have established, though much further along them—then what would these creatures have to say about the changes? I fell asleep idly pondering the matter, still conscious of the pale but darkening lake that stretched away beyond my feet, soft and deep with suggestions. In the morning, though, the sun rose red and insistent over the Arizona mountains and re-metalized the water, and the mystery had slipped away and the question of the moment was once again "Should I follow the lakeshore for a while or detour inland up that first side canyon?"

Some nights I slept far back from the lake. I would leave my lakeside lunch site in late afternoon or early evening and, with full canteens, strike inland. That way, I got a good start, in the cool of the day, on a long detour through country that seemed to offer a more promising route than the lakeshore. After an hour or two it would be too dark for me to walk with safety—not so much because I could no longer see where to place my feet as because I could no longer be sure I would avoid putting them down on or dangerously close to a rattle-snake (for twilight is the active time for small mammals and therefore for their predators). At this point I would camp in any convenient, level and reasonably attractive place.

By "attractive" I do not necessarily mean "having a pan-
oramic view or delicately harmonious natural furnishings" or
even meeting any other of the esthetic criteria I tend to look
for in a normal campsite. If those were met, of course, so
much the better, especially in bright moonlight. I did not
strain for them, though: the site would be little more than a
place at which I dined, slept and breakfasted. Yet each inland
camp I chose at the last minute, in failing light, had its
charms. Almost any camp in open desert has, I find, a certain
attractiveness about it. There turns out to be something
clean, simple and refreshingly granular about virtually any
small open space once you roll out your bed there and sit
down and begin housekeeping. It makes no difference, or
precious little, whether you have chosen gravel or sand or
bare rock or even one of the flat, stone-inlaid plateaus called
"desert pavement." Perhaps it is a matter of the openness of
such vegetation as there may be. Or perhaps . . . But as you
see, when I try to isolate components, I run into difficulties.
I might even suspect that the notion of the attractiveness of
such places is entirely idiosyncratic—were it not that I once
received surprising third-person confirmation.

We were making a National Geographic movie in the Mojave Desert, in midsummer, and I was playing myself. After a
few nights in small, hot, scruffy desert motels I chose, rather
than checking into another motel with the rest of the crew, to
ask that they drop me off at some remote but convenient
roadside place where I could sleep in comfort and be up and
waiting, ready to be picked up next morning by the van-
borne crew on the way to our day's shooting. It was not only
that I preferred the idea of sleeping in the open, though that
was certainly the case; I also figured that by sleeping there,
on my own, away from people, I could next day come closer
to the feelings I wanted to have and to show when the camera
started rolling and I was supposed to be walking and camping

in the desert and in touch with it. I am not sure the crew altogether understood. The cameraman clearly did not. He was
an entirely city gent, immersed in the technicalities of his
craft—which he handled very well indeed—and contemp-
tuous of what he once referred to as "all this Boy Scout crap."

One morning when I had camped out as usual—on a
small gravelly plateau, perhaps twenty paces above a blacktop road—I overslept and was still eating breakfast when,
just as the sun rose, I heard the van pull up on the nearby
road. Seconds later I saw Eric the cameraman stomping up
toward my camp. His body language announced that he was,
as usual, overacting.

But when he saw me there on my miniature plateau, sitting up in my sleeping bag and leaning against the propped-
up pack, eating the last of my breakfast, he halted. For a moment he just looked. Then he moved forward again, more
slowly, and stopped just beyond the foot of my bed. By this
time he had shed his habitual air of irritation.

"Hm," he said. "Maybe you know something we don't,
after all. You made the right choice this time, that's for sure.
This is a whole lot better than the place we slept."

It seemed that he and the rest of the crew had checked
into a motel that turned out to be basic and dreary and dirty
even by small-desert-motel standards. And that night—an
unusually hot one even for the midsummer Mojave Desert
—the motel's air-conditioning system had failed. Eric and
the rest of the crew did not enjoy a restful night. Then he had
come up over the rise and seen me in my "Boy Scout" camp.

Now, that particular campsite had nothing special about
it. Nothing at all. I had settled for the first level and convenient place I found, out of sight of the road, that promised to
make the most of such natural air conditioning as the night
might offer. The site was just a small piece of open gravel broken by skimpy vegetation. It offered no specially fluent

curves, no delectable balances, no banked flower beds. In the morning light, though, I discovered with appreciation that I had, as mostly happened, chosen a clean, well-lit place for breakfasting. It seemed clear that the moment Eric saw me sitting there in the newborn sunlight, he too appreciated the place's attractions. And if Eric, of all people, understood (and after that morning his contempt for me seemed a tad softened), then I judge it to be clear, beyond all reasonable doubt, that the attractiveness I detect in such casual desert campsites is not entirely idiosyncratic.

In the desert, as in most kinds of country, it is at camps and lunchtime stopovers, when you are more or less stationary and silent, and therefore less intrusive, that you tend to meet other forms of life. In order to get to know your neighbors better, of course, you have to stay in one place for several days and nights. But if, as mostly happens, you cannot afford that luxury, you still find, in all but the most barren deserts, that you meet a surprisingly rich assortment of wildlife.

All through those rhythmic days above the dam, the animals—insects and reptiles, birds and mammals—kept appearing onstage. Their performances were far too subdued for commercial production, and rarely educational in any scientific or even direct sense, but in their quiet way they wove vital threads in the fabric of my days.

Mostly, the insects had undemanding, crawl-on parts. But then, that is the way it always seems when we look at the whole stage. The world of the insects (a form of life more widespread and in some ways more successful than our own) tends to fade into insignificance, even invisibility, when seen through the coarser eyes of our own life branch (which has had its own successes, certainly—unless, that is, you choose to label them disasters).

A brown grasshopper squats on a brown stone, superbly camouflaged; it is long and rakish yet markedly unexceptional, and its raised antennae somehow make it seem almost aggressively torpid. A heavyset beetle, its pitted, matt-finish black body washed in yellow modernistic patterns, patrols a wasteland of stones, mission unknown. A slim, all-black cousin seems similarly employed. Another cousin, sheathed in orange-and-black motley, tightrope-walks along a leaning flower stem to devour a yellow petal—and instantly suggests a vegetarian dragon, or perhaps a mobile paper shredder.

A bee buzzes into my lakeside camp. It lands on my right hand and, paying particular attention to the spaces between fingers, which I open for it, explores both the hand and the spoon I happen to be holding. I become aware of a sense of pleasure, curiously tinged with power, at knowing that provided I do nothing to anger or disturb the explorer it will— counter to panicky popular opinion—do me no harm. The bee, after investigating every spoon and finger surface and in spite of all the alluring scents finding nothing worthy of harvest, gives quick sequential once-overs to my left hand, my naked midriff, the closed plastic garbage bag and the foot of the sleeping bag, then buzzes off to pastures new.

On the second day above the dam—when I have decided not to walk in the evening, and then choose to linger on in camp next morning—I attend a rather longer presentation. A few feet from camp I find, in the warmth of late afternoon, a crater, eighteen inches across, with at its center a narrow slit into and out of which scurry the ants that have built the crater. Hordes of them are busy carrying up the inner slopes of the crater what to me are grains of gravel but to them must be huge boulders. The ants work fast, energetically. They dump their boulders just over the lip or partway down the outside slope. Only once do I see an ant, carrying a truly gigantic burden, discard it partway up the inner slope. In the cool of the following morning, with the temperature 52 degrees, the show still goes on—but only just. There are fewer laborers now, and even they move sluggishly. They carry their burdens to the top only rarely—and no farther than the inside edge of the lip. Many leave their loads—even minor loads— far down the inner slope. I take another drag at the caffeine-fix cup of tea designed to get my own operation moving.

During those days above the dam, the reptiles make only rare appearances, in small supporting roles. I meet no snakes, no turtles. But my boots keep sending lizardous base stealers racing around bushes so adeptly that even an alert and waiting rattler would have difficulty in—if you will permit a scrambled metaphor, not to mention a base pun—striking them out. Yet my most vivid lizard memory (conveniently rekindled by film emulsion) is of a dark olive ham, blue-spotted on top, yellow-spotted below, peering over the top of a boulder like a poorly trained infantryman.

The birds—a branch of life that took flight from the main tree when it was hardly more than a sapling (unless the revisionists prove right, and birds are really dinosaurs)—fill parts almost as low-key as the insects'. Every morning, or so it seems, at least one chorus-skein of geese flies over, heading north, up the lake. A mourning dove, departing a lone tree in a desolate basin, mourns. A raven flaps away over a ridge, black and craaaking. A large hawk with a red tail glides down to reconnoiter me; through binoculars, I see sun glint on the quills of its dark primaries; the hawk decides it should distrust what it sees, finds an updraft, soars quickly to sparrow size, dematerializes.

Some members of the company re-raise a question from Act One. Half a dozen big, black, redheaded, hawklike birds, the same species as the one that had watched me at the slough, sit statuesque and silent on a pair of dead trees, waiting, just the way African vultures wait—and I feel more convinced than ever that that is what they must be. Later, when a flock of small brown birds share my lunch place, I scribble down a peck of detail about bluntish bills and female breasts flecked brown and male ones washed with crimson, and regret yet again my nonbuying of a bird book and wonder if the scribbled notes will indeed, eventually, lead to an identification.

Down by the lake, a few members of the avian cast mount low-key cameos. A floating quintet of black troupers with big white bills—whom even I identify with confidence as coots —dive often and predictably, for some reason beginning each dive with a comical playing-to-the-gallery leap that for an instant lifts the plump little body clear of the water. Mid-afternoon: a blur on the fringes of my lunchtime alcove; and there, perched on an arrowweed stalk, less than four feet from my eyes, is a tiny olive and iridescent hummingbird, and I find I am smiling, the way you can hardly resist smiling when you meet any hummingbird close up. Another mid-afternoon: at the edge of my day's alcove, another hummingbird perches on an arrowweed stalk; it is very ruffled from having just bathed; as it spreads wings and tail in the sun to dry, I see for the first time in my life how the wings look when extended but not in blurred motion; they are very slender, very curved; in order to finish drying its feathers and shake them into place, the hummingbird keeps making odd little flights, including one 360-degree turn less than an inch off its perch.

During those rhythmic days beyond the dam there were also our cousins the mammals. As I walked first through the mountains and then across flatter, rolling country, they too appeared onstage—but, as with the other animals, only rarely and fleetingly, in short, undramatic scenes.

Deserts support many more mammals than you might expect. Most, though by no means all, are small species. I disturb the usual quota of desert ground squirrels, busily but warily harvesting around their burrows or diving back into them. Once, as I tramp down a sandy wash, a black-tailed rabbit bobs out from behind a bush, then stops half a dozen paces from my feet, and I stop too and watch the wind blow waves across its soft fur. Another time, with the light failing and my mind turning toward a campsite, I see, directly ahead, a coyote moving up a small hill that stands silhouetted against the pale western sky. I halt. The hill is highly photogenic: very conical yet nicely off-kilter, and discreetly dotted with bushes of various and intriguing shapes. The coyote makes full use of these props. It executes a slow cinematographic saunter up the hill's left flank, pauses for a moment at the very point of the bare apex, then sits down, deliberately, and holds that pose like a statue, facing directly toward its lone human audience. It sits so still that had I not seen it arrive my eye would probably have accepted it as another of the silhouetted bushes. For a long interlude we survey each other. The light continues to seep away. Then I remember practical matters. I move forward, once more hunting for a convenient campsite. When I look up at the hill a few moments later, its summit is bare.

I think it is that same night, camped in a gravelly dell, that I am several times brought half awake by mice investigating the dinner scraps adhering to my metal cup. I have set the cup on top of a pot, and my visitors' scurryings, gentle as they are, keep rocking the cup metallically against the rather battered pot lid. Eventually I come wide enough awake to switch the flashlight on and glimpse two or three tiny bodies blurring for cover. I reach out, shift the cup from pot to soft soil—and sleep undisturbed through the rest of the night. Next morning my cup has been harvested clean.

Because I spend only one night at that camp, my visitors remain anonymouse: I never really meet them. To get to know your neighbors, as I have said, you must linger for a while in one place.

Once, for good reasons,* I camped on seven successive nights in a shallow desert cave (a cave that also lay close to the Colorado River). I slept beside a ledge at one end of the cave, and among some stones near my bed lived a family of deer mice. The head of the family was Beelzebub, the mouse who came to dinner.

Beelzebub came to dinner my first night in the cave. Well, to be more accurate, he came just after my dinner, to *his* breakfast. When my flashlight beam first impaled him he acted like a very timorous wee beastie, but as he discovered the joys of the fragments left in an "empty" can of ham he began to brave it out more and more confidently. As he ate, I admired his big cocked ears and his sleekit, electrical alertness. I fell asleep to the sound of his soft scurryings.

After that, the scurryings were there every night. And Beelzebub grew steadily bolder. Soon, he hardly seemed to notice when I impaled him in the flashlight beam, and he would scurry close under my wrist to sample a piece of candle I had just put out for him. I began to offer him, while I was still eating, food fragments lifted from my cup. Night after night, as he kept appearing to share my meals, he grew more and more tolerant of anything I did.

Eventually—I think it was on my sixth evening in the cave—Beelzebub brought his wife along. At least, I assumed it was his wife. She was a size smaller than he and a great deal more timid, and after some deliberation I christened her Beelzebess. Soon, a third and even smaller mouse joined them: Beelzebaby.

On the eighth day I moved my bed outside the cave, again for good reason, and on a gravel patch in the wash below the cave's mouth I set up what I knew would be my final camp. That night, I was just finishing dinner when Beelzebub—who had found his way down forty or fifty feet of

* See *The Man from the Cave.*

trackless wash—arrived for what had become his accustomed breakfast.

"Good evening, Beelzebub," I said.

Beelzebub, as was his custom, said nothing, just got down to business. By now he was almost unrecognizable as the timid, light-shy creature that had come to dinner eight days earlier. He jumped up without hesitation onto the rim of my cooking pot—which I had floodlit by flashlight—then hopped down into it and went to work on the residual fragments of stew. To see what would happen, I rocked the pot, gently at first, then forcibly. Beelzebub did not even pause in his eating. And when, after he had scrambled out of the pot, I spooned some stew from my cup and put it in an open place and then, while he ate, began to stroke his back with a fingertip, he hardly turned a whisker. I began to stroke him with two fingers. Slowly, by small increments, I increased their pressure. Soon I was running my fingers along his back so hard that his legs were bending under their pressure and my fingertips could feel every detail of his backbone and tiny, whipcord muscles. Beelzebub went on with his meal. He did glance back a couple of times, as if not wholly approving of what went on—the stroking was by now more like a massage—but before long he seemed to accept this new phenomenon as a natural part of the odd but productive world that had recently opened up for him. Wondering just how far I could go, I let my fingers move further and further along his tail after every down-the-body massage stroke. At last they were sliding down its entire length. After one massage movement, I gripped the tail's tip, then, very slowly, lifted. Beelzebub went on eating. I raised the tail higher. Beelzebub's rear feet left the ground. Still no interruption in his meal. I went on lifting until, just for a moment, both front feet were off the ground too. Beelzebub continued his breakfast. I put him down. No visible change in eating arrangements. I waited for a few moments, then gripped the tail again and began lifting: rear feet up; then front feet up, too. Beelzebub went on nibbling. This time I lifted still further until he was dangling there, mouth suspended just above breakfast, so that he was no longer able to nibble. And now at last he reacted. He began to struggle—not fiercely, but in a comic kind of petulance. I held on. Still pettishly rather than angrily, Beelzebub bent his back and without undue haste climbed his own tail with his front paws. He reached my fingertips and—very gently, as if to admonish those offenders rather than hurt them in any way—bit one. He bit so gently that there was no danger of his teeth breaking my skin. But I let go. Beelzebub landed on all fours—and promptly resumed his meal. When I resumed stroking him and then lifting him a few times until his rear feet were off the ground, he went on eating without so much as a backward glance. And then, without warning, at a moment when I was not even touching him, he turned and scurried out into the night.

I switched off the flashlight and sat in the sudden darkness, waiting. But Beelzebub did not return. And next morning I left the cave.

In most deserts—or at least in most remote desert places of the kind that I tend to travel on foot—you do not meet too many members of today's insistent animal species: the one that is most painfully obvious almost everywhere, clear around our planet. But during those four rhythmic days above the dam I came across a considerable number of the species—or their droppings. The encounters covered a broad spectrum, from N to Z.

For a quarter of a mile above the dam I followed a fishermen's trail that wound along the lakeshore. I met no fishermen, but I had to step around one red bait container, several discarded plastic bags and a whole cemetery of broadcast beer cans. I passed a broken plastic bottle, too, bright blue, that hung high, deflowering a cactus.

As I picked my way through the mountains north of the dam I stumbled on two small, long-abandoned mining operations—now marked only by a few weathered posts and, in one case, angular scraps of old machinery scattered across bare rock like a rust-brown dinosaur skeleton. The relics rested silent under the sun, but as I walked past them my imagination peopled the place with the ghosts of salty, long-forgotten desert characters. (A correspondent pointed out to me recently that: "The desert distills men into types more surely than do our coastal climates.")

When I emerged from the mountains and moved across flatter, rolling country toward the first boat marina—deep inside the National Recreation Area now—less ghostly manifestations kept reminding me that I was walking through a human playground, not a wilderness. On the morning of the third day beyond the dam, because my supplies threatened to run low before I reached the marina, I was making good time along a road, far back from the lake—a wide, newly graded dirt road that was gross and ugly but undeniably useful—when far ahead, out over the plain, a dust cloud appeared. As I watched, still walking, the cloud gained size, definition and, eventually, a sound track. Then it had materialized, close up, into two black-shirted youths driving their raucous scooters like the wind. They raced past, departed my life and bequeathed me a cloud of brown, choking dust. Later that day, back beside the lake, sitting in a green lunchtime alcove at the head of a small bay, alone with the rhythmic waves, pollen-thighed bees and an occasional questing hummingbird, I was being largely successful in ignoring the roarings of boats out on the lake and of a plane high overhead, and even of somebody exploding something off to the north, when a bright red powerboat erupted into the bay, outboard blaring, its two young occupants yelling at each other, full throttle. Within ninety seconds the boys had silenced the outboard, continued to yell, cast their respective fishing lines, broken one of them, restarted the motor and barreled away out of the bay, still bellowing at each other like banshees. Later that afternoon, though, when I was on the move again but uncertain of how soon I could expect to reach the marina, a couple tent-camped with teenage daughter beside the lake gave me some needed sugar and white gas. At all these meetings, even the last, I was aware that I remained firmly on the outside, glancing in. In my notebook I scribbled an arrogant, self-satisfied comment: "Beware of the man who spends a lot of time on his own. He may make something of his life."

Next morning, exactly seven days after walking out of the dog-day town, I walked into the first marina. It was a shipshape establishment at the mouth of a broad wash, copiously backed by neat, geometric lines of mobile homes—a place as convenient and crass and soulless as all-hell-get-out. Judging by the steep bluffs that had been water-sheared in long straight lines along the wash's flanks—bluffs that spoke eloquently, for those willing to listen, of a raging flood that had swept down the wash no more than a few centuries earlier—the place would at some point indeed get the hell out.

The marina seethed with the insistent, heedless species. There was a small store and a restaurant, and I bought all the food and other supplies I needed and also achieved a change of lunchtime pace with a beer, salad and overdone steak. But I managed, without really trying, to stay alone in the crowd —still essentially outside, only glancing in. Now, I assure you that in feeling pleasure at remaining apart I was not being self-righteous. Not at all. It was just that the long sunlit days of silence, and the silent nights too, had attuned me to solitude, had left me a-jangle with crowds; and for the moment at least, I wanted to keep it that way. Solo backpackers and other solitudinarians will, I'm sure, understand. Others may not; may detect only a smug, holier-than-thouness. Too bad. If my disclaimer doesn't satisfy them, I guess all I have to offer is sympathy.

Just before leaving the restaurant I picked up a newspaper and discovered, five days late, that Martin Luther King had been assassinated.

Beyond the first boat marina, my already modest time pressures eased even further.

The map suggested that if I kept moving at the same pace as during the previous four days I should be able to reach the second marina in another four. But I now carried enough supplies for at least six. And once I reached the second marina there would still be no urgency. I'd have my long-planned options: I could head for home; or I could re-replenish supplies and amble on northward for another twenty map-miles. So I could slow down, effective immediately; could devote most of my mind to seeing, really seeing, the country I walked through.

That was the way it turned out. The new regimen indeed freed me. Above all, it freed me, somewhat unexpectedly, for more picture-taking.

Some years earlier I had belatedly perceived that worthwhile photography not only consumes large chunks of time but also tends to take the place of real looking—of printing scenes on the emulsion of memory. Since that day I had been weaning myself from cameras. On this trip, though, I had brought not only my Pentax but also a recently acquired set of close-up lenses. And between marinas I played with my new toys.

Now, play, at its best, instructs. And my new close-up attachments retaught me that although photography may often get in the way of seeing, it can on occasion open your eyes.

Mostly, on that leisurely, between-marinas lap of the trip, I photographed flowers.

Flowers are the springtime desert's prime glory. In a vintage year—which tends to occur about once in two decades —you have to be part-blind to avoid seeing the prodigal displays, even if you are racing down hardtop roads in an air-conditioned Detroit behemoth. In such a year, if you walk almost anywhere, but especially cross-country—as I had walked ten years earlier, mile after bedecked mile—then your progress becomes an ongoing parade, almost sinful in its teeming Technicolor plenty. Often, you cannot avoid crushing delicate blooms beneath your clumsy boots. Even in an average year—the kind I was now experiencing—you walk much of the time through lavish natural flower gardens.

I hardly seem to have mentioned the flowers I passed earlier in the trip. I have certainly done them no kind of justice: perhaps the extravagant displays of ten years earlier had inoculated me against a decent wonder. My notebook does record, briefly, the first cactus I had seen in bloom, back below the dam: a beaver tail, squatting there in customary dull green ungainliness but now proclaiming glory to the world from the top of one sad paddle; blazing it out with a single superb creation of curving, purple, beyond-porcelain-delicacy petals.

Now, free beyond the first marina, I kept experiencing not only glorious flower displays possibly matchable in other beautiful places but also some endemic to desert. One such variant materializes most often when you are crossing a barren mesa. You walk down into a hollow or pass a small plateau and by chance your eye comes almost level with the plane of the surrounding land surface. And all at once you are looking through a miniature flower jungle. You walk on, and discover, now that your eyes have been opened, that the whole mesa—the mesa that had looked so barren from a distance, and even as you began to walk across it—is clothed with a lacework of Lilliputian flowers. A lacework so dense, in spite of its delicacy, that it now conceals the body of the land. Afterward, you keep remembering what you have seen, and the new knowledge enriches your way.

At my second post-marina camp, where I lay over for a day, I spent four morning hours taking close-ups of flowers.

I shot ground-level side views, often against dark backgrounds, of routine riots of white "daisies" and yellow "dandelions" and "buttercups" and tall purple legumes of some kind. My new magnifying lenses gave them new emulsion-life. Through one of the lenses, a tiny, delicate flower, valiantly alone on a stony slope—an insignificant bloom I would assuredly have walked past without noticing—resolved into an intricate fretwork of five purple petals and five yellow-tipped stamens. Up on a nearby ridge, barren as the next, if not barrener, I dollied in so tight against one sprayed-out little plant that my field of view was filled with a jungle of succulent green, heart-shaped leaves and curling pink-and-white flowers that sort of stationary-writhed in grotesque shapes at the ends of delicate, juicy-looking, pale pink stalks; and now that I really looked I saw that these leaves and flowers and stalks were all thickly covered with white hairs—or perhaps it would be more accurate to say "tufts"—and that each hair or tuft held at its base what seemed to be a minuscule blob of water, so that the whole curling, writhing, surprisingly moist affair looked as if it ought to be growing underwater, in a tropical sea, rather than on a "barren" ridge in a sun-drenched desert.

In midmorning of that camera-ruled rest day beyond the marina it occurred to me to boost the power of my new lens toys with the small 10-power geologist's magnifying glass that

I always carry for prospecting and other reasons. The notion worked. Soon I was kneeling beside a little cluster, perhaps from a single plant, that seemed at first glance to be mainly small white flowers in full bloom but that on closer inspection, even by the naked eye, turned out to be so complexified by faded and also budding flowers, by living green leaves, by their dead, red-speckled predecessors and by a latticework of intertwined white tendrils apparently growing out of the leaves, that the whole, with its confused colors and structure, reminded me of a fussy Victorian parlor-table floral arrangement; and when I moved in for a shot with camera and close-up lens and the geologist's glass held in front of them I learned that each small white living flower was itself a complex and beautiful structure of dimpled pink and white petals surrounding yellow-tipped stamens that managed to be at once delicately slender yet ramrod straight, like beauty queens in a boot camp.

I do not want to suggest, though, that I spent the whole of that rest day crawling around behind my camera.

There is a particular kind of freedom that you commonly gain when you swing a pack onto your back and walk out and away for a week or so into wilderness, or something like wilderness. This freedom is a generalized sort of state, theoretically available to all of us all the time yet unattainable in the modern world, or at least rarely attained, even when we are on vacation: the freedom from external pressures to do certain specific things, often at specific times—getting up in order to go to work, for example, or just putting out the garbage because it's Wednesday. It is a well-known fact, comprehended by everyone who knows nothing about it, that once you get out into wilderness you break free from all such pressures. If you have ever been backpacking—or have even read with any care what I have been writing—you will know that, much of the time, this wilderness fact is, like so many, mere fantasy. New imperatives arise to imprison you: the plain impulse to walk that probably initiated your trip; the ongoing itch to cover miles; the pride that drives you forward to emulation of others' feats; the possibly valid urge to get to the next campground; or the entirely valid need to reach water or a food-replenishing point. It takes time, I find, to break free from these new, mostly ridiculous chains. Eventually, though, you can. The final break tends to come, obviously, at a moment when the urge or need to make spatial progress has subsided, for the moment or for good. Then, unexpectedly, you wake up to the fact that the freedom you imagined you would gain when you took your first step away from roadhead—the freedom you vaguely imagined you had been experiencing since that moment—is at last attained, in full. It is a good moment, always. But it is not necessarily a "big" moment. On that rest day between the two boat marinas it came to me, almost ridiculously but with great force, as I sat in camp taking my time, with absolutely no sense of urgency, about decanting another day's ration of powdered milk from its shop-bought foil package into the plastic container, once containing honey, that I use for squirting milk onto anything that needs milk squirted onto it. You could say, sure, that there had been other moments that were just as free, or apparently just as free, much earlier in the trip. Maybe. But it was as I sat there in my lakeside alcove, on the ninth afternoon of the trip, that I became aware of the freedom. Perhaps, come to think of it, what I have been talking about is not so much the freedom itself as awareness of it. Anyway, when the time comes at last and the event takes place, the thing to do is to wallow in it. That afternoon beside the lake, I wallowed.

I gave myself up, simply but totally, to the sheer pleasure —a pleasure that rarely moves up into our conscious minds —of just sitting and looking at a scene that stands with all its elements meshing in perfect concord. The elements of the harmonic desert mesh are much like those of the harmonic mountain mesh, but rather more open: gravelly gully interlocks with gravelly little spur; bright green creosote bush with gleaming open space; plant stem with leaves with crowning flowers. Always, though, in the pure form, the scene remains untouched by straight-line-drawing human hand. I suppose the pleasure we get from sitting and looking for a prolonged spell at such a simple scene is—though subtler and more absolute—of the same kind as the pleasure that flows in when we walk away from traffic and high-rises, or even sidewalks and bungalows, out into a green and easy city park.

That ninth day of my trip, after the knowledge of freedom had hit me, I sat in my lakeside alcove, innocent of clothes, and watched the wavelets breaking just beyond my feet and looked through the green archway of the alcove out over the wind-ruffled lake with its shifting pinpoints of reflected afternoon sunlight, and then looked beyond the lake at the stark dry mountains and sloping plains that stood in Arizona; looked at the plains and mountains that had all along been held separate, cut off, by river or lake, so that they existed in another world, divorced from mine, even though the rational part of my mind knew that they echoed—stone by stone, wash by wash, silence by silence—the desert I had been walking through. I looked at all these things and noted, in due time, the way green alcove archway and gentle wavelets and gleaming lake and parched brown Arizona plains and mountains, and the cloud-decked sky above them, all meshed into a perfectly attuned whole. I listened, too. I listened to the wavelets lapping gently just beyond my feet and to the insect buzz among the arrowweed and salt cedar leaves. And behind these sounds I clearly heard—lying almost physically over land and water, a long way off and yet so close that it seemed to touch my naked body—the huge, heavy, resonant, enfolding desert silence.

Early in the second evening at my layover camp I stowed everything back into the pack and walked on northward for an hour, then camped, with specific intent, near the mouth of a large wash.

The hour's walk had confirmed a lurking suspicion. From a distance, the last lap between the two boat marinas had looked as if it might offer very easy walking—across what seemed to be the flattest section so far of the plain that sloped down to the lake. Even from a distance, though, I had harbored doubts. I knew those flat, gently sloping desert plains. If you have to walk across the grain of the country—as I now had to, because of the lake's unnatural shoreline—the flatness almost always proves illusory. The plain is grooved—repeatedly, almost constantly—by small gullies, big gullies, huge washes. So you do not, as you might imagine, travel serenely across a calm, desiccated lake; you battle, hot and sweaty, from trough to wave top of a hurricane-whipped ocean that has congealed into sand and gravel and rock. My hour's walk in the cool of that evening had revealed, sure enough, just such an obstacle course: a constant succession of gullies and washes running at right angles to my path. And because of the relative flatness of the country, the lake sent long arms reaching back along them, deep into the desert. At their heads, some of these arms ended in bays bounded by cliffs a hundred feet high.

I quickly saw that a route along this stretch of shoreline, or even a short distance inland, was impractical. I would have to find a suitable wash—one that seemed to curl northward —head inland along it, and at the right moment cut back down another wash to the lake. It seemed to me that if I carried enough water and made the right choices, then one such detour, timed so that it lasted less than a day, should bring me back to the lake not far from the second boat marina. If I attempted such a detour, the important thing would be to get an early start, so that I broke the back of the day's walking before the heat bore down.

I camped that evening at the head of a big, shallow bay into which ran a wash that seemed to reach far inland and also to swing northward—though without a topo map I could not be sure. By the time I was ready to camp, a layer of dark clouds suggested a slight chance of rain, and therefore of a flash flood, so I chose a site not on the floor of the wash but on a low promontory at its mouth. Even in this excellent camp I spent—for reasons unconnected with safety—a mildly uneasy night. The air's oppressive sultriness may have contributed; but the prime disturbing factor was the knowledge that next morning I must make an early start. It almost always happens that way when I have not brought an alarm clock: I can wake myself before dawn all right, but my internal alarm keeps going off at intervals all through the night, bringing me half awake or worse.

That night, I set my "alarm" for 4 a.m.—and finally came awake at 4:05. The air still felt oppressive, and the moon, barely above the horizon, revealed clouds still covering the western sky. By flashlight, I checked my thermometer, left lying on the ground: 64 degrees. In my notebook I jotted, "Too hot for good walking day. Will prob be muggy." As I eased into wakefulness, the moon set. For the first time all trip, I had to prepare breakfast in real darkness.

My aim had been to finish breakfast, have everything stowed into the pack and be ready to start walking by first light, at five o'clock. I was twenty minutes late. And by the time I had filled a half-gallon canteen for the strike inland, retightened my boots and taken the first loaded step, it was

5:30, and behind me, far over the lake, a hazy sun was beginning to lip up over the Arizona mountains. Already it seemed to hint at scorching heat for what promised to be the longest inland detour I had yet made.

The first hour was indeed a long, rough drag up the sandy floor of the wash. At the start, my toes felt slightly sore, too, from wearing moccasins all through the previous day's layover. But the toes soon warmed up and the sun never really did. Not to the extent I had feared, anyway. By 7:30 I had turned up an arm of the wash that led, just as I had hoped, almost due north, and the clouds had shunted off to the south and the going underfoot had changed from soft sand to firm, gently sloping gravel and I had reached the head of that arm of the wash. When I halted for my hourly rest on a strip of bare, black-gray crest that had been my target all the way up the wash, I could see that my immediate route, across an almost flat plateau that was seamed by no more than minor gullies and broken only by straggly creosote bushes and scattered yucca and small volcanic boulders, promised even easier walking. I reset my sights, with reservations, on a notch between two low, distant hills. By 10:15 the notch seemed within easy grasp. I stopped for tea.

By this time I must have felt that the pressure was off, for I see from my notes that the tea break lasted an hour and a half. I spent that pleasant interlude in the shade of my red poncho, hastily rigged as a roof with nylon cord threaded through some of its grommets and tied to creosote bushes. My staff, thrust up at an angle through the poncho's neck aperture and held in place by its hood, kept the roof high and admitted every vestige of a pleasantly cool breeze. I was surprised to find the thermometer, hung in the shade, reading as high as 84 degrees.

When I walked on at last, refreshed, I no longer hurried. I passed through the target notch, angled along a ridge and found myself looking out over another plateau. I halted. The breeze brushed soft music from scattered cacti. Ahead, the plateau's stone and gravel surface stretched away bright and glaring beneath the noonday sun. There had been a time when I would have viewed such a place as barren and hostile; but now I comprehended, even at first glance, something of the complexity that underlay the barrenness, and understood that the apparent hostility lay in the eye of a beholder; knew that—provided I had water and did nothing stupid or unlucky—the open plateau, with its flat, easy walking, was my friend. And standing there on that high and open place, where there was no hint that man existed on the planet, I could once more hear, loud and clear, behind the gentle breeze, that huge and hanging desert silence.

After a while I strolled on across the plateau. When, half an hour later, I angled down a gully, I found that it led, sure enough, into a wash that promised to cut directly down to the lake. By 1:30 I was standing on the shoreline.

I shed the pack, stripped off boots and socks and shorts, dived into the cool water, swam a few strokes, turned and climbed out. And afterward, when sun and wind had dried and cooled me and I had set up camp in the day's alcove, with wavelets lapping just beyond my feet, I knew that the eight-hour detour, though far less demanding than expected, had done its job. The challenges—of the day, of the trip—had been met, the needs assuaged. The excitement of returning to the desert had worn off. For the moment, I had had enough walking. But whatever had been ailing me a month earlier when I stood in my shower, deep in ennui, no longer ailed. I was restored—and eager, now, to return to the other world.

At lunchtime next day I walked into the second marina.

The place was less elaborate than the first, but somehow a shade less impermanent. I went past the little floating dock with its cluster of boats, past the dusty red gas pump at its shore end, past the sloping ramp with its turmoil of pickups loading and unloading small outboard-powered cabin cruisers, and walked up into seething Easter-weekend crowds. I had forgotten it was Easter.

In an open space near the small green cafe, two young blond Adonises, tall and sunburned and muscular, were tossing a football to and fro. When they saw me, pack on back, they aborted their Unitas dreams and came over and asked about where I had been.

They seemed to understand about coming back into the "real" world.

"Yeah, there's a newspaper stand over there," said one of them, pointing. "But if I was you I wouldn't read any of 'em. There's rioting, all over the country."

"Because of Martin Luther King?"

"No," said the other Adonis, suddenly dark. "Because they've nothing better to do."

I went into the cafe and with marginal hopes ordered another steak. The lunch marginally fulfilled my hopes. Afterward, I phoned Las Vegas airport and made a plane reservation home for Monday morning, two days ahead. I figured that by Sunday evening the Easter crowds would have thinned, everywhere, and I would come back to the marina and try to hitchhike into Vegas in plenty of time for my plane next morning.

I put down the phone and went out into the sunlight and walked back through the Easter throng, past the dock and along the lake for half a mile until I found a pleasant little notch in the barren rocky shoreline. It was an insignificant spot, but arrowweed and salt cedar grew there, providing the necessary alcove. It promised to be as good a place as I was likely to find for a twenty-four-hour stopover.

After the marina, it was quiet in my green hideaway, alone once again with an alcove's curving archway and lapping wavelets and the wide, wind-churned lake and the distant Arizona mountains, now lying flat and supine in the afternoon glare. Sprawled out almost naked in the speckled green shade, I hardly heard the roar of boats entering and leaving the marina. I could even block out, most of the time, the cacophonies of a noisy party camped in the next bay and equipped with hydroplanes. As I lay there in the heavy afternoon heat I let myself drift back, slowly, over the last twelve days. The terrain had indeed turned out to be much tamer than the desert I normally chose, so I had faced no trenchant physical challenge, made no startling discoveries, experienced no new visual delights. In a sense, it had hardly been a desert trip at all. Not really a wilderness trip, either: only for brief interludes had I escaped the insistent animal. More than most trips, it had been languorous, uneventful, largely shapeless. Even such vague form as was now beginning to emerge seemed all wrong: its climax, or something rather like it, had come in the wrong place—at the slough, at the very start. And yet, now that it was over, I felt content. More than content. In spite of everything, they had been twelve good days. Very good days.

I dozed, woke, dozed again. And then, at one reawakening, I saw that, back behind my little niche, the sun had eased down almost to the horizon. Most of the shoreline already lay in shadow, but the sunlit, breeze-touched lake still gleamed like pewter. I dozed again, briefly, reawakened. Now shadow covered the lake. Its edges once more fitted the desert like glass. Beyond it, the shadows were reaching out across the Arizona mountains, and even the remaining sunlit slopes had begun to soften toward evening. In the next bay, hydroplanes continued to buzz like massive, raucous flies. But beyond them, out in the hidden desert to the west, and out over the lake and the distant Arizona mountains, I could hear, still hanging heavy, still lying almost physically over land and water, the huge, enfolding desert silence. Or perhaps, now, just an echo of that silence.

4 Less Than a Day's Walk

Please do not assume that before you can wholly enter green and secret places you must heave a pack onto your back and stride stalwartly out into the unknown. That is certainly the surest and potentially richest path. Yet down the years I seem to have harvested a very fat crop of memories from short, unladen walks.

Some of these strolls were around local corners, others in distant lands.

Three or four times a week, I take a brief, brisk walk up a steep hill near my home. Most days, I follow a narrow road that twists through woods. I go mainly for exercise and often walk with my mind folded into itself and therefore cut off; but the woods are always there, calming or stimulating me according to their mood and mine. In slanting sunlight, half-hidden glades gleam brilliant green. In a winter storm, the dripping trees dance dark and slow. At night, shapes and shadows and silences invite, repel. Once, near the top of the hill, I met a fox. Always, when I come back down, I am a subtly different person from the one who set out.

Occasionally I take my walk up another part of the hill. An old construction road, now pleasingly overgrown, skirts at a respectful distance the house of the man who has given me permission to climb his sector of hillside. Where the road ends, a barely visible trail angles up through a band of poison oak that is just dense enough to parry all but the most mulish pedestrian. Beyond, the trail becomes steep and diffuse and branching. My usual route runs up a little gully that is a soft and sloping sanctuary: bracken, three kinds of fern, contorted live oaks festooned with Spanish moss. Some years ago I used for a while to see, near the foot of the gully, children's footprints that led to a meeting place tucked away in dense brush; and just this morning I found, at about the same place, an inexplicable bright orange golf ball. But mostly the hillside bears no trace of any two-footed animals except me—only of the deer that created and maintain the trails. I rarely see the deer, though. In fact, I rarely see any other mammals, except ground squirrels, either while I am climbing the gully or when it ends and I strike out onto a steep, open, grassy slope. This slope is precipitous—the sort of place no sane human would want to walk. Within fifteen minutes I have reached the top of it and if I want to can angle off into thick woods— all ferns and moss again, cool and secretive; but generally I halt on the open hillside, pause for a while, and just look out over the flatlands. A hawk or turkey vulture may plane past. A ground squirrel may emerge from its burrow to investigate the strange intrusion. All around me, the grass plunges green, or brown. A half-gale blasts across the slope, or summer sun beats down. I think the elements—always keener in that high and open place—help amplify my changed perspectives. I know, anyway, that as I sit or stand and survey the familiar stretch of country from my eyrie, I sometimes discover roads and houses that I did not know existed, and always I find that I can look out beyond known landmarks to vistas hidden when I am living down below. High on that plunging hillside, I also seem to gain a sense of new relationships between the familiar physical landmarks. Between other landmarks, too.

I know I am lucky, of course. I now live in shruburbia. So enclaves of the natural world surround me. But even in cities—most cities, anyway—there are parks; and you can often walk along riverbanks or seashore or across pieces of "wasteland"—our term for urban land not yet consumed by Mammon. (You can also walk on concrete, of course, and have a great time, but that is a horse of a different gait.)

The two cities I most recently lived in both had, if you knew where to look, delightful byways. Close to my apartment in one city, a pair of parallel paths cut through adjoining blocks along the banks of small creeks that still ran "unimproved"—that is, undesecrated. Within five minutes I could circumambulate these paths and be back home, restored. For birds built nests along the paths' little green alleyways. Once, a possum, crossing from sanctuary to sanctuary, heard me coming when he was in mid-tarmac and played his curled waiting game until I was well past. Mostly, though, there was just the greenery. And mostly it was enough.

On the outskirts of both cities, within easy driving distance, lay big hilltop parks, ideal for longer walks. One summer day, two of us—helplessly and idyllically in love—climbed the "unimproved" side of one of the parks. Hour after hour we angled upward, pausing occasionally to look back over a panorama of grass-covered hills that rose smooth and curving and beautiful as my companion's breasts. We saw no people, only birds and deer—and plunging slopes and billowing grass and sunlight and open space and the steadily widening panorama. By the time we reached the paved summit, just before sunset, we had been cleansed and purified, and we felt sorry for the poor people who had driven up to that crowning place in cars.

Later, in the second city, I often made the ten-minute drive from my apartment to a smaller but still spacious hilltop park and would climb to the crest and walk alone along it. There, too, I found steep grassy slopes and open space, and air of the kind that makes you drag deep and meditate on the smog lying sallow over rooftops, far below. Details of the many walks I made along that crest have blurred, now, into a pleasing tapestry of grass and space and sunlight. The lone salient memory comes, curiously enough, from one of my rare walks up there after dark. The events were strictly atypical, too; but they taught me, by an unexpected route, something new.

That night, the crest was swathed in heavy clouds that hid what little moonlight there may have been, and in order to avoid using a flashlight I walked along the only stretch topped by a hardtop road. The road was closed to vehicles after dark, and I rather think to pedestrians, too. I had gone perhaps half a mile when I heard, up ahead and off to the right, somewhere deep in the dampness, a human cough. I hesitated, then kept walking. As I passed the place the cough had seemed to come from I peered into the darkness. Nothing but the night. I strode on. A dozen paces, and I found myself remembering that earlier in the day I had heard a radio report about an inmate who had escaped from a nearby prison. I quickened my pace a notch. I was wearing rubber-soled boots and my footsteps made little sound, but now I made sure I put my feet down very softly. And I began to listen. Still nothing but the night. Fifty yards down the road I halted, listened more carefully. This time I heard, faint but clear, footsteps. I strode on again, a little faster but still treading softly, telling myself not to imagine foolish things. It might be illegal to walk along this road at night, but other people had as much dubious right as I to do so. Twice within the next hundred yards, though, I halted again and listened. Still the muffled footsteps, still following. I began to peer off to the sides of the road, looking for an escape route. The road must have dropped a little, or the clouds have lifted a shade, for light from the city below, reflecting off the clouds, now mitigated the blackness, and just after rounding a sharp bend I made out, off to the left, a swath of some kind—no doubt a firebreak—that had been cut through thick brush, at right angles to the road, directly down a steep slope. Stepping even more softly now, I turned off the blacktop and began to ease down this Red Sea–providential route.

The cut was recent, and the soil almost bare, so the going turned out to be less difficult than I had feared, and quieter. Soon I was well below the road and feeling safe enough to stop again and listen. I am no longer sure whether I actually heard the man's footsteps go on down the road, but I know I quickly became convinced that he must have passed; and I felt sure—assuming he had indeed been following me—that it would be a long time before he realized he had lost contact. Still, I decided to play it safe. Perhaps, I thought, the track will branch, or I shall come out onto open grass and be able to circle back to the road. I moved on down the slope. Almost at once, the track forked. I turned left. Twenty minutes later I stepped back onto the blacktopped crest road.

I had thoroughly enjoyed my detour. The unusual experience of cutting through thick brush at night, in rather poor light, had in itself been mildly exciting. But the high points had been two close encounters of an illuminating kind. For from them I had learned, with immediate gratitude, and with a certitude no book could have imparted, that the broad white stripe a skunk wears along its back must surely have evolved as a warning sign to any other animal that close-encountered one of them, even in poor light: as soon as the intruder saw the stripe, standing out clear as a beacon, he could back discreetly off before the skunk had to use its nifty protective weapon.

Many of the individual day walks I have taken down the years, in a myriad places, now tend to merge into a blur. Incidents stand out, though, like stalagmites. Some of these protruding memories are slight and simple. In a pine grove, an orange fungus pushes up through dark, dead leaves, bearing on its plateau two pebbles and a small pyramid of soil with a crimson flower still growing from the apex. In the shallows of a creek, a very large salamander climbs laboriously to the top of a shelving rock, comes face to face with a very small trout, and turns back. A nestful of jays, almost ready to fly, squawk and scrabble with outspread wings on the circular lip of the only universe they have ever known, fluttering blue and beautiful as they beseech weary parents for yet more food; I stand watching, wondering what they remind me of—and realize it is a styful of pigs, jostling at the trough at feeding time as they importune the approaching pig man.

Sometimes the pictures that flick up are more general and less granular—and of places rather than events.

One of them can be called local or exotic, as you wish. On a return visit to my native Wales I spend a sunny winter's day walking to the top of a small mountain near the cottage I am staying in. The locals protest, wide-eyed: "But you can't go all the way up *there!*" It turns out to be a stroll, and by noon I am sitting on the summit and can look out across the mosaic of neat green fields and watch a toy train puff white-plumed in a wide, slow-motion curve around the base of the mountain. That is all; but the memory sticks.

At times, the pictures are of ostensibly ordinary places, uncluttered by events. Just frozen scenes, really, from widespread locales. A trail curves into a meadow that nestles small and green and private among dark trees; the trail skirts its edge, cuts back into the forest. A creek swings clear and cold around a granite buttress that might have been filched from a Gothic cathedral. An ancient oak, barnacled with lichen and Spanish moss and clearly on its last roots—as it has been for decades—arches smooth and eloquent over the entrance to a little oval basin.

Often, though, I find my mind roving back to quite different moments.

It is dusk, going on twilight, and the moon rises over the flank of a hill that two of us are climbing, on the outskirts of town. This moon is not only shocking yellow and implausibly immense but also engraved with a series of thin black horizontal lines. We stop and stare. And we go on staring—until at last we comprehend that between us and the lifting moon there rides a posse of power lines.

The sun is rising over rolling grassland and I am walking through light mist along the crest of one slope when I see, pasted vivid on the next, my own shadow. The shadow is huge, and outlined with a brilliant, pulsating band of brightness that fits snug around my moving outline, and I slam to a halt and proclaim, to the innocent hills, "Jesus Christ! I've got a bloody halo!"

As I have said, almost every day's walking generates an interval when your mind breaks free, soars, works as you wish it would always work. Not all the thoughts you generate are useful, though, let alone profound. Even when mildly memorable, some of them can seem, given their birthplace, to be downright quirky.

Walking in some place that has since faded from memory I once solved in a flash of blinding inspiration the profound problem of how to report, simply and economically, the essence of a basketball game. All you had to do, I saw, was plot a small graph that charted the fluctuating point-gap between the teams. Inserted at the head of a newspaper report, or flashed on a TV screen, such a graph would convey at a glance—far more vividly than the box score's dry statistics, let alone most written or spoken reports—the game's ebb and flow, its essential rhythm. In my magnanimity I hereby cast this pearl, free of charge, before the sports sty.

Once you start walking you are never safe from such brainstorms. Not long ago I took a short walk just after reading an article on quantum physics by Martin Gardner in *The New York Review of Books*. Gardner is a mathematician and writer who has commented delightfully on the books of Lewis Carroll, notably in *The Annotated Snark*. As I walked, my head must have been roiling with bizarre terms used in the article: recently discovered particles such as quarks (red, green and blue), bosons, tauons, gravitons, gluons and muons, not to mention "pointlike" leptons; concepts labeled "spin," "weak force" (carried by W and Z particles) and "flavors" that can come "charmed," "top" (or "truth") or "bottom" (or "beauty"); also such acronyms as CERN and GUTS and SUZY. Anyway, as I walked along, harming no one, there shafted up into my mind (much as the original apparently burst unbidden into Lewis Carroll's mind) the last line of a verse. And in due course of time that germ developed, step by step, into:

Malice in Wonderland?

"Just the place for a quark!" the Gardner raves
  As he dibbles each truth with flair,
  Disporting his force in the weaks of the waves
  With a tauon entwined in a snare.

"We must strive to disCERN all lepton spin
  As we hunt for the boson's mate:
  Any quirk in a quark is a graviton sin
  That brings gluon—a death worse than fate.

"As we search we should scour each field and fold
  Seeking quarks, from beauty through Z,

For unificationist theories hold
That a quark can house bosons—maybe.

"We'll pointlessly peer with our pointlike rhyme
In the GUTS of all SUZYs, too,
While riding eleventh-dimensional time
Down the meons and baryons blue.

"But the snare to beware of in every choice
Is the man down the road who with glee
Announces at last in a positron voice,
'Well, a quark *is* a boson, you see.'"

But don't get me wrong: your walking mind does not squirl only with what some people would call frivolities. It makes contact, through all five senses, with simpler, earthier issues.

You cross a creek that is tinkling Debussy—and catch the delicate scent of wild strawberries. You pause, pick a few. Then you lean back against rough, sun-warmed granite and savor their velvet sweetness and watch small white clouds scud by above green, whispering treetops that are suddenly telling you many things, but mainly that life can sometimes be awfully bloody good.

In time, as you begin to connect, you discern new resonances. Strolling in a city park, past some old buildings, you register the pattern of patched and therefore variegated shake siding, or of a supporting wall crafted from smooth granite boulders, then find yourself looking down on a flock of pigeons being fed by children and suddenly detecting, in the birds' crowded slate and brown bodies, echoes from the patterns you saw in the old buildings. Later, you again detect echoes in mussel beds left dry by low tide, in eucalyptus leaves lying haphazard on brown soil, in the straight trunks of the eucalyptus grove itself, in the close-up detail of pale wheat chaff piled in mounds in a farmer's field, even in the mounds themselves when seen against a backdrop of distant grassy hills that are also pale and rounded. Later, out beyond the man-world, you find yourself making similar connections between a desert cactus "garden" and a meadow painted orange with wild poppies; between a pattern of mud cracks in a dry lake bed, of erosion buttresses along a crumbling bluff, even of the charred and therefore squared-off markings on a burnt tree trunk. You stand looking at the nut-storage reticule bored in rough pine bark by industrious acorn woodpeckers: some of the holes are dark and gaping, others shine with fresh brown nuts; and all at once, reviewing these echoes, you find yourself recalling that variegated shake siding on the old park building. The element connecting all these things within their web is a delicate filament that hangs suspended between mind and eye, and it will, I'm afraid, not translate adequately into words. It is there, though, hanging, and once you have detected it you never lose sight of it for very long.

Sometimes, on a very short walk, you can cross world boundaries.

One gray and overcast, downcast day, I drove along a stretch of remote and rugged coastline toward a beach that could only be reached, I was told, by a trail down a precipitous, thousand-foot cliff. That was why very few people visited it. When I reached the cliff top, rain was falling, gently but with determination. Looking down at the ocean that has been called "the eye of the world," I could see it only as a somber suggestion, deep in a general murk. For a long time I just sat in the car and morosed, passing in review a parade of splendid reasons for not getting out. In the end, though, I pulled on boots and parka, and plunged. Outside, the rain felt soft and almost welcoming, as I had known it really would. But the farther I went down the cliff, the more deeply my boots squelched into the mud and puddles of the narrow, hanging trail, and although the rhythmic pounding of the waves grew louder, the grayness only deepened. The trail ended at last and the waves broke close and surging. Beyond their whiteness a turmoil of gray water merged impercepti- bly into gray cloud. Gray beach stretched flat and pallid along the foot of gray cliff. Even the swath of tangled logs that litter all our local beaches looked gray rather than brown. The rain fell only intermittently now but squalls kept gusting down the beach and drawing drab gray screens across it. In all this scene I could detect no sign of the hand or foot of man.

I turned right and began to walk along the beach. Except for the waves and the turmoil beyond them, everything lay inert. The beach stretched flat and unending: it tapered off at last, like the sea, without real termination, into gray mist. Above it, the cliff loomed stark and silent. At its foot, the swath of sea-roughed logs lay heavy, ugly—the sawn-off ends a badge of logging, not of natural events beside the rivers that had borne them down to the sea.

I walked on along the beach, as close to the water as I could, well clear of the logs, trying to forget them: logging angers me more than almost any other human activity. But all at once, out of the corner of my eye, I saw one of the logs move. I stopped, looked again. No doubt at all. Fifty yards away, at the foot of the cliff, one of the gray-brown shapes among the endless jumble was making spasmodic little move- ments. I lifted my binoculars. The log, suddenly bigger, still jerked and quivered. Then, in one of those sharp twists of vision that leave you wide-eyed, it turned into a sea lion.

I lowered the binoculars, began to angle up the beach. Soon I could see that the sea lion was very big. I came within twenty yards of it, paused, then moved forward again. The animal was facing away from me, toward the cliff, but I expected it at any moment to detect my presence. I was within ten paces and moving cautiously before I saw that its eyes were closed and realized that it was asleep—and that the jerkings and quiverings could only be the outward signs of inward dreams. Very slowly, I moved in closer. At length I stood no more than three or four paces from the broad, rounded butt of the huge torpedo. For a long time I just stood there, looking. Somehow, it had never occurred to me that sea lions dreamed; but watching the erratic, almost convulsive movements that kept twitching whiskered head and sand-flecked flippers and even the flank of the smooth, gray-brown body, I had no more doubt about what I was seeing than I do when I see a dog dreaming before a fire.

I must have stood there in the soft sand, just looking, for five or ten minutes. Twenty paces away, the waves surged and pounded. Occasional light rain squalls gusted by. They kept the sea lion's skin wet and glistening. I began to know the feel of the skin, the pattern of its blotches. But there is a limit to what you can get out of sea lion watching when the animal is asleep, even when it is pantomime-dreaming; and at last I began to talk, very quietly. It seemed not impossible that if I could wake the animal gently enough it might accept my presence as nondangerous and let me discover what it was like to stand within three paces of a conscious, noncaptive sea lion. Perhaps we could even converse, in our fashion.

My first quiet and soothing words clearly failed to penetrate the screen of sleep. I raised my voice a little, in competition with the waves; a little more. The sea lion's one visible eye flicked open. The head turned. And then, before I had registered any change in the eye's expression, the body reared up and twisted around toward me and the mouth opened. At least, I think the mouth opened. And I think it uttered some unfriendly sound. That is certainly the impression I now carry. What I know for sure is that the sea lion was no longer very big but gigantic—and that it was surprised, scared, hostile, menacing. But my recollection of precisely what happened in the first seconds after it awoke was, even at the time, curiously blurred. I had to reconstruct our physical movements later, from the story inscribed in the soft sand. Our foot- and flipper-prints showed that I moved sharply backward, stumbled a little, regained my balance, then retreated several more steps; meanwhile, the sea lion had continued its rearing motion, come down on all four flippers with its head pointing seaward—and kept going.

The rest of our meeting I can remember clearly. With an awkward and comic but remarkably fast motion, eloquent of panic, the huge animal flipper-flubbered down the sloping beach, slid into the water, switched from comedy to poetry, dove under a wave. Just beyond the first line of breakers it turned and looked back at me. For a moment it floated there, black head against gray water, watching. Safely in its own element, it no longer seemed more than residually afraid. After a while it swam slowly and in a gentle curve back to within a few yards of the beach. There, for perhaps five minutes, it floated, thirty or forty paces away, peering at me. At last, apparently tired of man-watching, it turned, swam seaward, vanished.

I walked on up the beach. Soon, I sat down on a log and ate my sandwich lunch. Rain squalls kept sweeping by. The screens they drew seemed less drably gray now; they hung translucent, almost diaphanous, filled with pleasing hints of mystery. Even the logs angered me less.

After lunch I walked half a mile farther up the beach, then turned back. I had passed the sea lion place and almost reached the foot of the trail when, out beyond the breakers, something caught my eye. I halted, peered, lifted my binoculars. The squalls had given way to a steadier moisturizing of the air—not so much rain as a fluctuating curtain of mist —and drops of water kept running down the binocular lenses, so that what I saw through them was blurred and distorted, like the view through a window during a downpour.

At first, all I could see, out beyond the breakers, was an anonymous expanse of roiling, white-flecked grayness. It was a fitful expanse, too: deep troughs between swells meant that much of the sea's surface was always hidden from my sight. I had begun to doubt the reality of the anomalous something that had caught my eye when another something appeared near the edge of the binoculars' field. Just for a moment a blurred shape, thin and vertical, hung whiter and more defined than the background of wind-whipped water; then it had dissipated and once more there was only the foam-flecked grayness. For long minutes I held the binoculars in place. Nothing. I lowered the binoculars, peered with pursed eyes. Almost at once, off to the left, for a long, rolling moment, there was a shape; a shape so obfuscated by mist and roiling water that it was barely more than amorphous—but was still somehow definite enough, as long as it lasted, for me to classify it as black, or at least dark, rather than white, and as vaguely horizontal rather than vertical. A moment later I glimpsed another shape, similar and yet subtly different, very close to the place the first had just vanished. And then from this second shape there rose another slender white column, more definite this time, so that before it too dissipated into mushroom shape and then nothingness I knew what I was seeing.

Ten minutes must have passed, while I stood there in the mist, peering out beyond the breakers—sometimes through binoculars and sometimes without them—before I felt sure there were two whales. And another twenty minutes must have passed before it dawned on me what they were doing.

It was difficult to judge, in that flat, mist-washed grayness, just how far from shore the whales were performing their dance. And the distance varied. But I would guess it averaged three hundred yards. Sometimes the mist thickened and the range seemed far greater; sometimes when the curtain lifted, or almost lifted, it seemed much less. Yet even in the clearest interludes there was a blurred uncertainty, a constant indefinition, to the dark, rolling shapes that kept breaking the sea's gray surface.

When I had patched together enough glimpses I knew that one of the shapes was larger than the other, and a different shade of dark. Eventually I also understood that the two subtly different bodies kept moving slowly around each other, so close that at moments they seemed potentially intertwined, like circling wrestlers. But the bodies did not move like fighters, opponents. They rolled and glided around each other in stately and beautiful harmony—companionable, affectionate, loving. There was something musical about the dance, even something erotic—and it seemed all the more beautiful for being played half-concealed, out there beyond the breakers, in slow-moving troughs, behind shifting, translucent curtains. Perhaps the sense of privacy was what triggered my empathy, and sudden comprehension: was what made me realize that that was how you moved—or imagined you moved, if you thought about it—during certain transported interludes.

But perhaps I did not understand, there on the beach, about the delectability of the half-concealment. For I attempted to penetrate the screen—as we logical, inquisitive humans nearly always strive to penetrate the unknown. I turned and walked back to the foot of the cliff and climbed the trail until I could look down at a steep enough angle for the troughs between the waves to be visible.

The view from my new vantage point was if anything a little more blurred: I had moved farther away, and the curtain of mist tended to be thicker. But now, with the sea troughs laid bare, I could see the dance more continuously.

And my last doubts vanished. The two whales were making love—or at least flirting, foreplaying.*

I stayed for a long time at my vantage point partway up the cliff, watching the huge, dark bodies of the two whales appear intermittently, far below; watching them glide and roll lovingly around each other—entwining, as it were, in mime. At last the gray curtain of mist thickened and blotted out the ocean. I turned and began to walk back up the trail. By the time I reached cliff top and car, the rain was once more falling steadily and with determination. But now only the outside world stretched gray and morose.

A day walk taken when you are traveling in a strange land can stand out vividly in memory. The reason seems obvious. Yet when I rummage among my memories, back down the years, I find that the prime imprint is not necessarily of exotic terrain. Not, that is, in a straightforward, because-it's-different sense.

In at least one case, the unfamiliar terrain turned out to be a negative factor.

I had stepped ashore, for the first and so far only time in my life, on the Hawaiian Islands, eager to taste the much-advertised local wonders. Doubly eager, in fact, because for a week I had been penned in an ocean liner—a mode of trans-

---

* That evening I phoned a sea mammal expert and he confirmed my judgment. The whales—gray whales—were at that time of year returning north from their calving lagoons in Baja California, and their regular breeding season was over. But whales—and other cetaceans—are among the few groups of animals, other than us, with the wit to recognize lovemaking as so delightful a pursuit that it should be indulged in, or at least played at, well beyond the childbearing imperative. They also possess the hormonal control, or lack of it, to practice what they dream.

The expert said he had never actually wondered whether sea lions dreamed, but now that he considered the matter he felt it highly likely they did. Almost certain, in fact.

portation I dislike but had to accept, for goodish reasons, on the first leg of a longer trip.

I stepped ashore, unavoidably, in Honolulu. Within half an hour I had been exposed to Waikiki—not the beach itself, as far as I remember, but its concrete shoreside accretions, which were more than enough—had found a Forest Service headquarters of some kind, had learned that a ranger was about to make a one-day foot trip into the nearby hills, and had arranged to accompany him.

To my surprise, I carry only vague memories of the hours we spent walking in the hills. The drive to trailhead, yes. And wide, sunlit skies. Beyond that, though, few details linger except a hilltop view of Pearl Harbor, distant but distinct, sprawling open and bleak beyond a broad, flat and barren plain. I felt, I remember, that it did not look like a place conducive to decent history. Almost all my memories of that day, I find, are equally subjective. And as joyless. For what remains imprinted, beyond my initial and overwhelming desire to get the hell out of Honolulu, is the impression of an island ravaged by man with even greater thoroughness and ugliness than is our current human custom.

But a curious thing has just happened: I have looked at the color slides I took that day. And this rather less subjective record of reality reveals a very different picture from that served up by memory. Now, photography, too, can lie. But the impression the slides carried away from the hills—or rather, as I now see I should call them, the mountains—is of unspoiled, often precipitous country, similar to but richer than a certain California coast-range wilderness that delights me at home. The pictures reveal small patches of forest, too, and close-ups of gorgeous flowers, some delicate and retiring, some brilliant and striking. (They also include a shot of the ranger apparently measuring trail mileage with a bicycle-wheel device. This was no doubt at least one object of his mission—and one I had completely forgotten.) Anyway, the point is that my photographs show beautiful mountain scenery, at times bordering on the grand, and I am left wondering why my memory recalls only rather cruddy hill country, degraded by man. It may be that I photographed, as we all tend to, only outstanding scenes. Or perhaps I felt disappointed at the lack of the lush tropical forest I had somehow expected from the islands. Again, it could be that the initial revulsion at Waikiki has never let my memory off the hook. Anyway, whatever I or a chamber of commerce may want to think, the uncomfortable fact remains that the memory I carried away from the island paradise of Hawaii—or, to be more exact, from Oahu—is essentially cruddy. Odd.

Another memory surfaces from later on that same long journey. By this time I was traveling on a six-passenger freighter—a sea mode I find incomparably more pleasant than an ocean liner but one that is now sadly almost a thing of the past. After eight or nine weeks aboard, the last six without sight of land, we docked at Victoria, capital of the Seychelles, a thousand miles off the East African coast—and walked ashore into a time warp.

At that time, no regular passenger ship visited the islands, and there was no airport. A flying boat did sometimes service a U.S. satellite tracking station, but you could apparently get aboard it only if you had done something for Lyndon Baines Johnson lately.

The islands' inaccessibility somehow fitted their history. The French occupied the uninhabited archipelago in 1744, but in 1814 the British took over. The resulting mélange had worked: the French knew how to live, the British how to administer; and the current inhabitants—a few French and British, many Indians, a preponderance of Africans—seemed to a visiting eye to live a life that was gay and charming, without chaos or even undue and debilitating laxity. My visit, mind you, took place in 1967. Soon afterward I read with sadness that the British had decided to put in a large airport—ostensibly to encourage tourism but clearly for strategic purposes. Ten or fifteen years later, sure enough, I was reading of political nonsense in the newly independent Seychelles, with comic-opera local coup and abortive, foreign-led countercoup. And not long ago I heard reports of a Russian "vacuum" fishing ship patrolling offshore and sucking giant prawns into extinction. But in 1967 civilization—except for the small and mercifully hidden satellite tracking station—had not yet infected even the main island of Mahé. Its only grating sign of progress was one brand-new, rather shame-faced Shell Oil sign above a gas station on the main street of Victoria. So you walked off the ship, as I say, into a time warp.

The walking proved delightful, both in Victoria itself and then when three of us drove over to the far side of the island in an old, standard-shift Austin taxi that was not in the best of shape, perhaps because the driver recognized only second gear and therefore used it exclusively. On the far side of the island we found, lifted straight out of Somerset Maugham, an unassumingly perfect little hotel on a long, white, palm-fringed, deserted beach; and I learned that, not far beyond this Eden, the road and its attendant straggle of human occupation ended and that then there was nothing but a foot trail along uninhabited shoreline.

Our second day on the island, I took off for the trail. But the straggle of human occupation turned out to be much more difficult to pass through than I had expected. I had to pause at a humble but neatly kept little house, shaded and greened by banana trees, built close beside a big, beautifully rounded granite boulder that was etched on its moist and shadowy underside by a swirling pattern of ferns and pale green lichen. Then there was a bigger, more European house with an external circular stairway in delicate metalwork and a matching, beautifully proportioned veranda. Next, a modern school, the incipient severity of its angular concrete stairway tempered and even given dignity by subdued coral-block walls and finely balanced metal rails, and by a swirling kaleidoscope of neatly dressed young girls of all colors. Another small house sat almost hidden behind a startling mass of what looked at first like too garish plastic flowers but turned out to be luxuriant plant leaves—green, yellow, red, brown and something close to purple. An African youth passed, a load of huge fish suspended from the stout wooden post he carried on one shoulder. An African girl, no more than seven, wearing a white, red-flowered dress and a wide, matching straw hat, coquetted across the road as if she were indeed in Paris. When the road and the people ended at last and I came to the trail, I was almost sorry.

The little-used trail wound through low shrubs around the curves of the rather barren, indented shoreline. Sometimes it snaked among granite outcrops that were as beautifully rounded as the one that had neighbored the neat little house; but these shoreline boulders had weathered so dark as to look almost black, and therefore much more severe. Where the trail crossed creeks, banana trees and other tropical plants formed small, protected groves of lush greenery, and beyond them, up at the heads of steep valleys, I could glimpse knobby, dramatically upthrust peaks. But mostly, as far as I remember, I walked along bleak hillsides, a hundred feet or more above the sea, and segregated from it. The day was pleasant enough, and after the restricted weeks at sea I certainly welcomed a leg stretching on solid soil. Perhaps, though, with the sea pounding away below and reaching out unbroken to the horizon, that part of the day was too similar to shipboard life. I know, anyway, that when the walk was over it lingered as one of those rare cases in which my memories of the man-world remain more vivid than those of the green world.

The opposite was most explicitly true for a few hours I managed to snatch, slightly footloose, on the Mongolian grasslands.

It was the summer of 1980. China had only just been reopened to foreign tourists and you could travel only in groups. All through the month during which our group of twenty Americans was herded across the breadth of the land—from Hong Kong westward to the Sinkiang desert, near the Russian border, then back east—I had been working on our guides, softening them up to the idea that at some point I might want to go off on my own for a few hours, on foot—just to get a different perspective. At last we reached Inner Mongolia, and as we drove into a small commune on the edge of the grasslands, three thousand feet above sea level, in which we were to stay overnight, I felt almost sure the time for my solitary walk had come.

Minutes after we had checked into our yurts—traditional Mongolian house-tents made from animal hides and felt stretched taut over collapsible wooden frames—I was walking westward across an open plain covered with short, close-cropped green grass. I walked in a straight line for no more than half an hour, and I walked slowly, for I was just getting over a virus infection that had poleaxed most of our group, one by one. But the reconnaissance focused my intent.

As soon as I left the commune securely behind I walked into silence. Real, untrammeled silence. It was my first such silence, I realized, since we had flown out of San Francisco: no one would accuse China of being the quietest corner of the world. Above me, fleecy flat-bottomed clouds cruised a wide blue sky. The clouds sent dark shadows scudding across the open, sunlit plain.

I climbed a low ridge and sat for a while watching the sun slip down toward the horizon. In the last moments before it set, the moving ribbons of sun-flooded grass between the cloud shadows gained an even greater richness. From a distance, these emerald-green ribbons looked smooth, almost sandpapered; in nearby swaths, each tuft of floodlit grass stood in rough-textured relief against its elongated shadow.

After the sun had set and quietness had fallen over the plain, I lifted my binoculars and made certain practical observations. Westward, beyond the ridge, lay roads and other human signs. The broad hollow in which our commune lay was hardly wild land, either: I picked out no less than seventeen scattered groups of buildings. But immediately north of the commune, beyond a river, rose a line of low hills, and they bore no man-made scars. By the time I stood up and began to walk back toward the commune in the evening silence I was almost sure I had found what I wanted.

Next morning, as the sun rose, I slipped out of our yurt into crisp upland air for another quick, confirming reconnaissance. I hurried through the northern outskirts of the commune, past free-ranging goats and rabbits, past chickens that pecked delicately at new-laid human feces, and headed out beyond the last of the long adobe buildings. The north walls of the buildings were sternly door- and windowless— because of bitter winter winds, I had been told; it was certainly easy, even in September sunshine, to understand how it would be on those open steppes once winter clamped down. I skirted a scattering of black cattle and came to the river. It was very shallow. Paddling across barefoot turned out to be a cold business but well short of bone-chilling. Minutes later I stood on the crest of the low green hills and could see, northward, a promise of the openness I had hoped for. I was back in the commune in plenty of time for breakfast.

Immediately after we had eaten I walked out northward again, canteen at hip, fanny pack stuffed with the special picnic lunch our guides had, after some initial reluctance, arranged to be put up for me.

Later, when I looked back on my little stroll over the grasslands, it seemed—as it so often seems with my walks in retrospect—that almost nothing had happened. Only twice, both times near the start, did I meet people. As I sat drying my feet on the far side of the river, a man and his two young daughters, herding a flock of sheep *en famille*, came smiling toward me, and although we lacked a mutually intelligible word we had an amiable and pleasing powwow. Later, when the virus weakness came flooding back and I sat resting in a shallow depression, out in the middle of rolling nowhere, a lone sheepherder appeared on a nearby crest, strode toward me, halted barely three paces away, and stood staring down at me. He was a scruffy, semi-shaven, middle-aged man, anything but amiable. He wore impenetrably dark sunglasses, a white cap, dirty black coat, thick gray pants string-tied at the ankles and thin socks and flimsy slippers. Slung across his back was an umbrella. In one hand he carried a stick with a roughly made metal scoop at its lower end. The man just stood there, almost within arm's reach, staring down at me. He stood there for four or five minutes—silent, blank behind his sunglasses—simply staring. Then, without warning or sign of emotion, he turned on his heel and walked back over the crest. A little later, when I moved on again, I passed him at a distance and learned that he used his metal-scoop stick to pick up stones and fling them at sheep that strayed from his flock, thereby encouraging them to move in a desired direction. Those meetings—with man and daughters, then with solitary man—were, as I say, the sum of my human contacts. But then, I had not come out alone in order to meet people.

One specific if mundane thing I had hoped to check as I walked northward was whether the grass, which around the commune had been cropped short and sparse, and had eroded into frequent bare gullies, would begin to grow longer and thicker and less deprived. In the course of the few miles I walked, the grass showed no sign of change, the eroded gullies no sign of abating.*

---

* Our guides had delicately evaded the thrust of our questions about what seemed a clear case of overgrazing around the newly static homestead of a people who centuries ago had adopted a nomadic way of life in order to prevent just such a situation. It had been a very dry year, the guides said.

As it turned out, I did not walk far, that semi-footloose day. The virus weakness kept forcing me to rest, and barely a strong hour's walk from the commune I stopped for an early lunch—and learned that in China you must not assume that because you have consistently been served hard-boiled eggs for sit-down meals you will get them cooked that way for a picnic lunch. I also learned, sort of, how to clean soft egg yolk from every cranny of a fanny pack. After lunch I dozed, woke feeling stronger, pushed on northward.

But do not let my litany of trivia mislead you about those hours I spent alone, out on the Mongolian grassland.

I walked free, in silence, beneath a wide sky, across open, rolling greensward. In the distance, half a dozen cattle moved slow and black up a curving, sunlit slope. At my feet, among wide-spaced tufts of grass, grew clumps of pink-and-white daisies and occasional dark blue "trumpet cups." Grasshoppers equipped with rich red rear ends rose before me and hovered against the breeze, clapper-rattling; buff-coated cousins rasped rhythmically. A larklike bird planed away, low; a swallow swooped close; high above, a skein of geese arrowed eastward. And always, all around me, I had sky and green grass, space and silence—and the wind.

At first there was only a gentle drifting of the soft, mid-70-degree air, but by the time I reached a long ridge that fell

---

Yes, it was true that about a hundred and fifty kilometers farther north, the people, although organized into communes, still lived the traditional nomadic life. And yes again, it was true, as we had been told, that three-quarters of the 340,000 Mongolians who herded their cattle and sheep on the grasslands now lived in permanent commune dwellings; also that they herded almost four times as much stock as they had twenty-five years ealier, before "the Liberation." And yes again, in spite of this fact, the guides said, the grass did indeed, as we imagined, grow taller as you went farther north.

At least, that seemed to be the gist of what the guides said—though we had learned by now that a mist of uncertainty permeated all the official information we got in China, especially from our eager guides.

steadily away to the north, the wind had an edge to it. Not long after I sat down on the crest of this ridge and began trying to absorb the vista that had opened up, heavy clouds came barreling down from the north. Rain squalls built distant gray parallelograms. Soon, thunder rumbled.

Yet the new somberness suited the new view. The plateau that rolled away northward, mile after mile, was now mostly a dark and almost leaden green, though leavened still by candlesticks of sunlight. Off to the west, one small dirt road soon curled away out of sight. Through binoculars I could just make out, within the first few northering miles, half a dozen small, isolated buildings. But beyond these minor warts stretched long, green, virgin vistas. Halfway to the horizon, a single dark mountain thrust up, indistinct at the edge of a rain squall, hopelessly out of reach, infinitely alluring.

It was easy to imagine, a hundred and fifty kilometers into that vastness, scattered groups of men now officially organized into communes but still living the nomadic life that Mongols had lived for centuries. It was less easy, somehow, to imagine that another two hundred kilometers north you would come to the Soviet border—source of obvious and edgy concern not only in Peking but also at "our" commune. For standing on that ridge, it was the somber natural scene that filled your mind. The distances. The vaulting sky. Beside them, the deeds of man wrinkled into pettiness.

And when I stood up at last and began to trek back toward the commune, I knew that as I sat looking out over that vast and silent vista I had moved closer to the land than I had been in all the escorted, vehiculated days of the tour that had swept our little group to and fro across the breadth of China.

When I summon up into memory a perambulation I took in Rio de Janeiro—perhaps the world's most beautiful

and vibrant human city—I find that there is no doubt at all
about a certain exotic place being the prime imprint.

I had just jetted across the South Atlantic. My last
glimpse of land had been near the start of the eleven-hour
flight, with the midday sun beating down red and harsh,
thirty thousand feet below, onto the startlingly barren sand
desert of what is now called Namibia. Hour after hour, then,
there was nothing but blank sea beneath us, and when we
banked in over Rio at last the city shone clean and brilliant
in a cool, early evening light—and I fell at first sight. I must
have seen, as we drifted in low and slow, the richly indented,
island-studded harbor and the gleaming, close-packed sky-
scrapers that appear on slides I shot from the plane; but what
dominated my mind—must surely dominate the mind of
everyone who has been there—were the granite domes that
thrust up, huge and smooth, not only around the city but
within it, so that they form a part of its megastructure.

During my five days in Rio I walked for many hours along
its streets and promenades and beaches, reveling in such
idiosyncrasies as sinuous-patterned mosaic sidewalks and in
the gaiety and panache of its people, especially the women-
folk. (An American historian whom I met on one of these
walks turned out to be a specialist on Brazil, and he offered
the mock-serious opinion that when the miniskirts then in
worldwide vogue had become a memory elsewhere, the
women of Rio would continue to wear them.) But the walking
hours that come jutting up from my memory are those I spent
on the Sugarloaf, one of those gigantic granite domes.

The Sugarloaf stands within the city, on one of the harbor's many arms. (It would be more reasonable, of course, to
say that the city has embraced the Sugarloaf—but adopting
our normal homocentric view probably conveys the situation
more clearly.) The dome rises steeply from the sea—almost
sheer in places—for 1,290 feet. It is "served" now—or was

at that time—by a combined funicular and cable-suspended gondola system that ultimately deposits you, already almost overcome by stunning views of city and harbor and surrounding mountains, in a tourist enclave perched on the dome's summit.

But there at the summit, I found, it was all man. Crowds leaned against railings, staring down at the city. In such a place you could only see: your other senses became sealed off. And even the seeing was superficial. You could buy beer, of course, and the harsh Brazilian wine, to ease you over the hump. I watched a scraggly little waiter, bored to extinction, tossing metal bottle tops over the edge of a parapet. A jaded young wife with a tight mouth kept glancing from the stupendous vista to the humdrum husband standing beside her. A thin, lonely-looking man seemed to be searching for a homosexual mate. Two girls chattered, high-pitched. But before long I found, somewhere, a reasonably concealed exit from the enclave. (I saw no explicit prohibition of escape out onto the natural granite; but authority tends to frown on such deeds of sanity, and once they have frowned it is less easy to escape their gaze, so if you are wise you look for ways to do what you want to in "innocence.")

Out beyond the enclave there was at first, growing in soil trapped in a ledge that seamed the solid granite, a surprising wealth of vegetation: grass, plants, shrubs, even good-sized trees. Almost at once, this vegetation cut me off from possible detection. It deadened the sounds of the enclave, too, so that I walked alone—over terrain that sloped only very gently. Once I had escaped, there were no indications, as far as I remember, that anyone else had done the same thing. (I am not really suggesting that nobody had done so; only that the miniature forest seemed—or at least seems in memory—almost pristine.)

The physical details of just what I did once I had escaped

the tourist enclave remain curiously vague. (All this happened twenty years ago, and I seem for some reason to have taken no photographs, up there on high, after the escape, to hint in a mere objective way at just what I did.) But I know that before long I came to the edge of the vegetation and there was only bare, rough, sunlit granite sloping away in front of me. I am almost sure I managed to make my way— very slowly, very carefully—for a considerable distance down the slope, in growing surprise at being able to do so. A part of me is convinced that I went a very long way indeed down that slope. I certainly remember sitting, at some stage of these or neighboring proceedings, on bare, sloping granite only a few feet above the ocean—but I think I must have traversed out to that position from the foot of the dome, before going up to its summit. It certainly seems difficult to believe that, although I know I spent a long time up there on my patrol out from the consecrated summit, I managed to climb more than a thousand vertical feet down the precipitous slopes of the Sugarloaf.

But these physical, itinerary details do not really matter. I know the important things. For I can still remember— graphically, potently—the feeling of freedom, out there on the sunlit granite that stretched deliciously rough and open and shining all around me but quickly became smooth and seductive as it sloped down and away toward the sea. The rock was clean and glorious, and the sky open and shining too, and wrapped so tight around me that there was no one else on the planet—except, of course, for those specks far below, in miniature streets and miniature boats, and they did not quite count. So I stood or sat out there alone with the air and the light and the sound of the sea, far below, surging white on gray rocks. Occasionally, though, gray-black hawks circled by. Once, quite close, there was a huge, thin-fuse-laged, streamlined bird with narrow wings sharply crooked amidships—a design as efficient compared with a crow's (if fast flight was what you wanted) as is a modern jet's compared with a biplane's. There were occasional silvery man-birds, too—tiny straight-line mosquitoes jetting to and fro, far above—but they took their proper place now: potentially seminal, but temporary.

Now that I have paused in trying to write down what I remember, I find there is little else to say. That day above Rio, no profound philosophical revelations descended on me. As usual, nothing happened, really. I do not even recall coming back "in." But twenty years later I still remember that interlude out on the open, sloping granite, surrounded by sunlight and air and a sense of unstoppable freedom. I remember it with gratitude.

There is one other day walk taken in a strange land that stands out in my memory. This time, the reason underlying the special nature of the walk is not really the exotic terrain itself but certain of its specific and particular qualities that are not immediately obvious to us humans but that draw its teeming population back, year after year, to precisely the same place. These inhabitants are the monarchs of Michoacán.

The plain, objective facts of the case—though they pale beside the reality—are remarkable enough.

Late in the summer of each year, as temperatures begin to fall, the big orange-and-brown monarch butterflies that are widespread and fairly common throughout North America set out on long journeys. Those living on the Pacific side of the Rockies migrate westward, to California. The remainder—a far greater multitude—funnel southward, into Mexico. There they congregate for the winter in dense, clustered colonies at a few isolated sites northwest of Mexico City, mostly in the state of Michoacán. All the colonies lie in mountain forests, about 10,000 feet above sea level. The number of resident butterflies varies from year to year, but a current estimate is 100 million.

In the spring, as temperatures rise, the monarchs begin to travel back northward—to Kansas, Minnesota, Saskatchewan. But no single individual ever completes the long double migration. A butterfly that in September moves south from a wood in Wisconsin may be replaced the following June, in the same wood, by its grandchild or even greatgrandchild. We humans do not yet know how a family pulls off this trick—how three or four generations succeed in finding their collective, successive ways two thousand miles south and then two thousand miles back north—in most cases to and from the same locality, even the same trees. But the key could be magnetism: imprinted in the genetic code of each monarch may lie a magnetized map of its personal migration route.

At their overwintering sites the butterflies tend to rest and conserve energy; but on warm days many of them take flight to drink nectar and water.

These bare facts pale, as I say, beside the reality. Or at least beside my personal reality.

I had traveled to Michoacán in early December to see the monarchs, and was lucky and privileged enough to visit an overwintering site with the man most responsible for protecting it against human progress. Two of his friends came along, too.

It was midmorning, and we had been walking for twenty minutes along faint forest trails, when my companions halted. At first I could find little to see. High among some of the dark and towering conifers hung huge pendulous clumps, black and inert, that my intellect identified as clusters of butterflies; but the forest shadow lay so deep that I might as well have been looking at swarms of bees. A few butterflies flickered among the treetops. Otherwise, nothing moved. After all the travel and expectation, this passive reality seemed faintly disappointing.

I was still fighting to deny the disappointment when my companions began to drift up toward a rock ledge, just above the site. I followed. The others seated themselves in widely separated places. I chose a little niche at the lip of the ledge. Each of us sat motionless, in silence—apart, alone, turned inward.

From the rock ledge I could look directly into the main mass of clusters—and I found them transformed. There were many more of them than I had thought. They also hung less blackly now: sunlight had begun to slant through the trees, printing each cluster with subtle patterns. The sunbeams continued to pour down more and more strongly, warmer and warmer, onto the monarchs, and all at once I realized that they had responded by exploding, silently, into pageant.

The space between ground and treetops now danced with butterflies. Yet the individual flutterings that filled the air merged into a single soft and aery motion that was not merely free of anything as positive as pulsation but flowed so dense and constant and random that I could not detect in it anything so gross as aim or even drift. I found myself recalling the silent, wayward sweep of particles through a physicist's bubble chamber; the calm, accelerated swing of planets across a movie screen. But this languid forest spectacle flowed vivid orange against the dark trees. And it was not silent.

The sound track emanated, I soon determined, from the rock ledge on which I was sitting. The ledge supported a straggly undergrowth of shrubs and flowers. Among them flickered a minor multitude of dancers who had strayed from the main pageant, and the beat of their wings against foliage created a low but sustained whisper, as if a gentle rain were falling on broad leaves. This sound furnished the mesmeric dance, high above, with a harmonious, enriching accompaniment.

The onward-swinging sun warmed air and pageant. I sat and watched and listened. Minutes or hours passed. My companions stirred into life. We held a brief, hushed consultation. They had been to this place before and would come again, and they understood my unspoken needs. They left to visit another, nearby colony.

Alone, there was a difference. The monarchs even seemed to trust me more. They began to settle—not in large numbers, but by ones and occasional twos—on my bare legs and wrists, on neck and face. The soft tickle of their fluttering wings massaged body and mind. Soon I no longer felt a mere onlooker; I began to let myself imagine that I had become a part of the pageant.

A monarch landed on the back of my left hand and sunned itself, quivering wings held wide. I resisted a temptation to reach out with the other hand and brush a finger over the velvety nap that clothed the wings. Another monarch slapped into my shoulder and stayed there, flickering, gripping the jacket's coarse red fabric, even more ephemeral and beautiful because it was too close for my straining eye to force into focus. The butterfly moved slowly along my shoulder, still flickering, still unfocused, and disappeared somewhere behind my neck

A small cloud covered the sun and a cloud of butterflies descended into my little niche. The sun reasserted itself. The butterflies responded, and as they struggled back up out of the undergrowth their wings beat against the foliage and the whispering, gentle-rain sound track surged, then subsided. Many monarchs remained, clinging to plants or resting on the stony ground. A few lay flat, inert. Among that vast and vital host—resting below and dancing above—the dead, though sad at first, spelled solid continuity.

I picked up one of the corpses. The black veins that seamed its wings were not, I knew, really veins: they were ducts down which there flowed, as soon as the butterfly emerged from the chrysalis and began to unfurl its limp wings, a liquid that set stiff and so held the wings rigid, like the spokes of an umbrella. I could now see that the "veins" were not black, either, but a deep, resonant brown. I could see how one section of an inner vein thickened into a small bulb that was a sex-linked male scent pocket. I could also admire the white-on-black mosaic bands that framed the wings, and the delicate dots and bisecting white line that decorated the humped head. I could even see that the head was covered with sleek brown hair, soft and seductive as a woman's.

Gently, I laid the dead insect back on the ground. Nearby, a bumblebee, solid and humdrum, investigated a lupine. A small black beetle crawled busily by. Apart from them and me, the sanctuary seemed to embrace no visible creatures except monarch butterflies.

I looked up. My dreamy and delicious state had softened all sense of time. Warm, unwinterly sun was now pouring directly down into the open space between rock ledge and forest, and I found that the space had filled with butterflies. They glided across the conifer background like animated daubs of orange paint across a somber canvas. My eyes lifted. High among the trees, the open space was all shafts of sunlight and offsetting shadow, and among these delicate columns the main pageant flowed faster, denser, stronger than before. Yet it remained diaphanous, and it still lacked aim or even drift, let alone apparent purpose. There *was* purpose, of course. There had to be. But my eye saw only a random and ethereal flow, and my intellect was on vacation.

A cloud obscured the sun; the dance diminished. The cloud passed; the dance revived. A new shaft of warm sunlight encouraged a group of dormant, clustering wallflowers to join the pageant and they surged out into the sea of dancers as a small but denser wavelet; it melted, almost at once, into the seamless whole.

Lifting my binoculars to examine the source of another such wavelet, I discovered a cluster that did not hang in a clump but clung like an arboreal glove to the surfaces of what I had thought were the bare branches and trunks of small dead trees. And now I unlocked the secret of those subtle patterns I had already noticed. Some monarchs rested with wings outspread; others, folded. The warm orange of the wings' napped upper surfaces contrasted with the paler, more shiny undersurfaces, and also with exposed patches of green lichen, to form a design as delicate as a Japanese painting. Yet the pattern moved: a few dancers were always coming or going, and they gave each cluster perpetual liquidity. I swung my binoculars right, then left: cluster after cluster after cluster. I began to grasp the awesome number of individuals that constituted this single colony.

I lowered the binoculars. Everywhere, the dance flowed soft and seamless—all through the space in front of my rock ledge, among the trees, even high above them. Something caught my eye. Far above, a jetliner glinted metallic. It drew a harsh white double line across pastel blue. Just for an instant I remembered another, grosser world. Quickly, I refocused the flickering, golden dancers. Among them, a lone, detached wing drifted downward like an autumn leaf, but lighter, so that its tremulous, sideslipping descent was beautifully, almost unbearably, slow. My eye followed it. A breeze carried the wing back over my head—and I discovered that the pageant had spilled out into an open space behind the rock ledge. I stood up and walked a few steps into this clearing.

Now at last I was in among the dancers. They flowed all around me, even lighter, more festive than before, and because they now danced directly between me and the sun, they glowed. They floated against the shining sky like luminous orange snowflakes—sculptured, living snowflakes—

that never fell to earth but hung suspended as they lilted to a beat both tenuous and profound. It was a beat I had heard before. Out in the other world I could sometimes, in quieter moments, discern that everything we know is dancing to a common rhythm. And all at once I comprehended: this ethereal parade that trembled against the sky above me was a rare and exquisite distillation of that dance of life. Our dance of life.

As I stood there, motionless, a cloud snuffed out the sunshine. The pageant's brilliance dimmed. The cloud stalled, coalesced with others, built to a gray rampart. The air began to cool. The dancers lost momentum. Yet gradually—so gradually that I remained unaware of a transition until it was over—their random movement acquired aim, purpose, even a target. They had begun a slow but steady drift back toward the trees. Quickly, the pageant thinned.

I walked back toward my niche on the lip of the rock ledge. I still knew, intellectually, dimly, that a temperature drop had dowsed the monarchs' dance. But the fact hung pale. And suddenly I realized that there in the forest I had called up none of the scientific facts I had so carefully researched. I had simply embraced the reality—and it had turned out to be almost holy, like a perfect act of love.

I reached my little niche. The open space in front of the rock ledge was empty. Among the trees, stray dancers still flickered; but the sea of quivering life had subsided. Dense, pendulous clusters once more shrouded the forest, like a black curtain. A few stragglers flittered through deepening shadow and stitched themselves to the curtain. But the monarch millions now hung motionless, waiting in the new cold for another sun.

I turned away from the stage. It was time to go. Time to rejoin that other, grosser world.

5 Beside the Lake

The meanings of a wilderness trip, and especially of a long one, will often surface slowly, layer by layer. You probably grasp the obvious lessons while you are still out there, walking. Days or weeks or months later, more layers may unfold, one by one. But the deepest meanings can linger for years in a kind of twilight; you know they lurk there, somewhere, but that is about all.

More than a decade ago I made my first and so far only visit to Alaska, and there are things I think I learned, or should have learned, from those three weeks that I have still not brought into full focus. Perhaps I never will.

Out beyond the Cessna's bright red wingtip, the canyon wall hung close. All I could see was barren black rock faces and, below them, even more barren glacial silt. Ahead, the glacier snaked away among dark, snowcapped peaks. Gray clouds lay heavy on the peaks, and a gray light lay heavy on everything. Even the glacier looked gray. The day before, I had peered out of the window of a Boeing 707 and seen vast snowfields and glaciers gleaming in brilliant sunshine, twenty thousand feet below, pristine white and inviting. Now, in that bleak grayness, the narrow glacier beneath us was so close that I could see all the deposited dust and untidy crumble of summer. It looked dirty, used, jaded. But at least, in terms of human use, it was virgin.

From the moment we had taken off, half an hour earlier, a little before 6 p.m., I had scanned the country below us intently, the way you do in new places. Long after we had outreached the last road tentacles around Anchorage, there still seemed to be straight-line marks of man, or at least a cabin or tent, beside each of the countless lakes that dotted the tundra.

I made some comment about it to Charlie Allen, my pilot. Charlie had been flying out of Anchorage for twenty-two years, I'd been told. He had once been a guide as well but had grown sick of the way many hunters behaved and now restricted himself to piloting his little Cessna 185 floatplane.

"Yes," Charlie shouted above the engine noise. "I'm afraid you're right. They call Alaska a wide-open country . . . but I don't. Not anymore. These days, there's people everywhere—thanks to aircraft, I'm sorry to say."

"But it'll be pretty private out at my lake, won't it?"

Charlie banked us around a bend of canyon and glacier. "If not," he said, "we could always look for another lake."

We droned on. The canyon pinched in to almost nothing. Ahead, the glacier merged with a flat snowfield. Soon, we were skimming over the snowfield. Clouds pressed close, ragged and streaming. Barren talus slopes and jagged peaks flowed past. Then we were over the pass and a valley began

to drop away ahead. We slid down into it. There was no glacier now, and the valley's rounded flanks were covered with
pockets of vegetation. Suddenly, off to the right, in one of the
pockets—almost level with the plane, seemingly just beyond
the red wingtip yet utterly ignoring us—a lone grizzly
browsed. It looked disappointingly small and unthreatening.

"Maybe," said Charlie. "But don't forget we're a good
quarter-mile away."

The valley began to open up. We swung right-handed
over a ridge, nosed down into a side valley. There was more
vegetation now, on the steep gray talus. On one slope there
were five white dots, too, that Charlie assured me were Dall
sheep. We swung close, and I could make out brown horns,
even stubby white tails. The sheep ignored us.

We droned on over steep, broken terrain. Each side valley and hollow seemed to cradle at least one lake. Then we
had banked sharply and were slanting down toward what I
was already thinking of as "my" lake.

Twenty-four hours earlier, when I stepped off the jet in
Anchorage, I had no idea where I would be going. But a
chance introduction from back home to a state Fish and
Game biologist, Ray Kramer, led to a long one-on-one talk
with him and then, next morning, to a session at a wall map
in a busy corridor of the department's HQ. This session was
punctuated by much field-forged advice from passersby.
Given my stated priorities—assured solitude, a good chance
of fair weather, terrain that offered walking variety, and
maybe some fly-fishing (all very much in that order)—opinion among the corridor experts soon coagulated in favor of a
certain lake, 2,500 feet above sea level, a hundred miles from
any road, yet within reasonable charter-flight range of Anchorage. I might see a few caribou hunters, said the experts,
but the lake was five miles long and more than a mile wide
and I should have no difficulty in being very much alone.

"But what happens if some s.o.b. comes and tries to camp on my doorstep?" I asked Ray Kramer.

"Depends how ornery you are," he said.

Now as we slanted down toward the lake, motor almost idling, I saw that everything was as it ought to be—was just the way my one topo map had foretold. From the lake's western end, an outlet river snaked intriguingly away across lake-studded tundra. A mile above this outflow, two matching spits of land curved out across the water toward each other —clearly the remnants of a minor terminal moraine. (The glacier that had created them still existed, in reduced form, back up in the steep, dark mountains that cradled the head of the lake.) On the north shore I could see the plateau that had attracted me on the map because it promised easy walking—eastward to the mountains and also westward, down the river, toward greener country.

There were two things, though, that the map had not prepared me for. The lake—soup-thick with glacial silt—was, even in that lowering gray light, a milky but startlingly vivid turquoise. And the land—whether lakeshore, tundra, plateau or mountain foothill—had a uniformly gaunt and barren look. I think I had expected more lushness, and at least a few trees.

We banked to the left and angled down toward the campsite I had picked from the map—the spit of terminal moraine that curved out from the north shore.

Almost at once, Charlie said, "Damn!" and pointed.

Near the base of the spit, standing out from the gray-green tundra like a five-ball all alone on a pool table, sat a large, round, bright-orange tent.

Charlie swung the plane south, toward the matching spit on the other side of the lake. "I could put you down there," he said. "Good place for pickup, too. I could come in one side or the other, according to the wind."

We continued to angle down. The seconds ticked past. I

felt their pressure; felt the pressure of Charlie's needs. It was already past seven o'clock and he was no doubt thinking about dinner. I glanced right, toward the river. From that height, that angle, it looked fordable. So with luck I would still be able to reach the "walking" plateau—the plateau that led, downriver, toward greener country. Perhaps, even in that first moment, I had already set my sights.

"Okay," I said.

Ten minutes later we had unloaded my gear onto a stony beach near the base of the spit. We confirmed that Charlie would pick me up twenty-one days later either at this same place or, if I chose to move camp, not too far away—though I would be ready two days early in case there was a threat of the first big autumn storm, due just about then, and Charlie thought it wise to get me out. We also reconfirmed ground-to-air signals. Then Charlie taxied away, out into the lake, and took off. Soon, the little red-and-white plane vanished over a ridge. A soft silence flowed in behind it and I stood alone on the curving pebble shore of the spit; alone at last in wide Alaska, with three weeks of solitude stretching out ahead.

I sat down on a wooden box of supplies. From the ground, the place looked even more barren than from the air. Grayer, too. A blanket of heavy cloud hung barely a thousand feet above the lake. It hid the peaks that I knew must lie to the east; only the bases of their mountains bulged out below the clouds, black and somber. All around me, I could see only flat tundra and the slopes of tundra-covered ridges and then, cutting everything else off in a straight gray line, the ceiling of soft but stern cloud. At least, I told myself, it was not raining. And for the moment there seemed to be no insects. In my planning I had accepted that I might have to wage almost incessant war against both rain and bugs, but had judged that such annoyances would be a small price to pay for the certainty of solitude.

I spent the first hour reconnoitering for a campsite. With

one exception, any place on that flat, bleak shoreline seemed about as good as another. The exception was a willow thicket bordering a small creek that flowed into the lake a hundred yards from our landing place. There, running water and windbreak willows promised amenities. But just before he left, Charlie had mentioned, with studied casualness, that the willow thicket looked just the kind of place a grizzly might use as cover if it wanted to see what I was all about, and before I walked over to reconnoiter it I strapped on the leather shoulder holster and heavy revolver that Ray Kramer had given me that morning.

From the start, Ray had fed me a stream of bear stories. To cap them, he confirmed a report I had read in that morning's paper: an unarmed photographer, camping alone, had been chased out of his tent by a grizzly and eaten; only a few gnawed bones remained. "Look," said Ray, "I know you don't hunt and don't usually carry a gun, but I'm frankly not happy at seeing you go out there alone without a weapon of some sort. Why not take my revolver? It's a .357 magnum and packs a good clout, and I find that in its shoulder holster it doesn't get in the way, even with a big pack on your back. You likely won't need it—but you never know."

His words—and Charlie's—still hung in the forefront of my mind as I walked toward the willow thicket. It is always like that, I find, when you move into the arena of a new danger that is potential but not necessarily present. It had been like that in Africa when I first began to watch big game, on my own and often fairly close. Your heart beats more quickly and audibly, your breath pumps short. In time, you get over it. This is not to suggest that you get indifferent, careless; but eventually the quivers go—until the potential danger becomes clangingly present. The quivers were there, I have to admit, as I walked toward the willow thicket. After all, I had never met a grizzly—*Ursus horribilis*, as he is genially

labeled—and was torn, the way one usually is, between desire for a new experience and fervent hope that I'd be spared
it. Spared it at unhealthily close range, anyway. As I walked,
my mind kept moving down to the heavy revolver hanging
snugly under my left armpit. I might not be totally convinced
that in a real encounter it would do any good, but it certainly
felt comforting.

I need not have worried. Close up, the willow thicket
proved not only empty but entirely innocent-looking. There
were even signs that somebody had at some time camped
there. At the very mouth of the creek, thirty paces below the
last willows, I found a network of game tracks: many animals,
as they passed by, clearly swung down to the shoreline, no
doubt to avoid the potential dangers of the thicket. That, it
seemed to me, was a solid reason for not setting up camp
at the creek: much better to live far enough away to watch
the animals' passage, not in a place I would undoubtedly
scare them.

In the end I chose a site fifty paces inland from the place
we had unloaded the plane: a patch of flat, raised, well-
drained ground, covered with only a fur of green growth, that
lay sandwiched between the wide strip of lakeside pebbles
and a shallow but richly vegetated gully. From this site, a low
gravel bank at the end of the spit hid the orange tent, which
I could from most other locations see all too plainly over on
the far side of the lake. Within an hour I had pitched my blue
two-man mountain tent and had extracted enough from the
three backpacks I had brought, and from the auxiliary tin can
and wooden box, to prepare dinner. I took my time over dinner. And afterward I just sat quietly in the failing light.

By this time the flat, bleak spit looked even bleaker and
grayer. It would probably take longer than usual, I decided,
to sink into the solitude of this new world; to sink deep
enough for me to grasp its realities, or at least its subtleties.

And there was more to it than place. This camp was different from most first camps. The crossover from civilization had been absurdly abrupt. I had had no walking, this time, to oil body and mind and help ease the transition from one world into another. There was another thing, too. For months I had harbored a premonition about this trip. I knew, as one always "knows" with premonitions, that the fears were groundless; but somehow I had never been able to thrust them totally away. The light over lake and tundra faded toward a deeper gray. Yes, I decided, my ridiculous premonition was probably part of the trouble.

I crawled into my little tent. The night was still surprisingly warm. I had done no more than pull the unzipped sleeping bag loosely over me before I fell asleep.

I woke to find the tent shining bright. I crawled out into the day. The sun hung high in a cloudless sky and the world beneath it glittered. My turquoise lake seemed to radiate light. At its head, mountains thrust up black and beautiful to sawtooth peaks. Among them, clinging to precipitous clefts, gleamed snowfields and small glaciers.

At the mountains' foot, the vegetation began. Moist and glistening, it girdled the lake along both shorelines in a brilliant and broadening emerald swath that in the distance looked smooth and soft and strokable as a cat's nose but developed, closer, an intriguing depth of tint and texture. At my feet, the texture focused into filigree, the emerald into a pastiche of greens and browns and pinks and even purples.

Standing outside my tent in the warm sunlight, still half asleep, I think I smiled back.

That first morning, with the grayness banished and three weeks stretching bright before me, I took things very easy. There was no sense, really, in worrying about the transition business. I could leave that to the silence and the solitude. Above all, to the solitude. It must have been almost ten o'clock before I began breakfast.

I was still drinking the last cup of tea when a floatplane droned in from the south, roared low overhead, circled out into the lake, landed, taxied toward me and grounded a hundred yards away, at the mouth of my creek. I sat firm. Two young men got out, walked a few yards into low scrub near the creek, and then returned to the plane carrying two metal cans. They set the cans down, began walking toward me. I stayed put, scowling. "Depends how ornery you are," Ray Kramer had said.

The men turned out to be very pleasant young fellows. They had only dropped in, they said, to pick up some gasoline cached a week earlier. My fears allayed, I unscowled and allowed myself to talk. Within half an hour the pair had taken off and left me to the sunlight and silence.

It had been a disturbance, of course. If you seek solitude, any human presence, by definition, disturbs. But at least the young pair had not meant to camp on my doorstep. So I had not had to test the validity of Ray Kramer's advice, and I was glad of that.

The next twenty-four hours were hardly models of wilderness calm. Three or four small floatplanes passed nearby. Another came in low, reconnoitered the lake's entire shoreline, then departed. One landed near the hidden orange tent on the far shore, then took off again, cutting through the silence like a chain saw. Twice, the thump of rifle shots reverberated across the water. I cannot deny that these invasions distressed me, and during those first twenty-four hours I seemed to get very little done—in part, perhaps, because of a mild sore throat and light-headedness. I did make a tour of my domain, though: I strolled to the end of the spit, inspected its low terminal ridge, then strolled back again. Afterward, I revisited the willow thicket and cut myself a walking staff. I always like to have one for backpacking, and especially for river crossings. Later, I fished for a few minutes, halfheartedly, at the mouth of the creek. But mostly I sat naked beside my tent. The sun shone benignly. Except for a brief spell at dusk, a gentle breeze seemed to keep the insects grounded. At intervals, as I sat there beside the tent, I think I told myself that I was busy organizing equipment. Sometimes, I guess I was. But mostly I just sat. And by midafternoon of the second day, when my mild but persistent light-headedness had at last faded away, the space and the sunlight had begun their work.

Now that I look back, though, I realize that there was more to it than just space and sunlight. I guess there always is.

While cutting my staff, down in the thicket, I had looked up and seen the way a single small willow stood alone, etched sharp against the black rock of distant peaks. Later, back at camp, I happened to look up again and see, just as unexpectedly, the way one of the peaks supported, like a halo, a single fluffy white cloud.

There were other, different yet similar moments, too.

About noon on the first day, a large, heavyset brown animal came cantering noisily along the pebbled shoreline. It had big velveted antlers, and I immediately assumed it was a caribou. It splashed across the mouth of the creek, antlers held high, and headed directly toward me. Through binoculars, I saw that its hooves were large and splayed. Could it, I began to wonder, be a small moose? I was surprised and ashamed to find I could not be sure where the precise differences lay.

When the animal was no more than fifty yards away it became suddenly and obviously and almost comically aware of my presence, for it abruptly dug in with all four feet, slid and pivoted in one clumsily effective movement, then began to canter back the way it had come. Every few yards, it turned its head and checked me. When it reached the creek it swung right and continued its westward trek, still out in the open and still moving at no more than a lazy canter. When it disappeared at last over a fold in the tundra I found myself left with that humbling uncertainty about whether I had just seen my first caribou (other than from the air, in the Northwest Territories of Canada, twenty years earlier) or my first moose.

Just before sunset that first day I was watching the light begin to ignite the peaks at the head of the lake when out of the corner of my right eye I glimpsed movement. On the lip of the gully, just beyond my tent, a large porcupine was wheeling around, its quill fan extended in a prickly dish. The porcupine flubbled slowly but determinedly away, down into the gully, rolling like a tug in high seas. Once safely on the floor of the gully and nine or ten paces away from me, it lowered its quills and sat down, facing into the almost level sun's rays and sniffing the westerly breeze. From time to time it looked me over. It had a big black schmoo of a face, curiously amorphous; and with its forefeet hanging loosely in front, slightly bent, and all quills now lowered, there was an unexpectedly soft and vulnerable air about it. You could almost call the creature cuddly. I realized with some surprise that this was my first close-up of a porcupine at peace with the universe rather than high-quilling for cover.

I sat very still, peering down into the gully. The porcupine seemed almost half asleep. Its eyes kept drooping shut —and thereby rendering its face even schmooer. For several minutes it sat quietly, just sniffing the breeze occasionally and keeping loose tabs on me. At last it began to move away, along the gully floor. The vegetation in its path varied from a few inches to more than a foot tall, and in junglier sectors the porcupine—its body stretched out now—almost vanished. I stood up and eased forward for a photograph. At one point, when the creature was out in a clearing and I could not have been more than four or five paces away, it stopped and inspected me with care. Then, having apparently reconfirmed to its satisfaction that I was harmless, it moved slowly forward again. It moved, as I say, with its body outstretched, and although I could still detect a vestige of a slow, lazy sea roll, I would at least flirt with truth by saying that its progress was now a snaky slink. What is more, the rather shapeless and vaguely cuddly creature had somehow become a convincing, three-foot-long, Hollywood-style mock-up of a shaggy mammoth mouse—or perhaps of a dried-out beaver wearing a combed-back mohair coat. Even more surprisingly, the black schmoo mask had been transformed, by some means I could not even begin to explain, into a pointed, ratlike face furnished with short brown hairs. (Please do not dismiss this alleged metamorphosis as a figment of the imagination, possibly induced by a lingering light-headedness: my photographs have confirmed most of the details.) Before long, the porcupine vanished into a clump of dense vegetation, and as it did so the sun sank below the horizon and shadows claimed the little gully.

I turned back toward camp. The shadows had claimed the whole flat spread of lakeside tundra. But beyond my tent—up at the head of the calm lake, and mirrored in it—the peaks and their fluffy cloud caps had been transformed: the last sunlight had painted everything—rock, ice and cloud—with its delicate pale pink magic. I stood where I was, still standing in the gully, deep in evening silence, until the night's curtain of shadow had moved up to end the performance.

Next morning, the therapy continued. Another caribou (unless it, too, was a moose) cantered across the mouth of my creek, paused to inspect me—antlers high and proud, sunlight catching pale rump and shaggy "beard"—then cantered

on westward. In the course of the morning I managed to
identify—with the aid of the bird book I had at last bought
—some small, slim birds that seemed vaguely familiar: European wheatears, which I had last seen on the East African
savanna. A pearl-gray arctic tern glided past, almost within
arm's reach—delicate and graceful as a Japanese print. And
by the end of the morning the arctic ground squirrels, which
would at first appear only long enough for me to catch
glimpses of their slim brown bodies, had gained enough confidence to stand bolt upright for minutes on end, so that I
began to see sharp black eyes taking my measure and small
forepaws hanging limp and appealing over soft, downy
chests. By midafternoon I had been sufficiently weaned from
the man-world to get down on hands and knees, naked in the
hot sun, and examine the fur of green growth that barely covered the patch of flat ground on which I had camped. Its detail amazed me, the way such filigrees always do. Towering
up an inch or more above the main mat of greenery were scat-
terings of squat and sturdy little plants with thick glossy
green leaves, several startling pink succulents and a few delicate purple flowers. The underlying mat was constructed,
my close-up eye discovered, of tiny intermeshing leaves,
densely packed. This was, I tentatively decided, the caribou
staple known as "reindeer moss." As far as I could determine
from an inspection of the vegetation's lakeside margin, it had
probably been the first life-form to colonize the region's bare
pebbles and rock after the glaciers withdrew—and so had no
doubt initiated the whole current overlayer.

I was busy and happy at this investigation when yet another floatplane swooped overhead, low. It swung out over
the lake, touched down and began to taxi toward me. I stood
up and adopted as ornery a pose as I could muster. I think I
was vaguely aware, even then, that from the plane I must
look a little strange: a naked, hirsute figure, standing there

on the barren shoreline with hands planted aggressively on hips and neck thrust forward. But I was not really overacting. Not even acting. Already, even before I was sure, anger had surged up, hot and uncontrollable.

The plane continued to taxi slowly shoreward. It seemed to be heading toward the mouth of the creek; "my" creek. Soon I could read the white inscription on its red tail: "Rust's Flying Service." By the time its floats grounded gently, a few paces beyond the creek, I had a pair of shorts on and was waiting. As soon as men began to get out and unload packs, I orneryed forward.

I think my first words were: "I trust you are not going to camp here, right on my doorstep." I would like to think that the question was icy but controlled. I know, though, that from the start my voice shook, and that it refused to come under control. And when one of the men—there were three, aside from the pilot—said that they certainly were going to camp, and camp right there, I launched into a tirade about privacy and the size of the lake and regard for other people and goddam privacy and the size of the bloody lake. Once I got started, my language would hardly have passed unbleeped on any TV program. I knew, even as I let the words rip, that I might have done better to start things off, as I would normally have done, with a calm and reasonable approach; but my anger, short-fused in advance by Ray Kramer's advice, had taken over.

The protest never looked like working.

I had barely launched it when the spokesman for the trio (he was a dark-haired man of about forty—the others were a teenager and a graybeard) broke in: "No matter what you have to say, we're staying. We've camped here for the last two years. Right here. On this very spot. This'll be our third year. It's our camp, I tell you, and no matter what you have to say, we're staying."

"Three years?" I said. "I've been dreaming of this trip for five years. Maybe ten. Dreaming of being alone out here." But I think a part of me heard, even as I spoke, the metallic, true-believer edge to my voice.

"Well, I tried to keep it polite," said the spokesman.

I snapped something about his words being polite, maybe, but not his actions. Hell, surely he could see that his party would disturb me just by being there, by the noise they made if nothing else.

"We won't make any noise. We're not that sort of people. We'll only be here four days, and you'll find we don't really trouble you at all. We'll be off hunting by five-thirty every morning and we won't be back till six, and by that time we'll be so tired we'll just eat dinner and go to bed. Why, you won't even see us unless you use your glasses."

"Look," I said. "While you've still got the plane here, why don't you taxi down to the river and camp there?"

"What, and walk all that extra distance for hunting? No, this is our camp, I tell you. This'll be our third year. No matter what you say, we're staying."

In the end I just turned on my heel and left.

I stalked past my camp without breaking stride. But even walking clear around the spit, fast, did not cool me off. Before I got back to camp there were two tents—a yellow A-frame and an orange blister—down near the mouth of my creek, slap on the line the two cantering caribou had taken.

By that time I had made up my mind. An Episcopalian upbringing had taught me that Christians get their kicks by turning the other cheek. I do not. When justice and the occasion demand, I believe in the tarnished golden rule: "Do to the bastards as they have done to you."

At five-thirty next morning there was no sign of movement in the enemy camp. It was seven o'clock before the troops looked ready for deployment. At 7:05 I strode, fully equipped for a long day's campaign, around the edge of their camp—because it was the natural route, or so I told myself. As I passed I snarled a half-stifled "Morning." I do not think I got a reply. Beyond the two tents, I headed directly up the ridge along the narrow valley down which "my" creek ran— the valley that I judged was the enemy's most likely hunting ground for the first day. As soon as I had gained suitable cover I looked back through binoculars. The three men stood clustered together, rifles on shoulders, studying a map. When they folded the map and headed west, across the flat tundra at the foot of the ridge, I smiled. It was eminently possible to imagine that I had already forced a change of plans.

For half an hour, still in thick cover, I watched the men walk westward, spread out in line—and noted with mixed pleasure and anger that they passed close to the river campsite that they had spurned. When they turned south, up the slope of the ridge, I felt reasonably sure I knew the way they meant to spend the morning. I followed, keeping out of sight when possible behind folds in the tundra.

I will not itemize that day's hassling. In retrospect, I am by no means proud of what I did. In any case, the morning was hardly a resounding victory—though when the trio stopped for lunch at last on a low rise and kept scanning ahead through their rifle scopes, as if preparing for a stalk, I moved around their left flank, out in the open, blowing a whistle and waving a red handkerchief so that neither they nor their prey could fail to be aware of me. But when I angled across the hunters' front all I could find was a big rock harboring a colony of nervous ground squirrels. I did the best I could. Slowly, using what little cover there was, I moved forward to within thirty paces of the rock; then, planting myself in full view of the hunters, I began to study the squirrels through glasses. And I went on studying them, studiously. Before long, the enemy retreated, back the way they had come. It was a good moment. I could not be absolutely sure, though, that it had been my tactics that forced the retreat.

The afternoon went better. The hunters began to angle further up onto the ridge. I divined their intentions perfectly, outflanked them, and then, as soon as they split into two parties, moved into position in front of and in between them. Now I held perfect control. When the hunters stopped, I stopped. When they moved ahead, I moved. All the time, I knew and they knew that I would scare off any caribou in our path. It was beautiful. Best of all was the knowledge that they could not be sure, beyond shadow of doubt, that it had all been intentional. In the end they gave up. They retreated down the ridge and walked slowly back toward their camp.

I sat on a rock in the sunshine, filled with an unholy sense of triumph, and watched them go.

In retrospect, as I say, I am by no means proud of what I did that day. Even at the time, twinges of doubt kept tickling what passes for my post-Christian soul. In my notebook I scribbled, "Feeling MUCH better. Worked it out of me (you miserable bastard, you!)." But the fact remains that I did feel much better. Very much better.

After I had watched the hunters return safely to their camp I sat for a long time up on the ridge, flushed with victory. The sun beat down and the world was very quiet. After a while I discovered that through glasses I could see, far to the north—fifty miles away perhaps, or even more—a wall of black, snow-checkered peaks. Beyond them rose more peaks, a jumble of black and white and softening blue that ranged back and back and back until haze and doubt at last took over. This huge mountain mass covered a vast arc, left and right. And sitting there on the silent ridge with the sun striking warm on my bare shoulders, I began to grasp for the first time something of the immensity of Alaska. But then a plane droned in from the west and roared across my front, almost at eye level, before slanting down onto the lake. It taxied in to the orange tent on the far shore. Ten minutes later it roared back again, cleaving silence and solitude.

When it had gone, I began to study the river. Through glasses, looking steeply down, I could assess likely fording places. The most obvious one was at the outflow of the lake, across the boulders that were an old terminal moraine and now formed the lip over which the water flowed as it metamorphosed from lake into river. Distant views of fords can be deceiving, but it seemed to me that for most of the way across the water would be shallow enough to wade; a narrow gut near the center of the lip, though, looked as if it might well turn out to be too deep. Two or three hundred yards below the outflow, a series of angled rapids seemed to offer a better bet. Farther downstream, I could find nothing very promising. I let my glasses linger briefly on a big willow thicket that swathed a side creek, dark and brooding, a mile or so below the lake; then I let them swing on westward, tracing the course of the river across open, treeless tundra, far beyond the point at which I could have detected a ford, far beyond the boundaries of the single topo map I had brought. I let my eye follow the line of the twisting silver thread until it vanished among converging, folded hills. Then I scanned idly, left and right, trying to guess through precisely which gap, created by the hills' foldings, the river passed. And suddenly, unexpectedly, I found myself looking, through one of the gaps, at the tips of some trees.

Now, the tips of a few trees, seen many miles away, on the far side of a range of hills, not to mention a broad and rushing river, do not normally rivet your attention. Yet the moment these trees swung into view I found myself gripping my binoculars, tight. And all around me, it seemed, a deeper hush had fallen on the silence.

The trees were conifers, and I therefore knew, although I could see only their tips, that they must be spruces—the only conifer species, I had been told, in this part of the country. The tips of these spruces were neatly pointed and they stood black against green hillside. There is nothing very unusual about such a combination, of course. Yet I found myself staring at the tree tips hungrily, savoring their blackness and shapeliness and the way they pointed so cleanly at the sky. It was almost as if I had never seen a tree before. And after a few minutes it occurred to me that I had indeed not seen a tree—except for straggly little willows in the occasional thickets, and they did not really count—since Charlie Allen had left me standing alone, three days earlier, in the flat, unbroken landscape that surrounded the lake. (The landscape was in fact anything but flat and unbroken; but at that moment I was thinking in terms of the barrenness—to the distant eye—of tundra and ridges and mountains, and of the "walking" plateau on the far side of the river.)

Three days without trees can, of course, hardly be called a famine—unless you have been starved of something else, too. But I know that when I came down off the ridge at last and began to walk slowly back toward camp, my mind carried the memory—sharp, vibrant and filled with promise—of those dark, pointed spruce trees. And in the days that followed, the picture of them, barely visible through that gap in distant hills, kept sliding up, unbidden, into my mind's eye.

That evening and for the next two days I left the hunters alone; but I could rarely forget them. Even when they were not fishing near the mouth of my creek, yelling sporadically at each other, I hardly needed glasses to become aware of them. It was not just a matter of the yellow cone and orange blister standing slap on the converging game trails. From time to time, raucous laughter would spill out from the tents. Once, there was a fusillade of .22 rifle fire. On the second day, too, a Rust's Flying Service plane came back, noisy as ever, to deliver extra gear. Later, on a swing through the willow thicket when the hunters were away, I found a scattering of fresh human turds left the way no true outdoorsman would leave them: close to the creek, unburied and decorated with soiled, unburned toilet paper.

The day after my hunter hassling, it rained. All morning I lay in my tent, reading and trying to push aside thoughts about what it must have meant when I heard, quite close, two heavy-caliber rifle shots and then the murmur of excited voices. In midafternoon I walked through gentle but steady rain along a mile of marshy shoreline to the river's outflow and fished sporadically and at the same time reconnoitered for a crossing. I waded halfway across the lip of the bouldered outflow without going over the top of my thigh waders, but when I came to the narrow gut I had seen from the ridge I could tell at once, even in that gray light and slanting rain, that, although the gap was only a few feet across, the water would indeed be too deep and fast-flowing to wade. But at the very edge of the gap a sturdy grayling took my fly, and soon I was admiring once again the delicate blue sheen, suffusing head and fins and scales, that I had not seen for twenty years and had almost forgotten.

I fished for an hour, maybe two, and—even given the importance of not being Ernest—it was good, down there by the river, alone with the rain and the water. But when I walked back into camp there were two figures hogging the mouth of my creek, fishing and yelling at each other.

Next day the rain stopped and the clouds lifted a little, and I wandered for an hour or two up the valley that cut into the ridge above my camp—the valley that held my little willow-clothed creek. But I wandered rather aimlessly. I was just waiting, really. On the way down, I skirted the hunters' camp. From a heavy wooden frame hung the butchered carcasses of three caribou. I stopped and made an effort to be

civil, even mildly friendly. The hunters did not exactly encourage me, and I did not blame them for that. But as I was
about to leave the graybeard made what may, or may not,
have been a genuine response.

"That day back there," he said, jerking his head toward
the part of the ridge on which I had moved ahead of them
and watched the nervous ground squirrels on their rock.
"Did you get some good pictures of that wolverine?"

"Wolverine?" I said.

"Yeah. Big one. So big I thought at first it was a bear. We
watched it for a long time. Right close to the place you went.
I figured you was stalking it and must have gotten some real
good pictures."

"No, I was interested in other things, and I didn't see it.
I didn't have a camera with me, anyway."

"Maybe just as well," said Graybeard. "If you'd of stumbled on it in that cover you'd likely have gotten more than a
good picture from it." He laughed and turned back to his
companions. They continued to avoid my eye.

All three of them were busy with fishing rods around a
shallow man-made pool beside the creek, trying to snag with
bare hooks half a dozen grayling that they had clearly caught
in the lake and imprisoned there. While I watched, one of
them snagged a fish. He lifted it out of the water, tore the
hook free from its belly and dumped the struggling bar of silver on top of others in a big black plastic bag.

"Want to take a few of 'em home alive," said Graybeard.
"So's they'll be nice and fresh."

Once I had confirmed that the plane was due back about
four o'clock next day to take them out, I left. But as I walked
back to my tent I wondered whether Graybeard had been
telling no more than the truth about the wolverine or had
been imaginatively getting his own back. If that was it, then
I have to admit he succeeded. I am still wondering.

Next day, the Rust's Flying Service plane arrived a little

early, but even before it touched down I had in my hand, ready and waiting, an envelope containing a note, signed only with my initials, that read, "Dear Mr. Rust: If another of your planes disregards reasonable privacy and lands in my back yard—at my present —— Lake campsite or any other—you will soon be reading about it. And you might see that as poor publicity."

As soon as the pilot stepped ashore I walked down the beach, confirmed that he could personally deliver a letter to Rust, handed him the envelope, turned on my heel and walked back to camp. There, I sat down and prepared to watch with satisfaction as the hunters departed. Only then did I see that, in addition to the pilot, two newcomers had debarked from the plane and were now unloading packs and camp gear.

The anger flooded back, hot and uncontrollable again; fiercer, this time, for having been duped into abeyance. I stood up. I had taken a couple of strides down the beach before I stopped, walked back to camp and sat down again. The anger was too red. I had to keep myself away from the new intruders. Besides, haranguing them would do no good: the outgoing party would have told them about the surly character down the beach, and if they had been the kind of people with any regard for other people's privacy they would surely have gone elsewhere of their own accord. It also occurred to me that remonstration just might drive them down to the river—and I had already more or less decided to move there myself. So I sat motionless, and fumed.

When the plane taxied away the newcomers stood watching it. They were both tall men, wearing green slacks and shirts and green peaked caps. As soon as the plane had vanished over the ridge they began to walk along the beach toward me.

Once it was clear they meant to talk, I advanced a few

paces to meet them: I wanted no damned strangers in my camp. But although my opening salvo was curt I managed, this time, to restrain it a little: "I have to say that I can't pretend to welcome your presence."

The two men halted. One was perhaps sixty, the other around forty. The older man smiled. "So we heard," he said.

I did my best, but they were both so pleasant, so determined not to be pushed into rudeness, that my attack faltered. From the start, though, they remained adamant. They were going to stay for a week. They had camped in this same place the year before, back among the willows. And they had flown all the way from the East—one of them from Chicago, the other from New York. So they frankly could not buy the idea of my "squatter's rights." In the end we agreed to differ, more or less amiably, and they went back down the beach.

Within a few minutes I was following in their tracks. They were beginning to carry their gear back into the willows. I offered to help, then said, "Look, I'd like to apologize for my behavior. I'm afraid I was very angry—and still am—but there was no need for me to be so rude."

The older man took off his glasses and began polishing them. "There's nothing to apologize about," he said. "I quite understand how you felt. But I don't think you'll have too much to worry about. We're very quiet folks. We're here to hunt caribou, sure, but I'm a bit of a naturalist, and something of a photographer too, and one reason we like to camp back in the willows is so that we can watch the ptarmigan come right up close. So we understand, really. Nothing to apologize about at all."

I told them, then, about the two animals that had cantered past, before the other hunters arrived. They assured me that they had undoubtedly been caribou. Moose were quite different animals, "built more like cattle."

When it became obvious that they would genuinely prefer to carry their own gear and set up camp alone, we checked that our plans for the next day would not clash and I walked back along the beach. For the first time in four days, it seemed, I noticed the sparkling turquoise surface of the lake. And while tea brewed I took a quick, in-and-out-before-any-damage-done swim in the ice-cold water.

There was one thing I wanted to do before moving camp down to the river, and early next morning I climbed the ridge above the spit and turned east and went on up toward the world of rock and glaciers.

It turned out to be a day of light and shade. At first the sun shone, and near the foot of the ridge I discovered a delectable hidden garden, its lush grasses and flowers still bedewed and gleaming. Up on the crest, I found I could look back once more across lake and outflow and snaking river to the folded hills; but although I was almost sure which gap to train my glasses on, the angle seemed to be wrong and I could see no dark, pointed spruce trees. The panorama was impressive, though. I had deliberately left Anchorage with only five rolls of film, so that I would be forced to look at Alaska much of the time and not be tempted too often into merely photographing it, but at the crest I paused, as I did several more times that day, and busied myself for a while with the camera.

Soon, the ridge merged into a plateau that sloped up to the foot of the mountains. As I walked toward them, clouds began to form around the sawtooth peaks. Quickly, they slid down to cover the lower slopes. Before long, swirling mists kept enveloping me. It was good, though, to stride unhindered across that bleak and rolling tableland. An hour of it, and I felt cleansed, freed, keyed. But then, out of the mist to the south, spread wide across the stony grayness like attacking infantrymen, came four men. One of them passed me within half a dozen paces. We exchanged a few words. They had been flown into the head of the lake the evening before and were going to hunt the high country, camping up there for two or three days. The man was pleasant enough; but I had not gone up into that place to seek the human species. And as I climbed toward the nearest peak I could see—when the mist lifted briefly, as it did from time to time—four red packs moving slowly northward.

It took me an hour to climb the peak. Near the top—with the mist now boxing me inside a small, square, black-walled room that moved up as I moved, like a Stygian elevator floating free of all earthly objects—I found, in the center of a windswept saddle, a small, bleached skull. At first, I imagined it must have belonged to a Dall sheep: they were, I thought, the only animals likely to live up in such a place. But when I examined the skull more carefully I saw that it hardly looked like a sheep's. More like a rodent's, I decided: from the front of the mouth, top and bottom, set separate from and far in advance of the main teeth, protruded the remains of paired, still-yellow incisors. But I could think of no suitable rodent candidate with a five-inch-long skull: neither beaver nor porcupine, it seemed to me, would choose to live up in that world of rock and ice. In the end I just slipped the skull into a pocket.

I lunched up there on the peak. Around me, mist-curtains rose and fell, unveiling and then abruptly snuffing out brief and tantalizing half-vistas of sunlight and shadow that kept resculpturing rock and snow and ice and yawning space. After a brief postprandial doze I scrambled across a talus slope to the foot of a broad but shallow glacier.

Now, I am used to visiting glaciers only at around fourteen thousand feet above sea level, and at that elevation your mind can rarely grapple with any but the most basic notions. That afternoon, though, at little more than five thousand feet, my mind was functioning normally. And when I stood in the middle of the gray and apparently barren chaos of boulders at the glacier's foot, looking at an unexpected little cantonment of lichens and mosses and plants and even knots of grass, I found myself seeing it as a vivid exemplar of how life recolonizes the earth after an ice age; and also, essentially, of how land-life first colonized the bare-rock continents. That was another of the day's lighted moments.

When I had scrambled down to the foot of an immense, big-boulder moraine that took me two or three hours to cross, I passed the base of the peak I had climbed. Looking up at it through a chance break in the mist, I saw two human figures up on the summit. The figures waved to me and then began their long climb down. I hurried on across the sloping plateau: unless I made good time it would be dark before I could reach camp. Half an hour passed before it occurred to me that the two men on the peak might have been my new neighbors, who could possibly have changed their plans, and that if so they would be hard put to make it back in daylight. So when I came down at last to our little spit—with daylight to spare, as it turned out—I checked their camp. They were home all right, and tired but happy. They had already killed their first caribou, a cow, and without thinking I blurted out that on my way back down I had seen a cow caribou with calf—and at once wished I could withdraw the words. To cover my embarrassment, I took from my pocket the skull I had found up in the barren saddle.

"Can't make up my mind what this is," I said. "Looks like a rodent, but . . ."

The older man took the skull and turned it slowly over in his hand. At last he said, "Might be a small beaver. A wolf could have taken it up there. They just love beaver, you know, and they'll sometimes carry things for miles. Yes, I wouldn't want to be sure, of course, but it could be a beaver all right." He handed the skull back and looked down at his still half-extended hand. "You know, I've been thinking about your problem. Wanting to be alone, I mean. Been thinking about it all day, off and on. And it seems to me that the answer would be for you to come up here before the hunting season starts. That way, you wouldn't be troubled by other people."

And afterward, as I walked slowly toward my own camp, easing into the first shadows of the night, it seemed to me that back among the dark willows near the mouth of the creek a new light now burned, small but bright.

Next morning I made a reconnaissance. I walked the marshy mile down to the river and found a good campsite a couple of hundred yards below the outflow. From it I could see neither the lake surface nor any of the lakeside tents. Above the line of the outflow, though, the lake-head peaks, with their stark, ice-clad rock walls, remained as visible as they were from my camp on the spit. The river tumbled and whispered past, and the new campsite abutted a twenty-yard stretch of perfect dry-fly water. I had brought my fishing tackle, and within five minutes I had caught two big grayling. That seemed a pleasant bonus. But what the new site promised above all was elegance. It stood on a slight rise and so commanded wide vistas; and all the lines of landscape meshed, far and close, in the kind of concordance that is very hard to explain but that stands clear and dear to the heart of anyone with a feel for such things.

That afternoon I moved camp. It was because of just such a possible transfer that I had brought three backpacks, and what promised to be a chore turned out to be a surprisingly joyful affair. All afternoon, as I packed heavy loads along the lakeshore, I sang and lilted. Having good neighbors had made a difference, of course. Had made a lot of difference.

And now that I was moving to a secluded place, escaping at last from the turmoil that had come to seem inevitable on that original spit of land (not to mention on the far side of the lake, where a plane-fed tent colony had now sprouted around the original orange one), I could look back and find everything that had happened almost funny. Clearly, I had misjudged the outdoorsman's attitude, here in Alaska. I should have known that the hunters would not see solitude as a part of it all. They came for other things. Perhaps I had been oversensitive about my privacy, too, and so had made a series of unfortunate circumstances worse. I was by no means sure about that; but now, for the first time, it at least seemed worth considering. And as I packed my third and final load around the foot of the lake and turned into the last lap, with the sun already easing down onto the horizon, I found myself remembering the story of the oversensitive British Guards officer who, when asked what it had been like at Dunkirk, put his nose in the air and said, "But my dear, the noise! And the people!"

Five minutes later the river came in sight. On its far side, directly opposite my new campsite, there stood—red-shirted and garish against the bare, bouldered bank—three people, fishing. Almost at once, one of them whistled. I could not be sure whether the whistle was for me or for a companion who had strayed downstream, but I promptly put my ex-British nose in the air, ignored the people's very presence, and stalked stiffly to my goal.

Before long, though, the fishermen retreated upstream, toward the hidden orange-tent colony. The sun set red and reassuring. Its light warmed the wide and whispering river. After dinner, I sat quietly outside my tent with the stars and the night and the silence.

In the morning it was still peaceful, there beside the wide, sunlit river. I got up late and fished for a while at the foot of my new front garden. When I had caught three more good grayling I carried them back up to the tent and began to cook brunch. Soon I was leaning back against my pack and eating their firm, fresh flesh.

That morning, though, the planes seemed even busier than usual. Although the lake's surface was out of my sight, I could see them coming and going. One small red machine landed somewhere near the orange-tent colony, took off again and landed near my old camp on the spit; soon it came roaring so low over my tent that I could see the passenger's face as he peered down. I sat stiff and upright, in no way acknowledging the intruders' presence, hoping they could see my scowl. When the plane banked back upriver and landed just above the outflow and then, out of sight but very much within earshot, apparently taxied to shore at the point nearest to me, I decided that it probably carried game rangers checking on licenses and bags. My resurgent anger gave way to a sort of amused resignation. There comes a time when you have to roll with the punches. The rangers were, after all, only doing their job.

Moments after the plane's engine cut, two figures appeared up near the outflow and began walking toward me. Before long I could through glasses see Alaska Fish and Game badges on the sleeves of their brown uniforms. I took my fishing license from its plastic bag, then went on eating. There was, after all, no need for the interruption to last longer than necessary. I was still eating when the rangers arrived. I smiled and, without getting up, offered my hand. We shook. As we did so I noticed that in addition to Fish and Game badges each man wore on his chest a silver star inscribed "State Trooper."

"I guess you want to see my fishing license," I said, and held it out.

"Well," said the smaller of the two troopers, "it isn't really what we came for, but now we're here I may as well take a look at it." He studied it briefly, handed it back. "What we came about, Mr. Fletcher," he said, "was the note you sent Mr. Rust."

"Good God! That! But why?"

"Because it could be construed in many ways."

"Many ways? How?"

"Well, we get some nuts out here, you know. Real nuts, some of them. Even shooting at planes. And Mr. Rust thought you might be threatening to do just that to his planes—and saying he'd read about it in the papers afterward. So he turned the note over to us."

I must have looked astonished.

"Of course, there could be other explanations."

"There certainly could. I assure you that was the last thing I had in mind. If I'd said in the note that I was a writer, maybe that would have made a difference."

The troopers glanced at each other. "Ah!" said one of them. "It certainly would."

I explained how I had come to the lake to find solitude— and had perhaps paid too much attention to Ray Kramer's casual and well-meaning "depends on how ornery you are." I was extremely sorry to have precipitated such a brouhaha; on the other hand, I still felt I had a legitimate beef and therefore didn't really regret my general position. "After all, I came here for peace and quiet. And I did my best to get good advice about a suitable place. But this lake is like a bloody airport."

The smaller trooper nodded. "I can sympathize with you," he said. "Up to a point, anyway. But you must understand that Henry Rust had some reason to be alarmed. By the way, I think that was his plane that came in just now, farther up the lake, and he may be down here shortly."

We chatted for a while—about how they had felt sure they had the right man when they saw me sitting stiffly up-

right as they flew over my camp; about the economy mea-
sures that had forced "cross-training" of some state troopers
as "Fish and Wildlife Enforcement Officers"; and about the
latest weather report. ("Promises more like this," said the
bulkier trooper, gesturing at the cloudless sky. He smiled.
"So it'll likely turn bad.")

I offered my guests tea.

"Thanks, but we'd better finish our business and get
going. We're sorry to have disturbed your lunch, anyway.
But we'll need a brief written statement from you. There's
this report to file, you see, and we've got to close it out."

So I sat there in the sunshine with the tundra wide around
me and the river rushing past, and wrote a statement for the
police files. "I came to Alaska for solitude . . ." I began. The
body of the statement was conciliatory, expressing regret at
the way things had turned out. "But," I concluded, "I still
like hell want my privacy."

While one trooper read the report quickly, the other said,
"I hope you won't get the idea from all this that Alaskans are
inhospitable. You just hit the wrong people under the wrong
conditions. I think you'll find that most Alaskans go out of
their way to welcome strangers."

When I had reassured him, he seemed happier.

The other trooper finished reading my statement. "One
final thing," he said. "I'm afraid I'll need your Social Security
number."

I looked at them and laughed. "My God! When things
have reached the point that you get asked for your Social Security number out in a place like this, I'm not sure there's all
that much hope for the species." I also explained that I could
never remember the damned number; but we found it on my
fishing license (which rather seemed to suggest something,
too), and we were standing up and shaking hands when a
plane landed, out of sight, up near the troopers'.

"Probably Henry Rust," said one trooper. "I think you'll

find he's a most reasonable man. At least, he usually is. I only hope he doesn't make a liar out of me this time."

A man appeared, up by the outflow, and began walking toward us. When he arrived I held out my hand. "My name's Colin Fletcher."

"I'm Hank Rust."

We shook.

Rust was a shortish, bearded man, essentially inscrutable behind big sunglasses.

"I guess I'm semi-repentant," I said.

Behind the sunglasses, Rust appeared to be relieved. "Well, I'm glad to hear that."

And we went through the whole thing again. After the first few minutes of explanation, Rust seemed to understand my point of view, and I found myself wishing I could be sure that in his place I would have been as reasonable.

He did say, at one point, "Mind you, if I'd been here when you wrote that note I might have suggested you consult your lawyer."

"I'm afraid I'm not much of a man for lawyers. I'd probably have said . . ." I made a suitably obscene gesture.

Rust laughed, slightly.

Soon afterward he took a wristwatch from his pocket and began to put it on. It occurred to me that he had come prepared for a fight. But in the end he virtually apologized for having turned the note over to the police. "You see, I'm not equipped to deal with this sort of thing—and these fellows are. Besides, they weren't emotionally involved."

Just before Rust and the troopers left, I happened to mention in the course of discussion that one reason I had moved down to the river was the hope of fording it and gaining the plateau on the far bank, where the walking would be easier. I did not mention the spruce trees. Rust immediately said that he would be flying in three days later to pick up the two hunters at my old campsite, and that if I had not found a crossing by then he would be glad to move me across to the far side of the lake—provided, of course, that I was all packed up and ready.

"Well, thank you," I said. "I really appreciate your offer, especially in the circumstances. And I might just take you up on it."

We shook hands all around, very amicably, and Rust and the troopers walked away together toward their planes, talking as they went. I watched them go. It was impossible not to wish I could hear what they were saying.

When both planes had taken off and there had been time for peace to begin seeping back over the tundra, I found myself running the confrontation over in my mind. I suspected, now, that Henry Rust had come out of it better than I had. In future he might be more careful with the instructions he gave his pilots about landing clients in other people's "back yards." But I would be more careful about ornerying off into first-strike attacks, and about sending tart but ambiguous notes to strangers. All this could no doubt be seen as communal gain. But it also occurred to me that, at a more purely personal level, I might have to rescrutinize my faith in the tarnished Golden Rule. This time, it had brought me a week's hassle, ending with two state troopers and a plaintiff on my doorstep. And that was hardly what I had been striving for. So it was just possible that after further careful consideration of all pros and cons I might have to admit that maybe, just maybe, my former co-religionists were onto something after all, pragmatically speaking, when they turned—or at least extolled a turning of—the other cheek.

And as I sat there alone beside the again peaceful river, that salutary note seemed a fitting one for what I suddenly saw, with a relieved and surprisingly firm conviction, had been a natural conclusion to the first chapter of my visit to wide Alaska.

6 More Than a Day's Walk

Four more days passed before I set out in search of the spruce trees, and during those days I at last began to touch the things I had come to Alaska to find.

Around my new camp—its concordances confirmed now, though I would have been hard put to say how—the local ground squirrels soon grew accustomed to my presence. When up on deck—on watch, scanning the horizons of their universe—they stood very erect and very still, so that sometimes the tundra around me seemed dotted, at a discreet distance, with small, pale, sawn-off fence posts; but if I was looking into low sunlight it would incandesce the little animals' coats and they would set me thinking instead of huge furry caterpillars hanging suspended, limp among the grassheads, from invisible trees.

From time to time, families of ptarmigan paraded confidently across the nearby tundra, then erupted into spurts of brown-and-white flight. High overhead, geese commuted up and down the valley in tremulous skeins. Small birds visited, at respectful distances: wheatear, pipits, sparrows, warblers. It was while I sat watching an orange-crowned warbler, trying to let myself pretend it just might be the one that habitually wintered in my garden, that I met the resident short-tailed weasel.

He was investigating the heads and entrails of several grayling I had cleaned on some lichen-covered riverside boulders—a full fifty yards below camp, to avoid attracting bears within prejudicially close range. At least, I think the weasel was investigating the fish. He was certainly within point-blank whiff-range of them when I first saw him. But for the next half hour he devoted his energies to playing games with me. That was how it seemed, anyway. He would come quicksilvering toward me, more mercury than mammal, pause on a boulder summit to squat and scratch outstretched neck with blurred paw, then dart on, only to flick to a halt on another boulder and stand scrutinizing me—body poised ready for instant relocomotion, pink feet firmly planted, pink forepaws held halfway up clean white shirtfront, white-rimmed ears cocked, sharp black eyes peering inquisitively out from pointed, bewhiskered, chocolate-brown face. Then, faster than my eye could follow, gone. Gone below, under a boulder. Seconds later, up again, five yards away. Back toward me, even curiouser this time. A boulder-top pause for a brief but luxurious rubbing of belly along rough lichen, his whole body ecstatically outstretched, from tip of black nose to black tip of tail. Another flick forward. A longer, stand-up, white-shirtfront inspection of me—this time, barely three feet from my moccasins. Then gone again, flashing down into one of those dark sub-boulder caverns. And so it went on and on, minute after delightful minute: flick forward, neck scratch, lichen belly rub, stand-up inspection of odd intruder, dive into cavern. And in between, more and more often, playful quicksilverings across boulder tops. Long before our half hour together had ended, I discovered that I could summon my playmate up from his caverns, or bring him toward me from his play, with a faint, high-pitched whistle. Well, could almost always do so. But at last there was a time when he failed to emerge again from his cavernous underworld, come whistle or patient wait, and all I could do was walk slowly back to my own shelter, sad that the play was over as well as elated that I had been onstage.

There was the earth to watch, too. One morning I woke to find the tundra white with frost, and although the sun soon banished it and the day shone summerlike again, something had changed. The grasses had grown darker, older. The carpet of leaves lay flatter, and tinged with red. The last lingering flowers had shriveled, almost gone. And when I looked downriver, the tint of distant slopes confirmed that the year had moved on.

Now that the human turmoil had ceased and I had the time and peace to do nothing—or, rather, to do something with the absence of other things—I could more easily detect the earth's slower changes.

Even back at the first camp, when I looked at the curving terminal-moraine shore of the spit and at the long, parallel, lateral-moraine ridges that bulged beneath the vegetation along both flanks of the valley, I was able to comprehend, cerebrally, the icy fingers that had so recently shaped this land. Now, down by the river, there were moments when these signs, and others, too, stood out so vividly that I could almost hear the vast masses of blue ice grinding past overhead—out in every direction—as they moved, foot by foot, year after year, down huge, ordained corridors.

The nights were different now, too. After sunset on the day of the Rust confrontation I sat outside my tent and watched bloodshot sky paint sliding river. It brushed a different, delicate shade across each rapid, riffle and pool. As the sun swung slowly northward—below the horizon but still dragging the rim of its flaming chariot wheel across the sky's hem—the tones of the painting grew darker, richer. I sat on, cocooned against the cold (hooded down jacket, down pants, down booties), watching the show and eating.

For dinner, instead of my normal cooked entree, I served tomato soup, sliced salami, dehydrated milk shake, a chocolate bar and assorted nuts. I am aware that this menu scarcely suggests a gourmet's delight. Contemplating it now in cold blood and retrospect, from the pillows of civilization, even I remain unmoved; but I know that there beside the river it was, because of its very break from the norm, a celebration. A celebration, I think, of breaking free at last. And as I sat eating, snugly warm, I rejoiced: at the bite of rich, cold night air dragged deep into lungs; at the stars blazing by their myriads, the way they blaze in desert skies; and at the way I could still follow the rim of the sun's chariot in its northward turning. The wheel was sinking, though. And its flame had now died. Only a paleness remained. I watched a shooting star bisect this paleness. Then I became aware of another light source, farther right, almost due north. It too was a faint white dome, curving across the sky. Slowly I became aware that this arch was growing, as if a huge, well-lit city had begun to spring up, even as I looked, somewhere far up in the arctic. Then a second, fainter band began to appear, circling the first—and I realized that, for the first time since I had spent a summer in the Northwest Territories of Canada, twenty years before, I was watching the aurora borealis.

This time, the lights—the northern lights—were not colored, the way I remembered them. All I could see—then, at the beginning—were two huge bands of white light arcing across the northern sky. And this double arc stood firm. At least, that is how I remember it. But I see I have used not only the word "arc" but also "arch" and "band" and even "dome," and this seems to suggest a shifting phenomenon. So although I remember that in the beginning the bands of light looked almost as if painted across the sky, perhaps this memory arose only by comparison with what followed. For after a while the bands began to break up. They re-formed into vertical beams, and these beams began to dance across the line of the vanished curves. The beams moved slowly and majestically, yet at the same time lightly, ephemerally, so that even then, at the beginning, the whole northern sky was like a vast, cosmic, *son et lumière* performance for which you could without difficulty supply your own Bach. It is difficult, perhaps impossible, to apply measurements to such phenomena: they are too ethereal for mundane treatment. But our minds are channeled in linear grooves, and in my notebook I jotted down that the lights covered "100's of miles—whole N. sky."

The performance went on and on, minute after minute, until I lost touch with time. Intermissions came, when the dancing beams re-formed into the original, almost static arc, or into the double arc. Once, I remember, they created a third band, faint but far out, almost directly over my head. Then the bands would break up again. Delicate shapes would once more move across the vacated curve. Sometimes the shapes mimicked musical notes, bunched on a written stave. But the bundles were never static, like written music: they shifted and sang, like the tips of violin bows in a symphony orchestra; and they moved to rhythms more subtle and quivering and undivinable than those of any music that man has yet written. Sometimes the shapes looked like searchlights, massed or single, probing the night sky; but still they danced to those subtle rhythms. Sometimes the shapes were not shapes at all—just shifting masses of pale light that throbbed and pulsated. No, that is wrong. They did not "pulsate": nothing so regular and predictable; they waxed and waned and welled and quivered. Yet always, no matter how its forms kept modulating, mutating, the light remained white and simple and pure.

Toward the end, the shapes became curtains. These curtains swept across the sky in luxuriant folds, shifting and refolding—always about to reveal something stupendous but never actually doing anything so gross, so crass, so unethereal. And sometimes, at the most exquisite moments, the curtains were not curtains at all but only the hems of curtains, still moving across a vast sweep of sky in undulating folds but reduced, now, to their gossamer limit. They swayed, the hems of these curtains—or perhaps they were the hems of diaphanous dresses—and they shimmered and almost audibly sibilated. And all the time they were contracting and dilating with small, breathless, trembling shifts of shape, as if half frightened, half filled with delight. For a long, ecstatic interlude, the quivering light dominated the night sky. Then, very quickly, the climax had come and gone. For a while there were lingering throbs and subtle movements. Then there remained only the two original bands of light arcing across the sky. The bands were fainter now, as if tired. All at once I was tired, too. And although I had decided two hours earlier, almost at the beginning of the performance, that I would sit outside all night and watch, I turned and crawled into the tent, into my sleeping bag.

Next morning I set out to confirm that the way to the spruce trees lay open. Or at least that the first obstacle was passable.

After an early breakfast I pulled on my thigh waders and walked a hundred yards downstream to the broad, broken-water place that on the day of the hunter hassle had looked from my stance on the ridge like the most promising ford. I did not, to put it mildly, want to swim across: the water temperature was 52 degrees and therefore not merely uninviting but probably dangerous for anything except a rather brief immersion.

In less than half an hour of slow, tentative wading down and across a complicated series of bars and riffles—during which my willow staff provided invaluable third-leg service —I had found a safe and surprisingly easy route and had stepped dry-shod onto the far bank. I stood there for a few minutes, looking across flat tundra at the line of rolling hills that blocked my westward view—the line of hills that was broken by a series of low, folding gaps. Then I stepped back into the river. The return, angling up and against the current, proved only marginally more difficult. By the time I stepped back onto the left bank I had no doubt that even with a heavy pack I could manage the crossing, both ways.

With the one apparent barrier between me and the spruce trees surmounted, I did not go back to camp and begin preparing for my journey. Instead, I walked on downriver. Ostensibly, I went because I told myself I ought to look for an even better crossing place. After all, if the river rose while I was away I might have a hell of a time getting back. But the real goad, when I turned downriver, was my premonition.

Even on marginally hazardous trips I had occasionally suffered premonitions of a sticky end. None had ever been particularly strong. None, obviously, had proved particularly fatal. But ever since the moment, months earlier, when my long-planned trip to Alaska had at last hardened into probability, I had felt in my bones that something final was going to happen to me up there.

My sane, logical components kept coming up with sane,

logical, pooh-poohing explanations: the challenge of a huge and unknown land; the oddly pointed remarks of two different friends when they heard I meant to go, as usual, on my own. Such things, I knew, were enough to have started my whole train of thought. But the knowledge did little to help. As time passed, the premonition, if anything, gained strength. I had no idea what form the danger might take— though grizzlies kept peering out from the dark canyons in which such fears lurk—yet by the time I left home there was a part of me that did not really believe I would ever again walk in through my familiar front door. Only "a part of me," though. My sane, cool, cerebral sectors continued to dismiss the whole thing as childish. The childish, human, irrational corners counter-objected. "Listen to *us!*" they whispered. "That's only your head talking through its hat. Listen to what *we* are saying! Beware!" But most of us, FDR notwithstanding, fear fear itself, and my sane sectors responded, repeatedly, "Don't be a damned fool. Ignore that nonsense. You simply can't live that way. Of course you must go to Alaska —or you'll never do anything again. Just go." So I went.*

That morning, after I had crossed and recrossed the river just below camp, my irrational segments kept warning that something might happen if I ventured into a dense willow thicket, a mile or more downstream—that same thicket my glasses had lingered on, the day of the hunter hassling, when I studied the river from my stance on the ridge. Even then

* Nonbackpackers will no doubt regard my premonition as an intimation of idiosyncratic cowardice. But I suspect that experienced backpackers will understand. I find that many of them admit, if asked, that they almost routinely wonder, when they walk out of their front doors for a long trip—or at least for a solo trip to some rugged or remote place—whether they will ever walk back in through that door. They know, of course, that the thought is base and probably baseless. But they still, just for a moment, wonder. And sometimes, they also admit, that moment has a way of lingering in their minds—and of reemerging at intervals throughout the trip.

it had looked very broad, swathing its little side creek—very dense and decidedly dark; and somewhere deep down the irrational voices had murmured. But now the cerebral sector was counterattacking. "Crazy!" it said. "Why, you simply can't let them get away with it, or you'll never do anything. Sheer cowardice, I tell you. Go! Just go!" So, as usual, I went.

I went at no great pace, searching with focused care for a ford, detecting nothing remotely like one. In due course I looked up and found myself a hundred yards from the big thicket. I hesitated, then walked slowly toward it. Ray Kramer's heavy six-shooter—its shoulder holster strapped outside my shirt and fitting so comfortably that I rarely noticed it—all at once felt reassuring; but I kept remembering one of the bear stories Ray had told me, back in Anchorage. We had been standing in the corridor outside his office and he had pointed at a photograph hanging on the wall. It was a shot—by no means a horrendously dramatic close-up—of a female grizzly with two cubs.

"One of our guys took that," Ray had said. "He was one of the few people in the department that didn't carry a gun of some kind in the field—and it was almost his last picture. He saw the bears from a ways off and had plenty of time to move clear, but decided to hang around for a good shot. Right after he'd taken this one, Mama came for him. By the time she reached him he was already fifteen feet up a spruce, and thought he was safe. Now, you mustn't believe the stories that grizzlies can't climb trees. This Mama went up after him. When she was still a couple of feet short of him, though, she began to lose her grip. But just before she fell she reached up and one claw caught in the lace of the guy's boot. So she pulled him down with her. She mauled him pretty badly. Among other things, tore his scalp nearly off. He played dead, though, and after savaging both his arms pretty severely, Mama left. He survived, but only just. Things got better, and he's okay now—but he still carries the scars. The point is, it seems likely that if he'd had a gun, even a decent-caliber revolver, he might have been able to kill Mama as she came up the tree."

So as I approached the big thicket, the heavy six-shooter under my left armpit felt, as I say, reassuring. A small plastic whistle hung around my neck, too, on a length of nylon cord. Ray had suggested I carry it there and blow it whenever I moved through thick cover. Grizzlies mostly took off when they heard a whistle, he said, and just about the only dangerous bear was one you surprised, up close. In addition, I was carrying—for brewing tea—an ordinary tin can with a baling-wire handle and also, clipped to my belt, on my right side, a steel Sierra Club cup; and I had already practiced tapping these two together. The sound of metal against metal—even a very faint sound—seems to scare off most truly wild animals. One East African dusk, a big herd of elephants had drifted close to my bogged-down car. They were upwind, and seemed unaware of my presence. There were young animals among them, too, some so small that they hung close to their mothers' towering bulks. When the nearest elephants had moved to within about a hundred and fifty yards, and my adrenaline had begun to pump, I tapped a spoon gently against the side of the car. Slowly, without panic but in clear response, the huge black shapes began to swing away to the right.

In spite of my fears, the thicket turned out to be a pleasant and interesting place. When I was still a hundred yards from the first willows, I saw a caribou standing half-concealed in a clearing. I began to stalk it. Wind and cover were in my favor, and soon I was crouching at the edge of the clearing. The caribou—a young animal, with no branches on its velveted antlers—was now lying down, body upright, legs tucked under. Through glasses I could see the veins standing out on the soft brown fur of its face. From time to time it would give a low, flat grunt, remarkably like the grunts I had often heard from wildebeest, or gnus, on the East African savanna. And when I at last moved forward in an attempt to get even closer, using very sparse cover, and the caribou detected me and scrambled to its feet and dashed away, its startled grunts sounded even more wildebeestial.

I moved on toward the creek that bisected the thicket. The cover thickened. I began blowing my whistle, then tapping cup against tin can. In that quiet, sun-speckled place, it seemed an almost sacrilegious act. It was reassuring, though, and I went on doing it. Before long I came out into more open country between the several stony branches of the creek. The whistling and cup-tapping did not seem to have done undue harm: very soon I saw a big caribou with huge antlers stroll across the main creek bed and settle down for a siesta in a willow clump.

Otherwise, nothing much happened during that day's patrol. I built a small fire and brewed tea in the wire-handled tin can. I sat watching sunlight, birds, more sunlight. I went on downstream for another mile, braving more thickets. That was all. But when I got back to camp in midafternoon, bearing the knowledge that another vault of my premonition had been faced, and faced down, the river seemed to sing more sweetly than when I had left, the sun to shine even more brightly.

That evening I fished purely for fun in the delectable stretch—half pool, half run—at the foot of my garden. I used only dry fly and cast only into difficult places. I caught four big grayling and because I had eaten enough fish I returned them all.

During dinner, and for long afterward, I sat watching another *lumière* performance in the northern sky. It was just as ethereal and almost as exciting as the first; and I was treated to no fewer than three shooting stars. At last, half an hour after midnight, I crawled inside the tent. For the first time since arriving in Alaska I slid fully into the sleeping bag and zippered it shut: the temperature outside had already fallen to 28 degrees, and it seemed likely that the open bag, pulled loosely over me, the way I had been using it, might not be warm enough. Before I fell asleep it occurred to me that this day, the eleventh since Charlie Allen had dropped me on the spit, was the first on which I had seen no other human being. Perhaps, I thought, I would now be granted true solitude.

Around eight o'clock next morning, five figures appeared on the opposite bank, walking down from the direction of the hidden orange-tent encampment. I was doing chores outside the tent, stark naked (in the shade, my thermometer read 40 degrees; but there was no wind, and in the sunlight it felt pleasantly warm, provided you did not hold one side of your body in shadow for too long, kept moving and were furnished with a good coat of body hair). The figures on the far bank spread out along the river, fishing. I clad myself in shorts, against the crowd. Soon I noticed a pair of hunters on the far bank, too, squatting on a knoll almost directly opposite me. For an hour they kept studying through their rifle scopes something on my side of the river, apparently almost in my back yard. When they vanished at last I walked to a hillock not far from my tent. Two hundred yards away, a big caribou was browsing out in open tundra. I stood watching it through glasses. After a while it saw me and trotted upriver. Only when I turned away did I see that the hunters were back on their knoll. As I walked back to camp I kept my eyes averted from them. Before long they shouldered their packs and strode off. They went downriver, westward, toward the rolling hills, toward the spruce trees, toward "my" country. I spread a plastic sheet in front of my tent and began checking onto it the things I would need for a week's journey.

By midmorning a line of dark clouds was sweeping in from the southwest. I began to hurry my preparations. But when the first drops fell I was still not quite ready. I piled everything back inside the tent. Within half an hour a steady rain was falling.

It rained, with minor intermissions, for forty-eight hours. Most of that time I lay in my tent, reading. The weather kept the fishermen out of my territory, but it seemed, if anything, to encourage the hunters. Distant rifle shots kept thumping across the tundra. And early on the second morning I was startled out of half-sleep by a loud crack-thump, very fast, very close. The crack came from directly upstream, on my side of the river, the thump from the far bank; and I guessed immediately what had happened. Almost at once, another crack-thump confirmed the diagnosis. By the time I stuck my head out of the tent, two men were hurrying down the far bank, obviously looking for a crossing place. As they came closer I saw that they were the two hunters that the day before had glassed my back yard for so long from the knoll on the far bank—the hunters I had inadvertently cheated of their prey. And as I watched them wade a rapid—they both wore waist waders—then pass close to my tent with eyes riveted upriver, and finally, up near the outflow, lift in triumph from concealing vegetation the limp head of a big caribou, I had to admit that rough justice had been done. In the end, they had killed in my front yard. And for more than two hours I was almost constantly aware, as I lay reading, that if I looked out through the triangle of the tent's open entrance I would see that it framed a picture of the two hunters crouched in the gray rain over their dead caribou, hacking. They waded back across the river at last, with bulging packs, and left me to read in peace.

The little book I read during those two rainy days was *Should Trees Have Standing?* by Christopher D. Stone, a lawyer.* It proposed that "natural objects such as trees, mountains, rivers and lakes should, like corporations, have legal rights." A U.S. Supreme Court opinion had already cited this once unthinkable idea, and I found the main essay—written in plain English, not dense legal prose—absorbing and even exciting. What stirred me most deeply, though, was a short final section on what might be called the philosophical or even religious implications. In it, the lawyer transcended mere law. He quoted not only Kant and Hegel but also Jacques Cousteau and Carson McCullers, and it was an extract from a McCullers short story, "A Tree, a Rock, a Cloud," that lifted me, as I lay there in my little tent, into a not altogether explicable state approaching beatitude. In its final discussion of the urgent need for a world religion and the "myths" (in an altogether undemeaning sense) that every religion must offer, the book roused me to a kind of mental orgasm: "What is needed is a myth that can fit our growing body of knowledge of geophysics, biology and the cosmos. In this vein, I do not think it too remote that we may come to regard the Earth, as some have suggested, as one organism, of which Mankind is a functional part—the mind, perhaps: different from the rest of nature, but different as a man's brain is from his lungs."

Now, I know I cannot expect you, supplied with only this brief summary of what I read, to generate any of the euphoria I felt that rainy day in my little tent. But it does not matter. All I am asking and hoping is that you accept that for a spell I was "high." That matters.

Just as I finished, in early afternoon, the essay that is the core of the book, the clouds lifted enough for me to begin my journey in search of the spruce trees. At least, that is how I

* Now published by Tioga Publishing Company, Box 50490, Palo Alto, California 94303. 1988 edition, softcover, $7.95.

viewed events at the time: no more than a lucky coincidence. But now, looking back, I am inclined to doubt that during the previous two days there had been altogether valid reasons for my failure to get going. The weather had several times shown promise of clearing. Once, the clouds had lifted enough to reveal new snow cloaking the mountains. But when the peaks vanished once more behind new mists and the rain began again, I had gone back to my book. I am not totally convinced, now, that when I finally made the decision to go, the weather had turned decisively better. Perhaps it was simply that with the book finished and my spirit soaring I was ready at last: no longer did any effective voting sector of me want to put off, for whatever dark reason, the journey that much of me had all along been hungering for. Anyway, the fact is that I at last made up my mind.

It would, I felt sure, take me more than a day to reach the trees, and I did not toy for very long with the idea of postponing the start until the following morning. As soon as I had stuffed a few last-minute items, including the book, into my pack, I moved outside into the damp but brightening tundra and battened down my little tent, tight. Onto its front guy line I tied a plastic bag holding a note to Charlie Allen—telling him, just in case something went wrong, where I was going and the latest I expected to be back. I told him, that is, as best I could: my only map ended a mile or two west of camp. In the note I avoided, as I had been avoiding in my notebook—even, when I could, in my thoughts—the phrase "going west." Given the premonitions, that seemed too much like tempting fate.

At last, at 3:35 p.m. on my fourteenth day alone in wide Alaska, I heaved the heavy pack onto my back and began to walk toward the spruce trees.

The rest of that first day went well but unremarkably. Thanks largely to the willow staff I managed, though heavily laden now, to ford the river without difficulty. On the far bank I spent almost an hour reorganizing the pack from a semi-waterproofed, river-crossing conformation into its normal tactical mode, with load distribution and ease of access the prime criteria. Finally, I lashed the hip waders in an undisciplined gob on top of the already overflowing pack and headed westward across flat tundra toward my first landmark—a huge rounded boulder, standing alone, that had been dumped on the plain by some long-departed glacier.

The pack felt oppressively heavy and the going proved rough. The staff helped, though, and I was pleased to find that, even wearing the pack, I hardly noticed the heavy revolver in its shoulder holster. From the start, route-finding turned out to be a subtle and absorbing business, but by the time I had angled across the flats to the first rolling hills and climbed close to their crest—and thereby moved beyond the margin of my map—I had at least begun to learn the local rules. The route-finding was, as always, a continuing, feedback process of judging from experience whether a certain color or texture or conformation of ground was likely to mean impenetrable barrier, horrendous obstacle course, normal slogging or even something that you could in benevolent moments call good walking. As everywhere, the trick was to tap local knowledge. In this case, the obvious source was the caribou. But I had to remember, the way you always must, that the natives might not be going the same place I was going, and that even if they were, their motives might be different from mine. When I found that a likely and well-defined trail repeatedly and frustratingly petered out into untracked mossy wilderness, I had to remember that what I saw as a mossy wilderness might to a caribou look like a sumptuous dining room; so I had to remember that if I always lived within a stomachful of starvation, or at least of hunger pangs, and were walking down a corridor that kept opening up into dining rooms filled with tables bearing sumptuous dishes, then I too would often forget for a while about where I was going and would detour to one of the many vacant chairs. As an experienced caribou I would, with luck and practice, soon pick the trail up again, anyway. And even if I failed I could be reasonably sure that before long I would run across signs that somebody else had gone my way, trailblazing. For me, firmly in human form, what all this added up to was that I must expect to keep losing the trail and having to probe in likely places before I picked it up again.

By seven o'clock I had mastered the rudiments of this local route-finding and was up on the crest of the bare rolling hills that folded over, far ahead, into a gap; into the gap that I hoped was the right gap.

Behind me, when I looked, I saw clouds still clinging to the mountains. Gray veils of rain kept sweeping across their foothills. But ahead, beyond my gap, blue sky fed expectation. And around me, now, stretched a new world. A barren, bracing world of skyline ridges, lakes held secret in shallow pockets and placid, wandering caribou. Soon, a wedge of dark cloud came sliding through my gap, refeeding fears. Light drizzle fell. I strode on, into uncharted country. From far behind, faint but still deadly, came a single rifle thump. But then a shaft of sunlight split the cloud, a rainbow arched down, and westward, look, the land was bright.

I camped at dusk near one of the small, secret lakes. It was a barren place, really—just a windswept tarn with its almost dry bed a mosaic of cracked brown mud. Gray clouds hung low over the bare, encircling slopes. After dark, no moon softened the night. There were no northern lights. But I had rolled out my sleeping pad near another big and rounded rock, on pale green "reindeer moss" that was as soft and springing underfoot and underbody as a thick, ancient lawn, and when I had strung up my white plastic tarpaulin so that it formed a cozy but open-ended cubicle I had a very comfortable little camp. The unknown always breeds excitement, too, and although I had in the last light been unable to see very far ahead, I knew that next day I would reach the gap.

From the start, the next day indeed turned out to be different. I woke late. And I did not leave the half-dried tarn until after one o'clock. I still cannot fully explain the dallying. Even at the time, I think I was vaguely puzzled by it. My muscles may have been a little weary: it was some time since I had carried such a brute of a load, and the evening before I had walked hard for four hours across rough, rhythm-disrupting terrain. I did not feel tired, though, that second morning. Yet despite the nearness of the gap and the promise of those dark and pointed spruce trees there was no sense of urgency in me. The threatening weather, with dark clouds scudding eastward before a chill wind, may have had something to do with it, I suppose. Anyway, the fact is that after a leisurely breakfast I sat watching the weather, re-sorting equipment and, as my notebook lamely records, "taking it easy." But the notes also say "sort of savoring aloneness," and this may be more relevant. For up on the crest of those bare and rolling hills, with the wind blowing clean and cold—and with the big lake long gone, the mountains almost hidden and the river valley now far below—I had, without shadow of nagging doubt, finally broken free. So perhaps it is hardly surprising that I should have lingered to relish my new, assured solitude.

Once, faint and so far off that the sound did little more than jostle memory, a rifle thumped. Later, a herd of caribou drifted past, cropping moss and lichen. Several of them passed close enough for me to see again, through glasses, veins and arteries standing out on their brown faces. But that was about the extent of the events that took place outside me, that rather odd morning by the tarn, that morning with its curious air of unreality, that morning on which I seemed, even more than usual, to be masterless of my fate. And for a long time I was not aware that events were germinating inside me.

I am not sure at what stage of the morning the first germ appeared. I have no recollection of any ordered preparatory line of thought, and until the first words welled up I do not think I had an inkling that I was about to generate something. That first surprising germ is there in the notebook, though, all by itself, unconnected to anything else, lying in front of me now as I write. It is word-perfect and correctly punctuated, so I probably pulled my copy of *Should Trees Have Standing?* out of the pack and copied the passage direct; on the other hand, it may be that, because of the words' beautiful rhythm, I had memorized them. What I wrote was part of the quotation from the Carson McCullers story. A cranky, decrepit old man sitting in a streetcar cafe beside a twelve-year-old boy, a stranger, suddenly asks whether the boy knows "how love should be begun." The story goes on:

> The old man leaned closer and whispered:
> "A tree. A rock. A cloud." . . .
> "The weather was like this in Portland," he said.
> "At the time my science was begun."

I do not think I knew, as I wrote this passage down, just why I was doing so. But it is clear from what follows in the notebook that very soon I was scribbling ferociously, filled with a beautiful if ridiculous certainty that what I wrote was good; filled, what is more, with a barely acknowledged awareness that it was not I who wrote but someone writing through me. The details of what I wrote do not matter now. The point is that from that moment my state of mind changed. As soon as the first fine frenzy of writing had abated, I struck camp and continued walking westward; and for most of the rest of that day, and all the next, I lived a cloven, schizoid life.

On one level I lived a normal, down-to-earth, one-foot-in-front-of-the-other, physical existence: I walked westward across rough tundra and saw caribou and clouds and rocks. But on another level that was mostly much more real—by which I suppose I mean that it gripped my mind more firmly—I lived above this little figure striding westward and so could see not only the tundra and caribou and clouds and rocks that surrounded the figure at any given moment but also all those worlds surrounding him at every moment since Charlie Allen had deposited him beside the big lake, fourteen days before. This second, elevated, semi-omniscient self could also see—clearly, but at first only in disjointed cameos—most of the whys and wherefores and even thuses that lay behind both these onward-flowing worlds, supporting them and finally giving them meaning.

Now there is, I suppose, a sense in which all of us have for brief spells lived this kind of binocular existence; but that day I left the half-dried tarn and walked on toward the gap in the hills, I walked in a more curiously divided state than any I had ever experienced, even imagined. For that day I was overseer, too. I was at the same time a third entity, standing apart from the little figure walking across the tundra and also apart from the other being that hung elevated slightly above him. This overseer monitored them both. And from time to time he muttered, in slightly baffled amusement—out loud, to the open tundra—"How very odd!"

As they walked, all three levels of my being were filled with growing excitement. The earthbound man, picking his way slowly across rough terrain, quickened to the thought of the gap that was coming closer and closer. The being that floated above him, still composing furiously in his head and sometimes in his notebook, responded to the experience of monitoring the walker, and also to the joy that always flares up when a newly germinated seed promises to mature into satisfying flower. And the overseer delighted in the new experience of double monitoring. At least, I think that is how the division went, that second day west of the lake, as my three selves moved forward together through our separate but interlinked and even merging worlds.

In the physical world, we moved through a gray and lowering light. And in that understory of events, down on the tundra, progress was at first ordinary, mundane. I began to climb a rise. A lone caribou trotted across the skyline. I angled down toward a long, somehow surprising little lake. Lunch beside this lake. On again, along a steep ridge. From it, looking out over a wide vista, an awareness that the whole tundra was tinted now with red; a renewed awareness that the season was no longer summer.

For a spell, then, the overseer—at least, I think it was the overseer, but it may have been another of us—could look back beyond the reddening tundra, back beyond the orange-tent encampment on the shore of the big lake, back beyond all the big human cities of the planet, back to the way the planet had been fifty-odd years earlier. In that larger world, too, the seasons had changed. For fifty-odd years earlier, when I had been born, our species had seemed—to many human minds, anyway—to be living in halcyon, sunlit days; if not internally, then certainly in our relationship to the rest of the world. Our dominion over the rest of the world, as sanctified in Genesis or as assumed in such Christian heresies as Communism and also in most, though not all, the other major, more or less functioning religions, was still accepted without thought, let alone question, by the vast majority of people. But that was fifty-odd years ago. Now it was no longer summer in that world, either.

I strode on over the reddening tundra. Soon I was slanting down off the ridge and up a long, slow slope toward what seemed at last to be the entrance to the gap. Clouds racing across the sky in windswept skeins. Off to the right, a squirrel up on his bridge, on watch, casing me, then vanishing. At my left shoulder, soaring on an updraft, seven noisy ravens. And always, every yard, the separate, conjoined three of us: the monitor; the hovering scribbler; the earthbound walking self—each of us smiling, each of us as excited, in our own way, as a child.

Almost at the gap now; at the pass. No clear crest. Just an easing around a corner and the slow unfolding of a new valley. But now, no doubt responding to expectation, the earthbound walker shed subservience; became once more the dominant member of our trio. My eyes remained riveted ahead as they devoured each detail of the unfolding tundra slope on the far side of the valley. The wind blew cold on my left cheek. I strode on. No trees yet.

Then, at last, over on the far side of the valley, the barren tundra began to unfold a line of something—or at least the suggestion of a line—that was dark and different. A dozen more steps, and there could be no doubt. Along the hem of the still-unfolding slope grew a few small, dark, pointed spruces. I glanced at my watch—to log, I suppose, the instant of fulfillment: 4:53 p.m.

From that moment I began to move less urgently down the slope of the pass. There was plenty of daylight left, I told myself. I would walk down into the valley, taking my time, and camp.

As I began my descent, the earthbound walker took total command—and held it for the rest of the day. The floating self whispered a few final lines it had scribbled, then fell silent, melted away. The overseer evaporated.

I walked down from the pass, angled out onto a spur. The

valley continued to unfold. Before long its floor lifted into full view.

The stretch of valley that I could now see formed a natural bowl with a river winding through it. This bowl, held cupped between low hills to my left and a black upriver gorge, measured perhaps six miles by three. No sound disturbed its calm. In all its length I could detect no sign of man. The dark spruce trees, semaphoring to me a week earlier through their gap, had not lied.

The winding river often lay hidden between steep banks, but near the center of the bowl lay a small sunken crescent and within it I could see tumbling water, turquoise-gray or white and glistening. The lines of the sunken, secluded crescent had a certain subtle harmony. Steep, curving slopes hemmed the crescent in and seemed to shield it from the outer world, inviolate, as if it formed a separate little kingdom. On the floor of this crescent-kingdom and on its slopes grew phalanxes of tall, dark spruces, taller and fuller by far than the small trees I had glimpsed from the top of the pass. Some of them clustered in dark, mysterious clumps. Others thrust up singly, like black swords. Yet even in that day's gray and lowering light the trees seemed to be pointing, promising, softening the tundra, warming me against the wind. They stood as trees should stand—clean, elegant, autonomous.

I sat down beside a hillock and, part-sheltered from the wind, looked down through glasses into the little crescent-kingdom. At that range, even in such drab and dreary light, the open spaces between the trees looked flat and green and smooth, like manicured parkland. Here and there, caribou browsed. As I scanned, my glasses kept swinging past a dense mass of trees, across the river from the crescent. This mass stood round and humped as a citadel—huge, dark, impregnable—the sort of place that might conceal anything. It made no difference, though. Even in that first moment, I think I knew where my journey would end. My outward journey, anyway.

From the start, I thought of the little sunken kingdom as "Eden." The word is there in my notebook, scribbled while I still sat beside the windbreaking hillock, exploring the valley through glasses. Even at the time, of course, a part of me knew better than to pay any attention to maunderings about "kingdom" and "citadel" and "Eden." Another part of me fortunately knew better still.

I began to feel chilled, even part-sheltered as I was from the wind. I lowered the glasses, stood up and began to walk down into the bowl. A dozen caribou browsed placid along a spur. An old beaver dam curved across a narrow side-valley. When I reached the floor of the bowl there were bushes bearing black berries, ripe for bears. It was much warmer down there, out of the wind.

I walked in among the first, scattered spruces. They stood dark and beautiful, and much taller than I had expected. I stopped to savor them. But the savoring did not really work. They were just trees. It did not matter, though. What they had signaled and I had come to find, it now seemed, was this valley with its secluded crescent-kingdom.

Without warning, and for no apparent reason, I began to feel weary. My ambitions contracted. I would go only as far as the first visible river bend, I abruptly decided, and camp at the edge of my crescent-kingdom, on the brink of Eden.

Reaching the bend took far longer than I had expected: without a map, I had misjudged the valley's size. And as I weaved my way across flat but trackless tundra a new wind arose and black clouds crowded low over the southern hills. The sky grew very dark. I found a good, protected campsite under the lee of a steep bank. It stood high above the river, but a small creek piped water into my back yard. By the time

I had battened down my white plastic tarpaulin into a sturdy fortress, the wind was shrieking overhead, above the bank, and rain had begun to fall.

It rained all night, steadily and heavily. By a dispensation of providence, it rained all the next day too, and I was able to sit or lie hour after hour in my little white castle, with the rain drumming down on it, untempted to explore and therefore able to indulge without distraction the excitement that I found once more flooding through me as soon as I woke.

I did not know whether the idea that had germinated the day before, beside the tarn, would still look valid when I got back out into "the world"; but that rainy morning, with the excitement once more in flood, there was no question of not grappling with the resurging thoughts. Cloven and schizoid again, I worked all day at them, with the mundane me sitting or lying in my rain-drum castle but with the floating self back in command. So much in command that it remained barely conscious of the wet and windblown world in which the mundane self vaguely existed, at least intermittently. I am not sure if the overseer accompanied us that day, but I do not think so. All day, though, the floating self grappled with its task, and by nightfall the whole thing was, except for its conclusion, down on paper.

I slept soundly through a second night of rain. Come dawn, it was still raining: I remained trapped, free. Hour after hour I continued to lie under the tarp, polishing. All at once, in midmorning, I had the conclusion down, too—not fashioned yet, but already framed, blocked out, so that I knew where I was going. Then, without warning, I was written out, wrung, finished.*

---

* If by any chance you would like to see what I wrote—to see it in its finished form—try to get hold of a copy of *Backpacker* magazine #12 (vol. 3, no. 4, Winter 1975) and turn to page 50: "More Than a Day's Walk: A

The first, terrible, unfightable exhaustion passed, the way it always does; and although I continued for a while to sit there under the taut white tarp, leaning against my pack—released, content, leached of ambition—there at length came a time when I was ready as well as free to go out and look at the country.

Only then did I become aware that the rain had stopped and that the world outside my tarp was growing lighter. I crawled to the taller end of the castle, stuck my head outside. A cutting edge of blue sky had begun to slice in from the west. Above me, clouds still dripped a little, but the wind had died. In the new calm I thought I heard, just for a moment, a faint, curiously unpinnable humming noise that seemed to come from a distance but from no particular direction; it faded away, though, before I could be sure that it had ever really existed. Soon, the clouds had fled and the world sparkled.

I made some quick calculations. The journey back to the lake would, once again, be more than a day's walk, and although Charlie Allen was not due to pick me up until six days later I had made that promise to be ready two days early, in case the first big autumn storm threatened. So I could stay in this new valley for only two more full days. I therefore bestirred myself. Beneath new and energizing sunlight, I struck camp and moved upriver into the heart of my crescent-kingdom.

For the first day and a half in Eden, things did not go quite as I had planned. By the time I left camp, the sunlight had waned, a new grayness had spread across the sky and hardened into a threat, and the wind had caught a second breath. As I began to walk along the lip of the steep slope that enclosed the sunken kingdom—close up, the slope had be-

Story in 20 Stanzas." I find I still have a soft spot for the story, but I should warn you, I guess, that some critics regard it as less than a work of genius.

come a gracious, curving escarpment, almost motherly in its protectiveness—I could see dark clouds settling over the black upriver gorge. The gorge looked even more ominous now, another place for premonitions, and I felt glad I would have no time even to consider accepting its challenge. Over on the far side of the crescent, though, the round and humped mass of trees that I had called the "citadel" still stood huge and dark and impregnable.

As I walked along the lip of the escarpment, a marsh hawk quartered low across the flat tundra to my right. A covey of ptarmigan scattered before it, frantic brown and white. The hawk sliced among them, then turned so quickly that I could not be absolutely sure, before it vanished, that it had indeed struck food. I walked on. A raven hovered at my left shoulder, suspended in its presumably more gentle world by the escarpment's updraft. Then I had moved up onto a slight promontory and the crescent opened out below me.

There was not, after all, much mystery about it. Not, I mean, the mystery of dark, concealed things. From this new, plunging angle I could see that most of the trees stood wide apart. So my eye could penetrate, dispel imaginings. The rushing river curved and twisted, white and turquoise, down broad and open channels. And yet, for all its unexpected openness, the kingdom did not disappoint me.

For one thing, it is wrong, really, to have called it "open." Although there were wider spaces than I had expected between the elegant, pointing, almost statuesque trees, vegetation crowded thick and tall. And its denseness lent weight, gave me pause. I could see no animals, down there on the floor of the sunken kingdom, but I knew now that there was plenty of cover for them. And I found that as I walked on along the escarpment's lip I felt a new respect. This was no manicured parkland but a raw, lean, pragmatic wilderness in which life muscled, defended, hit.

The wind continued to rise, the clouds to loom blacker. I found a way down the escarpment onto the floor of my kingdom and began looking for a campsite.

It took me two hours to find one. The vegetation grew even taller and denser than I had expected, so there were plenty of sheltered sites, many of them with water nearby. But when I found, at the first potential site, tucked in under a likely tree, the flattened bed and fresh droppings of what seemed to be a very large bear, I discovered that I was willing to camp only in an open place. I also began to move about with fanfare, blowing my whistle and drumming my steel cup against the metal of the revolver butt that protruded from its shoulder holster. Finally I chose a site high above the river, protected by another steep bank from the now howling wind. I pitched the tarp very low, very tight.

That night it rained hard and blew harder. Next morning the river ran gray, barely tinted with turquoise. Rain still fell. By midmorning, though, the wind's howl had subsided to a mutter. Now I kept hearing, at intervals, the faint, curiously unpinnable humming noise that seemed to come from no particular direction. I had heard it once or twice during the night, too, during lulls in the storm, and its persistence demolished my earlier assumption that it probably came from a light plane circling not far away. Now that I could hear the hum more clearly I decided that it did not sound the way I remembered a diamond drill rig sounding. Perhaps somewhere beneath the gaunt surrounding hills, in huge caverns cleft from solid rock, there lurked a Martian service base for flying saucers. In such a conspicuously man-free place, that seemed almost as likely a source as any other for such a mechanized-sounding noise.

Soon after noon, the rain stopped. I set off to explore my kingdom.

Down on the floor of the crescent, beside the river, the

clumps of trees that from the escarpment had looked so widely separated once more stood thick, palpable with possible surprises. In the "open" spaces, vegetation often crowded so tall and jungled that my fishing rod became an entangling nuisance. I threaded my way through it, fanfaring with the whistle and accompanying with cup-on-gun-butt percussion, like a whistle-happy referee doubling as a bomb-happy timpanist. Even then, I chose the most open routes. The river kept dividing into separate channels, and when I found a minor, half-dry one that cut through the heart of the crescent, I began to walk up its wide, stony bed.

I had gone perhaps fifty yards up this channel—no longer fanfaring, because it was so open—when off to the right, in one of the gaps that kept opening up between trees, something moved. Its color was so close to that of a bleached tree stump on almost the same line of sight, and its movement so slight, that I had almost missed it. I lifted my binoculars. The pale antlers, flaring wide from a barely visible brown head, looked bigger and more heavily spiked than those of any caribou I had seen so far. I fine-focused my glasses. The brown head swung slowly to one side—and there glinted into existence, as if by magic, a huge, pale, suspended slab. It was as if a six-foot-long two-by-twelve plank of fresh-cut spruce had materialized in thin air. Even before my eyes had fully recorded that the wooden plank was really bone, that it was not flat but concave, and that stout, curving tines sprang from its outer edge, I knew what I was seeing. Then the brown head had swung further around—and the pale slab flicked out of existence. But now, because I understood what I was seeing, I could make out the dark underside of the slab and the thick round horizontal bar of bone from which it sprang. I could also see that the curving tines along the outer edge of the huge paddle formed a fearsome arsenal of offensive weapons.

The animal swung its head away from me and slowly,

placidly, began to move forward. But the head, browsing down among bushes, soon swung again—and a second pale slab glinted into midair existence, wavered, flickered out. Then the massive brown rump was there, high above the bushes, solid and square and strong—but with an incongruous fat stub of a tail. The beast continued to move slowly forward, at right angles to my line of sight, feeding as it went.

I lowered my glasses. The moose was about two hundred yards away, near the far side of a big clearing. The wind blew steady from the right, almost exactly across my front. And to my left grew a wedge of tall spruces with its forward edge protruding into the clearing. I took two pictures, then eased left, toward the trees. They gave good cover, and once I was among them I moved forward slowly but with confidence. Within five minutes I stood beside a tree at the very tip of the wedge, barely a hundred yards from the moose.

The huge pale paddles of its antlers—still glinting board-like and almost white when they caught the light, then turning and flicking into near-invisibility—now looked unnervingly solid. The biggest tines in their fringing phalanxes were at least a foot long, and stiletto sharp. But the moose was still browsing peacefully. Ray Kramer had said, "Caribou never come for you, moose very rarely—and then only during the rut." I could no longer remember when he had said the rutting season began; but the brown body still half concealed among bushes and small trees did not seem, in spite of its bulk, to pose any kind of threat.

I shot another photograph. The moose continued to move languidly—browsing, easing left. Soon, he melted away behind a large spruce; for agonizing moments I did not know if I would see him again. Then he had moved clear of the tree. Almost at once, he paused to feed on a low bush.

Now only his legs were hidden. For the first time I could see the whole brown body, massive at the shoulder, muscled like a Brahma bull, square and powerful and bulldozer. I could see thick black mud, still wet from a recent wallow, caking the body's lower half. Could see ruffled patches of fur on the upper coat, where the animal had licked with its tongue or perhaps rubbed with its antlers. Could see the long "bell" of skin and hair that hung from the throat—dewlap fashion, but too far forward, and not continuing down the neck the way a normal dewlap does. And now that the animal stood in perfect profile I could also see—and be surprised by it, though I cannot imagine why—the curiously drooping muzzle that I had long known, from photographs and drawings and perhaps even from zoos, was the moose trademark.

The inoffensive, almost downtrodden impression conveyed by this sad-sack muzzle—perhaps abetted by a patch of pale fur near its tip that at first glance looked like ludicrously oversize nostrils, and by the way the big, sad eyes were set so high in the head, overshadowed by those towering antlers—removed the last of my lingering apprehension. This odd, lugubrious, rather comic animal would surely harm no one. I relaxed, shot two more pictures. Whether the moose heard the camera's clicks or whether I had grown careless in my new confidence and made some obvious movement, I do not know, but suddenly the beast was alert; had turned his head and was looking directly at me.

Head-on, the moose had Jekyll-and-Hyded. I was no longer looking at a sad and harmless comic. I faced a solid citizen: overly solemn, perhaps; "square" as more than a bulldozer, no doubt; impassive most of the time, I felt sure; but once aroused, deadly determined. Without question, not somebody to trifle with.

The moose continued to stare directly at me. I stood very still. Minutes ticked past.

From this head-on view I could see that the eyes were in the right place after all: sensibly and serviceably sited, well below the bulging fore-bone of the skull. From this fore-bone protruded the powerful horizontal bars of the antler base, and from these bars sprang the two massive paddles. With the head held high and turned toward me, both paddles now caught the light. They gleamed like plowshares—or perhaps more like swords. Giants' swords. I guessed now that they measured sixteen inches across, not twelve. I had been wrong about the tines, too: the biggest of those curving, stiletto-sharp weapons were at least two feet long. Between the antlers, the moose's ears now stood pricked. To their right, the body had not moved. Had not changed position, that is. But now it, too, was alert: more menacingly muscled, even more profoundly square.

The moose took two paces toward me, stopped. Now body as well as head was pointing, poised. Externally, I remained immobile, frozen. Inside, my heart pounded. I had been wrong about the "hundred yards," too: it now seemed more like sixty. When was it Ray Kramer had said the rut began? The nearest spruce was plainly unclimbable, dammit. Too dense by far. The clump of trees behind, maybe. I seemed to remember their being thinner, almost straggly. But I could not turn my head to check. Not yet.

The bull continued to stare, fixedly. More minutes ticked past. He was taking an unconscionable time over the business of deciding. It was a decision I had often watched being made. A wild animal, unused to meeting humans, meets one of us without a clear introduction, so that uncertainties abound. The animal, by some process not necessarily at all like the cerebration we go through in similar situations, at some point makes up its mind whether this new phenomenon should be fled from, ignored or attacked. Sometimes the decision comes quickly. But not always. You can often sit tight and almost watch the dice being rolled. Whatever the decision—flight, casual acceptance or a charge—it is rarely reversed (unless, of course, the decision is acceptance and you later behave in unseemly fashion).

For his ballot the bull moose appeared to have set up a very canny, deliberate committee. But at last he turned and resumed his slow movement to the left. He seemed somewhat reassured. Yet I still had no sense of a final verdict. Intermittently, the animal continued to browse. But his languid air had gone. From time to time he would stop and look for a moment directly toward me. After a while I saw that his slow and apparently unplanned forward progress was taking him in a steadily tightening curve; that before long he would arrive downwind of me; and that he would then be uncomfortably close.

I began to retreat. I eased to my left rear, toward the trees just behind me that I had now checked were indeed thinner and almost straggly. I moved, of course, only when the moose was moving. At such times, with his head back in profile, he was once more the harmless comic. But I knew better now. And each time he turned his head and looked me over I got a reminder of his true, alternate, Mr. Hyde nature.

Before long I was in among the thinner trees. One of them indeed looked eminently climbable by a man with vivid motivation. Not by a man carrying a fishing rod, though. So before easing between two trees that stood no more than five feet apart, I left my rod outside the canopy of their lower branches. My final position, midway between the two trees, gave me not only good cover but also a feeling that those huge antlers with their protruding tines would not be able, for all the power driving them, to penetrate that fastness of trunks and branches. Still, you could never be sure. And when I studied the climbable tree more closely I realized that although its major branches indeed formed excellent rungs, the smaller branches and dense twigs might well snag the paraphernalia I was carrying slung around neck and waist—

fishing bag, camera, binoculars, whistle, steel cup—and so leave me snared like a fish in a gill net, a few feet above the ground, well within moose-tine range. Had I not known I would feel an absolute fool as well as a stark coward if I stripped myself of all the encumbrances at this early juncture, I would probably have done so. But I was, after all, not even sure that the rutting season had begun. At least, I think that is what I told myself. Besides, Ray had said that even during the rut moose only rarely attacked.

By the time I was comfortably established between the two trees—well, fairly comfortably established—the moose had moved almost directly downwind of me, and to within fifty yards. His progress had slowed, and every few yards he looked toward me; but he kept moving forward. The underbrush around him was now very short, so that I could see all of him except the hooves. His lower legs were dirty white. I could pick out color variations in his rough brown coat, and on the antlers, too: the blunt top of each paddle was tinged pale brown. And through binoculars I saw that his eyes—no longer at all sad and languid but alert and suspicious—had baleful red rims around their big brown irises.

The moose came to a halt and peered at me intently. He made a tentative forward movement, stopped, edged away to his right, stopped again. His committee was clearly back in session, and proceedings seemed to have reached an impasse. The massive animal made several short, indecisive movements, forward, then back. After each of them he would stand stock-still—directly facing me, outlined against dark spruces, ears pressed back. I found myself marveling at the bulk of his huge, muscled neck. After one of his pauses he moved forward, still tentatively, to the top of a low bank. The gap separating us cannot now have measured more than forty paces. I became aware that my heart was pounding again, my breath coming shallow and fast. The moose went on standing there, half sideways, at the top of the bank, still a monument of indecision.

This time there was not, as is usually the case, any single moment of clear decision. Not one that I could detect, anyway. But eventually the huge animal turned and began to move directly away from me. He moved faster than before, but at no great speed. He reached the edge of the clearing, kept going. He did not look back. The last I saw of him was that huge rack sailing through the trees at a steady, dignified pace.

For several minutes after he had gone I stood where I was among the spruce branches. When heart and breath had resumed their normal rhythms, I reversed out of the trees, picked up my fishing rod and began to walk back toward the open, stony channel from which I had first seen the flicker of his antlers.

As I walked, I smiled to myself. I had often been puzzled by people who professed to have been deeply moved by the sight of their first moose. It had always seemed to me that such an uncouth and rather ludicrous beast was hardly the kind to provoke genuine rhapsodies. But now I understood. Sheer bulk had something to do with it, of course. So did a certain wild, untamable . . .

I stepped out of the last bushes onto the open river channel—and as I did so I glimpsed movement among trees on its far side, seventy or eighty paces away. For an instant I thought the huge antlers belonged to another moose. Then I saw their shape more clearly. I lifted my glasses. The antlers were in velvet—and were, if not the biggest caribou rack I had seen, then very nearly the biggest. Certainly the biggest I had seen so close. The animal beneath them looked, by comparison, almost inadequately small. As I stood there, the caribou wandered out of the trees, directly toward me. He began to angle down a steep bank into the channel, and I could see that he moved his right rear leg stiffly. He was very thin: the rib cage showed clearly.

At the foot of the bank he stopped for a moment, then turned his head and, holding his lame leg off the ground, began to lick it. Because of the way he held his head, I found myself looking at the antlers from behind. They were huge: tilted sideways as they now were, their lower tips barely cleared the stones of the channel bed. Seen from behind, with their spreading terminal tines out of the way and no longer confusing my eye, the basic structure showed very clearly: three pairs of branches, each pair successively longer, more curving and more widely spread; each branch broadening and flattening near its tip into a small palm from which spread three, four or five tines. On the upper branches, some tines were a foot long, slender but strong; on the lower branches they became progressively shorter, stubbier, sometimes rudimentary. The entire edifice was wrapped, skintight—base of branch to tip of tine—with a warm brown velvet nap that exactly matched the animal's coat.

The caribou stopped licking his leg and limped forward toward the creek that ran down the middle of the stony channel. Head-on, his rack was even more impressive. The upper branches curved high, wide and handsome—seven or eight feet apart at their widest, tips nine or ten feet above the ground. The second pair of branches pointed almost directly forward and curved only slightly. The third and final pair, below and inside them—pointing forward and slightly down, so that they hung over the nose and looked as if they must obscure the animal's vision—were virtually straight; and they grew so close together that the branches' inside edges almost seemed to touch. The whole magnificent, convoluted structure seemed almost too much of a good thing for the rather unpretentious animal that bore it.

The caribou came to the edge of the creek, stopped, drank. He still seemed utterly relaxed, totally unaware of my presence; and when he had finished drinking he began to wade across the strip of shallow water that separated us. But after three or four steps he stopped again, out in midstream, and looked directly at me. I waited. Clearly, this was his moment of decision.

Fortunately, I stood almost directly downwind of the caribou. From where he stood, too, my background was a confusion of trees and bushes, and I had been standing very still—though at judicious moments I had lifted and lowered my glasses and also taken four or five photographs. On the other hand, I was standing out in the open channel, and I was wearing a red-and-black-plaid wool shirt of the kind often worn by hunters so that they will be readily visible to fellow assassins. What is more, the caribou and I cannot at this point have been more than thirty paces apart. Yet after a pause of no more than a few seconds the animal moved forward again, directly toward me, still looking relaxed and confident. Clearly, he had decided that I was harmless.

He waded out of the creek, limped across a few yards of open ground and began to browse on a line of bushes, barely fifteen paces from me. As he began to feed, I shot what I knew was the last frame of the roll in the camera: I felt sure he would take fright at any moment, and it seemed crazy not to grasp such a close-up opportunity.

I had the telephoto lens on the camera, and by this time the caribou was so close that in order to frame the full antlers for a horizontal shot I had to cut his legs off altogether. After I had taken the shot, the animal continued, to my astonishment, to browse along the line of bushes that passed close to my left elbow. He continued to move—that is, directly toward me. From time to time he lifted his head and gave me a glance of mild interest.

My fifth and last roll of film was in the fishing bag slung at my waist, and it seemed obvious that if I made the movements necessary to take out the new roll, let alone load it, the caribou would bolt. So partly in mock exasperation at missing what would have been even closer close-ups but also in order to see what effect it would have at a range of a dozen paces, I said, in a normal speaking voice, "Oh no, fella—not closer, not *now!*"

The caribou turned his head and looked me in the eye. Mucus clung to hairs protruding from his left nostril. Halfway up his face was the scar of an old cut. Faint raised ducts curved irregularly up the branches of his antlers: arteries, no doubt, feeding the velvet. I could see now that the lowest pair of branches did not really obscure his vision. Not head-on, anyway. The incurving tines almost touched their opposite numbers—the tips of one pair, in fact, rested delicately on each other, like the tips of Oliver Hardy's fingers in one of his standard disapproval poses—and as a result each of the caribou's dark brown eyes had a clear forward view, outboard of branches and tines. These eyes were now inspecting me. For a few seconds they seemed to express mild distrust; then they turned back to the bushes. The caribou resumed his browsing.

After a moment's hesitation I reached down, opened my fishing bag, fumbled, found the roll of film, put it in the breast pocket of my shirt. The caribou browsed on. I began to change film. At first I did everything in slow motion. Soon, out of sheer desire to experiment, I was making no attempt to curb or even slow down my hand movements. The caribou slid me a few puzzled glances. Otherwise, he just munched —and took an occasional step forward along the line of bushes. By the time I had the camera reloaded we were no more than ten yards apart.

Now I could smell him. He had a rank, fetid, almost putrid stench. I wondered, briefly, if that was normal caribou body odor; perhaps a cut on the lame leg had putrefied. I could smell him, of course, because I stood directly downwind; so he would probably not yet be able to smell me. On the other hand, he had now moved into such a position that he was looking at me down the line of the open channel, and I knew I had no background of any kind within a hundred yards, perhaps several hundred yards. I was therefore about as well camouflaged as a lamppost on a sand dune. A lamppost that moved its hands. A lamppost that also clicked. For as soon as the camera was ready I began taking more photographs—and the shutter of my old Pentax clicks fortissimo. From time to time the caribou lifted his head and gave me one of his puzzled, vaguely inquiring looks. Then he went back to his browsing. He also edged even closer. By the time I shot my third frame on the new roll, even a vertical shot barely encompassed both his muzzle and the tip of one upper antler; and it completely excluded all antlers on the other side.

At this point the caribou lifted his head and surveyed me in detail. This inspection lasted a long, long time. At the end of it the animal did not turn back again to the line of bushes that passed close by my left elbow; he moved, slowly and rather vaguely, to a little island of low bushes that grew off to my right and began feeding on them. So he continued to advance; but now, instead of heading directly toward me, he moved at an angle. It seemed as if, although not in any way alarmed by my presence, he would on the whole prefer to avoid actually bumping into me. When he had browsed forward to the end of the island of bushes he lifted his head again and subjected me to another searching inspection; then he began to move away from me, still slowly and vaguely, out across the stony, open channel, toward the creek.

As soon as he had taken a few steps I could see for the first time why he limped. Something had wounded him, savagely. His whole rump was rough and discolored, probably from dried blood. Long gashes down both haunches had torn through the hide, but they seemed, with one exception, to have healed over. The exception was a wound on his right quarter. There, flesh showed red. He had another partly healed gash above his right knee, and the whole of his right leg, clear down to the hoof, was slightly swollen. I could imagine nothing causing such wounds except a grizzly.

It is possible that I uttered some kind of sympathetic lament; anyway, the caribou stopped when still only halfway to the creek, turned his head and gave me yet another probing inspection. But this one had a new edge to it. For now his whole body was alert. And all of a sudden, his eyes flashed white. For a long interlude we both stood still, looking at each other. Then, deliberately, and for the first time since sighting him, I moved my feet. I did not move them much: just a little experimental shuffle. But the caribou took off. He took off like a very slightly lame rocket. Within seconds he had splashed across the creek, surged up over the steep bank and vanished among dense trees.

As soon as I felt sure I would not see him again, I stepped off the distance between the place I had been standing and the nearest of the hoof marks he had left in the coarse sand between the stones: eight paces. Then I checked my watch: 6:15. As far as I could remember, I had first sighted the moose—from very nearly that same spot—around five o'clock.

I wandered slowly back down the winding channel, elated yet relaxed, calm and content. It almost always worked, this business of coming face to face in some special way with wild animals. I had often seen the results in other people, especially when it was their first time: their joy was transparent, lilting, beautiful to see. But the best thing about such meetings was that, no matter how often they happened to you, some special or new element could rekindle your excitement, elation and wonder. Size helped, of course; but it was not necessary. Cheetah, as well as elephants, had ignited me. A "new" animal almost always worked: the moose would probably have done so even without his bulk and impassive, unexpected, head-on solemnity. Extreme closeness was surefire, too; and if you had a high serendipity quotient that you nurtured, it was surprising how often an animal would come ridiculously close, the way the caribou had done.

Whatever the special element, such encounters always left you, I had found, with a sense of privilege. And provided you had something to give, they lifted you beyond the piffling, smoky world of man into a reality that was cleaner and surer. If it was your first vision of that reality—your first knowledge beyond mere cerebration, I mean—then amazement fed your joy. If you had been there before, no matter how often, it was like the lights being turned on again in an old, familiar guesthouse that you had begun to take for granted because it had been standing there for so long, unlit, at the bottom of your garden. That evening, as I say, I walked back along the open, stony channel feeling relaxed as well as elated, at peace with the world, content with what I had found at last in my crescent kingdom, asking no more. It even turned out to be no very big deal when, a short way down the channel, I saw another bull moose.

He stood in thick cover, off to the left, less than a hundred yards away. Through glasses I could see soft velvet on his huge antlers; but trees hid his body and he kept lowering his head to browse. There was no hiding his size, though, and for a moment I felt my pulse quicken, my lungs suck air. I was standing out in the open channel, already almost upwind of him, and very soon he lifted his head and looked directly at me. I felt sure he was aware of my presence, yet he showed no sign of alarm. Because the light was now very poor, and also to conserve film, I took no pictures; I moved, instead, until the wind was blowing directly from me to moose. The moose gave me a long look, then resumed his browsing. I banged my steel cup against the revolver butt. The moose glanced up, went back to his meal. I walked on toward camp.

For the first few paces I was aware that I must be alert for the noise of a big animal charging through thick brush: after all, it might already be rutting season. But the warning sounded only in my head. It did not tingle up and down my spine. After the first surprise of seeing the moose, my pulse and breath had, I am almost sure, performed perfectly normally. And I remember, clearly, that after I had walked about fifty yards I was shocked to find that I had forgotten all about the moose, let alone possible danger. I looked back. He was still there, feeding. Once more, I turned and walked on.

The first time is always *the* occasion, of course: inoculation mostly works, with joy as with disease. That evening, I was also eager to get back to camp and get to sleep: I wanted to make an early start next morning on the journey back to the lake. But I think the main reason I did not linger with that second moose was my sense that it was all over. I could go now. My crescent-kingdom, my Eden, had proved that it was not after all just another stretch of just another river valley. Not for me, anyway. It had fulfilled its promise. Its promises. The promises I had glimpsed first as small dark trees growing somewhere beyond a distant gap and then, from the pass, as a beckoning, mysterious parkland. It had indeed turned out to be—just as I had known, though I did not know exactly what I had known—a place inviolate against the outer world, a place in which I had found absolutely no sign that any other man had ever visited it (even though I do not think I really believed it had not been visited); a place in which something would happen. To most people, of course, it would not seem as if very much had happened, and it would as usual be useless to try to explain to someone who did not understand. It would sound hopelessly flat: "I saw my first moose, and a caribou came up to within eight paces of me." But it had been enough. More than enough. My premonitions had turned out to be benign, too, not malevolent. It occurred to me, then, that not once during my tour of the crescent-kingdom had I remembered the round and humped mass of trees on the far bank of the river—the dark shape that had seemed to stand so huge and impregnable that I had called it the "citadel." I halted and looked to my right, above the trees that grew on the far bank of the open channel. The humped mass was there all right. But even in the fading light it was no longer quite a hump, and certainly not a dark and impregnable citadel. Now that I had penetrated into my Eden, I could see long open spaces among the trees, and they broke the mass into thin, unthreatening swaths.

I walked on toward camp. For the first time since I closed the front door of my house behind me, nearly three weeks earlier, I felt confident that, plane crashes aside, I would after all walk safely back, in due course, through that familiar door. For the thing was indeed over now, accomplished. It had achieved the right shape. Even those first days had played their part—those days beside the lake when I had been denied the solitude I had come to find, and had therefore been held at arm's length from the reality of this new, wide land. For the denial of solitude had driven me into discovering this valley. So everything had, after all, been worth it: the waiting, the frustration, even the hassling. In the end, the place had produced. That, I think, is why, as I walked back toward camp along the stony channel, I felt so content. I had no right to ask for more. No need to ask.

Now, as far as I know, what I have just written is true. I am pretty sure that is how I felt as I walked along the channel.

How a part of me felt, anyway. But at the same time, in op-
position yet somehow not really in conflict, the sane, earthbound sector of me kept saying, "Bullshit! This sunken
crescent is just another stretch of just another river. Why,
look at it! It's not even all that beautiful. Not close up. Pretty
rough, in fact. What the hell are you doing, building all these
fantasies?" But the fact remains that as I walked on toward
camp I still felt content, relaxed. When I had at one point
to push through a dense thicket, I indeed blew my whistle
and clanged cup against revolver, but I did so with considerable bravado. As I began to cook dinner I found myself wondering whether I was glad or sorry that I had not met a grizzly
in Eden.

Next morning I began my return, across the hills and
back through the gap, retracing the journey that had indeed
been more than a day's walk. I followed, in reverse, much the
same route as the three of us had taken, moving at our different levels of existence, on the way out. But this time I
lived every hour, every minute, in the earthbound present.

By eleven o'clock I was pausing near the pass—though
out on a ridge this time—for a final look back at my kingdom
of Eden. It once more lay toylike in the bowl of the valley.
Beyond it, the citadel again humped dark and round; but no
longer forbidding. Up at the head of the bowl sat the black
gorge, unexplored and therefore unchanged. I smiled and
turned and walked on, through the gap and then across upland tundra now reddening fast toward winter. Down in a
small, hidden valley, along a string of beaver ponds, the mak-
ers' dens stood out like big, black, slightly flattened beehives,
and it occurred to me that they must act as beckoning bea-
cons to predators. I found myself remembering, with affec-
tion, the way the older hunter had held the bleached skull in

his hand: "A wolf could have taken it up there. They just love beaver. . . ." Soon, I thought I heard—but could not be sure—a rifle thump, very faint, off to my right, down in the "old" valley. In my notebook I scribbled, "You see what happens once you leave Eden!"

By two o'clock I was lunching at the same long and somehow surprising lake beside which I had lunched on the outward journey. Afterward, the day darkened. Clouds pressed in, scudding like gray warships before the southwest wind that now tore unchecked across the flat openness of the old valley to my right. The clouds coalesced. As the day tapered toward its close, the wind gained strength. It was not a cold wind, though. Provided I kept moving, I could still walk stripped to the waist.

By now I was beginning to understand some of the tundra's signs and portents. Its granite boulders, for example. Glaciers had dropped them haphazardly about the landscape—the only rock in all those rounded hills. I was getting used, now, to the way they would keep catching my eye from a distance. In that first moment, each blob looked as if it might be almost anything. Each time, of course, even as I lifted my glasses to check, I knew that this particular blob would indeed turn out to be nothing more than a granite boulder. But I still checked. After all, once every couple of millennia, one of them might turn out to be a mammoth or a diamond drill rig or a motel. Or, rather more often, on my own little calendar, a grizzly.

Knowing more about route-finding now, and taking a lower line along the edge of the hills, I made better time than on the outward journey. Just before seven o'clock, scanning far ahead through my binoculars—by now impossible to hold steady in the driving wind—I glimpsed, out across the distant flats of the valley, a tiny blue blur that was almost certainly my tent. By eight o'clock I was approaching a ridge that seemed sure to give me an unobstructed view of the lake, out over intervening flats. When I reached the crest of the ridge, I should be able to pick out the best route across the flats, ready for the morning; and once I had done that I would, although I still had an hour of daylight left, stop at the first water I found—still up in the hills, not yet back among the rifles. Perhaps, I thought, there would be another small lake just beyond the ridge. I walked toward its crest, aiming for a saddle furnished with an odd little playground of granite boulders. Although I was not yet exactly tired, it would be a good place to take a rest.

I was rather less than a hundred yards from the granite-boulder playground when into it, from the far side, without warning, romped a bear cub.

I stopped dead. I knew what would appear next. Softly, but loudly enough for me to hear the word above the wind, I said, "Jesus!"

What appeared next, though, while I still stood rooted, was a second cub.

If anything, that made it worse. With two of them to protect, would she not be twice as protective, twice as ornery? I turned and began to walk firmly but unhurriedly away from the playground. Within the first few steps I had pulled the big, heavy revolver from its holster. It suddenly felt very small, very light, almost frivolous.

I was walking at a slight angle away from the cubs: with luck, it should be obvious, even to an animal with poor eyesight, that I was retreating, and therefore posed no threat. I moved slightly downhill, over the most open and unstumblable route in sight, and this angle of retreat allowed me to keep an eye on events back at the playground and at the same time to make sure that, aided to some extent by the willow staff, I put my boots down in safe places. To my surprise, I am no longer quite sure how the wind blew; but I think it was still barreling in from the southwest, and if so then my move in angling away may also have been designed in part to ensure that Mama got my scent when still as far away as possible. At least, that sounds like a sensible factor to have incorporated in a good, calm decision, and it is not totally impossible that I incorporated it.

I had probably walked only about twenty paces—though several eternities had elapsed—before Mama appeared. Even on all fours, she dwarfed the cubs. And almost at once she reared up on her hind legs and peered directly at me.

I no longer know whether I was at that moment looking through binoculars—it seems highly unlikely—or whether I saw her there, erect against the skyline, with my naked eyes. What I do know is that, binoculared or not, I had developed tunnel vision. I have no idea where the cubs were, or what they were doing. I was not even aware, as I tend to be at pivotal moments, of such granular detail as the color of the foliage, the way the light fell or the angle of the wind. All I saw was Mama. She towered there, brown and indestructible, enormous, and she blotted out everything else. Any objective assessment of her size is bound to be suspect, but in that first moment I knew intuitively that she stood at least fifty feet tall. Don't let them kid you that King Kong is fiction.

At some point I had halted. I may have done so just before Mama appeared—because she seemed such a long time coming—or at the moment she appeared or, from shock, when she stood up. But I am fairly sure that for most if not all the excruciatingly prolonged interval during which she stood there against the sky—spread out like one of those enormous and deadly bearskins you still find occasionally on floors or even walls—I was, like time, standing still.

My first reaction was to record the spectacle on film. I think I actually leaned the staff against my body—the revolver, now shrunk to the size and heft of a .22, was in my left hand—and began to reach for the camera. Then I not only remembered the photograph on the corridor wall in Anchorage, and what had happened to that overzealous photographer; I also realized that the grizzly, standing erect and peering down at me, trying to figure out in her bearish way what I might be and what I meant and what she should do about it, was at that moment probably on the brink of making her wild-animal decision—whether to flee, ignore or charge; a decision that, once made, would be almost irreversible. I redirected my right hand, away from the camera. I reached down, grasped the steel cup dangling from the belt at my right side, moved it across my body, met it halfway with the revolver—which had just contracted to the size and apparent usefulness of a peashooter—and began tapping the two metal objects together.

The effect was almost instantaneous. Mama came down from the sky and in the same movement turned left. On all fours, she began hurrying back the way she had come, over the ridge. The cubs followed. Within seconds, the playground stood empty.

For several minutes I stayed where I was, letting pulse and breath simmer back toward normalcy. I also figured out what to do. It seemed clear from the haste with which she had turned and hurried away that Mama had decided I was bad news for bears. But I knew I must under no circumstances give her the impression that I was following her. Downhill, the way she had most likely gone, a nearby branch of the ridge cut off my view. She could be anywhere down there. It was also possible, though, that she had doubled back uphill and was lurking behind the ridge's upper extension. The one place she almost certainly would not be, I decided, was the place I had last seen her.

I allowed five minutes' cooling-off time. Cooling-off time for both of us. Then I advanced once more toward the playground. I advanced at the ready, staff now held in my left hand, cocked revolver in the right. The revolver, I could not help noticing, stayed rooted in its peashooter mode.

I would like to think that I walked firmly and resolutely toward the bouldered playground. But I distinctly remember that covering the hundred yards took a very long time, and I know that at one point, about twenty yards from ground zero, I became aware that I was moving, insofar as the heavy pack permitted, in a sort of token or Hollywood crouch. At a guess, I looked rather like Groucho Marx in madcap slow motion, and I have no idea what the hell I hoped to gain from the impersonation. As soon as I became aware of it I straightened up into a manly gait. At least, I think I did.

At long last, I walked onto the playground.

The slope beyond stretched innocent of bears. So did the entire visible landscape. By far the most likely direction for the family to have gone, I could now see, was indeed down-hill, into a dense willow thicket, a quarter of a mile away, that was the only cover in sight. I therefore continued on my east-ward line, along the contour of the hills.

As I walked, I stopped from time to time to glass the coun-try below. And at last I saw, though only dimly in the fading light, two brown shapes sort of semi-skulking down near the willow thicket. Perhaps there were, for an instant, three shapes. One of them, in any case, was far too big to be a cub. Between us stretched at least a quarter of a mile of sloping, open tundra. I slid the revolver back into its holster. And just before the last of the brown shapes disappeared behind a ridge I lifted the camera and took a hurried shot of the tundra in that general direction: even in such poor light I might with luck salvage some attenuated record of my first meeting with grizzlies—a meeting during which I somehow seemed to have managed to do all the right things.

When I had taken the photograph I walked on, alert for willow thickets. Very alert. It is amazing what a shot of adrenaline does for incipient tiredness—and as a reviver of premonitions. As I walked, though, it occurred to me that now, with luck, there were really only the planes left.

I camped as the last light failed, out on the flats, well clear of all willow thickets.

Next morning, halfway to the river, I met three hunters walking back toward the orange-tent campsite. Their pack frames bore bulky bundles wrapped in bloodstained white fabric.

"Got him late last evening, back down by the river," said one of the hunters, jerking his head over his shoulder. "How long you been gone?"

"Five or six days."

"Where'd you go?"

"Oh, back over those hills."

"See many caribou?"

I hesitated. "No, precious few."

"Been blowing like crazy here," said a second hunter. "Seventy, eighty miles an hour, easy. Blew our tent clear over. Blew so strong it even capsized a stand with caribou meat hanging on it. Big heavy wooden stand it was, too. South wind, and warm, so's the glaciers melted faster and the river sure as hell came up. She's going back down now, though."

The river was indeed higher than when I left, but after half an hour of strain and roar, waders slightly awash, willow staff working overtime, I climbed out onto the far bank. My little tent stood taut and shipshape.

I spent much of the next two days inside the tent, reading and writing. Outside, intermittent rain fell and a wind with a cutting edge whipped up the valley. The scudding clouds hung low and gray, concealing the peaks at the head of the lake. I knew I had been lucky, though. When I had accepted, in my planning for Alaska, that I might have to wage almost incessant war against rain and insects, I had judged that such annoyances would be a small price to pay for the certainty of solitude; but rain had been tolerably rare, insects never a problem. The only snag, of course, was that for much of my trip the solitude had turned out to be a caribou of a very different color.

During those final two days, whenever I patrolled outside the tent, I saw that the tundra was turning an ever brighter red. It was indeed, I kept thinking, no longer summer in this place, the way it had been when I came. But the lake seemed, if anything, even busier. Fishermen paraded up and down the far riverbank. Rifles thumped, all over. Planes came and went.

My last evening, the wind died. Clouds still concealed the peaks, but when I walked up to the outflow, the lake stretched mirrorlike and beautiful before me.

Next morning dawned clear and calm. For the first time in ten days, the sun showed promise of stable rule. I could see the peaks again, up at the head of the lake, black and white and epic. By noon I was sitting ready and packed in the little cove where the troopers and Henry Rust had beached their planes. The lake was now a sparkling mirror—the way it had often been those first days, just after Charlie Allen had landed me on the little spit. But from where I sat I could look across the mirror and see the orange-tent encampment. There must have been six or seven tents now, all clustered together. From them, carrying clear as Coney Island across the mile of water, came choruses of loud, empty-vessel shoutings.

Charlie Allen arrived just before five o'clock. Minutes

later, we took off. As we swung around toward Anchorage I looked westward for the last time, across lake and river. If I kept my eyes away from the tent cluster, it all looked much the same as when I had first seen it, three weeks before—except that the tundra was red now, going on brown.

Half an hour later, as we droned through the spectacularities of a forty-mile-long canyon, with a glacier once more dirty gray below our wingtips and Mount McKinley thrusting up white and spectral far to the north, I asked Charlie about the mysterious humming noise I had half-heard in my "new" valley. Could it have been a diamond drill rig?

"No," he said, shouting above the engine noise, "I don't know of any rigs out that way just now. But there's some kind of a military base at a lake just to the north, down in the forest, and you could well have heard some kind of machinery noise from there."

At six-thirty we touched down in Anchorage. By a little after eight o'clock I had managed to get a room in a new and spectral international-type hotel with long, empty, fire-doored corridors; had learned from the room-service waiter that President Ford had nominated Nelson Rockefeller for the vacant vice presidency and that in the room waiter's considered opinion Rocky had "the inside track"; had made airline reservations, two days ahead, for the flight home to California; had phoned there; and was soaking in a hot bath and double Johnnie Walker Black Label while I listened to the Budapest Quartet caress late Beethoven. By the time I went to bed, Sonny Jurgensen had at age forty thrown a gem of a touchdown pass—and the Redskins had still lost. By the time I fell asleep I felt I was halfway back.

I woke next morning to find the radio reporting that a week earlier, at a lake barely fifty miles south of "my" lake, a fifty-nine-year-old man had been killed and part-eaten by a grizzly. The story had only just broken because the man's widow had not been picked up by plane, as arranged, until the day before. But although I calculated that the incident had happened just about the time I left my lake to walk toward the spruce trees, the story did not seem to mean as much as it should have. I could not fully grasp it. It carried only a little more flesh-and-blood meaning than the routine reports of accidents and violence that we hear every day on the radio and can no longer, out of sheer self-protection, translate into too vivid reality. For I now hung suspended between two worlds. The transition had, even more than usual, been too fast for any current human brain to cope with. Too fast for my brain, anyway. Somewhere underneath, though, I knew I still had the dark spruces glimpsed through the distant gap, and the moose and the lame caribou deep in Eden, and the Mama grizzly towering like King Kong on the skyline. I had the sparkling lake and the sunlight, then racing, windswept skies. I had the northern lights. I had granite boulders and reddening tundra. I had "a tree, a rock, a cloud . . ." I had the hunters as well, and the troopers and Henry Rust. They were all there still, stored deep and safe and meshing. I had the meanings that lay behind them, too: the easy lessons that I had already grasped, and the other things that still lurked there somewhere, unfocused, waiting. I had all these to draw on, now, for as long as I lasted.

7 Among the Redwoods

Mist lay along the treetops, soft and gray. Down at ground level, the autumn afternoon had begun its slide into evening. I locked the car, swung the pack onto my back, crossed the blacktop parking lot, passed through a small gate and began walking down the trail. When I glanced up at the treetops I could still see the mist hanging there, soft and silent and timeless; but down on the trail the day was slipping away. I lengthened my stride. It was too late, now, to walk the eight miles to the Grove before dark. With luck, though, I should get far enough up Redwood Creek for a safe crossing from one world into another; far enough, perhaps, for me to begin fumbling for answers—or at least to frame the questions more clearly.

The trail ran straight and true. Ran too straight and true

to be good, really, for it followed the line of an old logging road. But time had already begun its slow work: thick green overgrowth had blunted the angularity, had softened the engineering scars. It seemed just possible to hope that the softening might hold a hint of an answer.

I had walked half a mile and was crossing a lush meadow when I met two young fellows, packless, hurrying back toward the parking lot.

"Going up to the Tall Trees?" one of them asked.

I nodded.

"It's well worth it."

"Good."

Then we had passed like ships, still smiling.

It was good, I found, to get such an unsolicited testimonial right at the start. It might even help focus my questions. In Tall Trees Grove stood the tallest known tree in the world, and also the third and sixth tallest. The Grove was therefore seen as the heart of the long, narrow appendix of Redwood National Park, known as "the Worm," which twisted southward along Redwood Creek—and it had been the prime reason for the park's creation, nine years earlier, in 1968. But the Grove was not merely unprotected from certain happenings beyond its boundaries; it was actively threatened by them. This threat was what had raised my questions. The immediate questions, that is.

I strode on through the fading light. Soon, the trail crossed Redwood Creek. The water was so shallow that I almost stepping-stoned across without wetting my boots. From mid-ford I could see, above the far bank, a hillside of virgin redwoods; could see colonnades of massive brown trunks vaulting like sculpture from the steep slope; could recognize the familiar fern-clad openness between the sculptures; could discern, even in that fading light, the velvety, moss-covered trunks of fallen giants; could look for the first time into the heart of the problem.

On the far bank the trail still followed the line of the old logging road. Here, the road curved along between creek and hillside through a natural green tunnel. When the road was built, many years before, the land on either side had been cleared, but thick foliage had now reclaimed the disturbed earth so densely that I walked enclosed, in a soft and silent world that seemed almost as timeless as the mist that lay along the treetops. The new growth was mostly maple and alder, tan oak and laurel, with a few small conifers. It was a landscape that in many places would seem rich and pleasing—in modern Pennsylvania, say, or modern Shropshire. But in this place, because of the majestic hillside redwoods —which even when hidden still hung in my mind—it seemed, for all its lushness, to be scraggy, almost tatty.

My nose detected a whiff of smoke. I halted. Down on a gravel bank on the far side of the creek, a man stood beside a red pack and a small, flickering fire. The distance between us was too great for salutation and the man's stance signaled, anyway, that he was no more eager than I for mere human communication. His little camp looked calm and serene, there beneath the vast, dark wall of trees that lined the far bank. I walked on.

Another mile, and I began catching glimpses of hillside through breaks in the green tunnel. But now, no majestic virgin forest. Instead, tangled, messy underbrush, with only a few half-size though still soaring redwoods. In some places, the hillside's dense green underbrush would have seemed rich and pleasing. In Shropshire, say, or Pennsylvania. But not in this valley, if you knew how it had once been.

I had not expected such a hillside within the Worm. On the map, the thin green strip had looked comfortingly inviolate. I had known that it extended for only a quarter of a mile on either side of the creek, and that logging continued on private land outside it; also that, because of certain things that had happened and were still happening higher up the watershed, such sanctuary as the Worm offered might in the long run prove illusory. So I was not expecting an unspoiled paradise. But I had not been prepared, somehow, to find that part of the Worm, other than the old road, had already been logged off. The rape had occurred a long time ago, of course—back when we had not yet acquired the power to tear things quite so ruinously apart. Now the worst scars had largely healed. But there was still no denying that the place had been raped.

The day eased into dusk. A crouching rabbit bobbed away into undergrowth. A pair of wrens flickered brown and tiny. Once, far ahead, a grouse stood serene and almost statuesque; then, without apparent motion, faded away. By the time I heard the tinkle of the little side creek near which I planned to camp—because Redwood Creek water was no longer drinkable without boiling or purification—daylight was melding into moonlight.

Just before I reached the side creek, the green-foliage tunnel that enfolded the trail sloped gently upward for a few yards and created, almost level with my eyes, a round opening backlit by pale twilight. As I moved forward, the opening grew larger. Then I had halted and was standing very still. Framed in the tunnel, outlined against the pale light beyond, coming toward me in languid slow motion—moving with a slow, almost liquid side-to-side roll that spoke of utter confidence in privacy and protection from such crass intruders as men—was a shape. A shape that was only just a shape; a shape that barely escaped being totally shapeless.

In that first moment, because of some trick of the light—aided perhaps by the way the opening had been growing larger, and by the eye-level nature of our confrontation—the shape had no real size. The creature could have had the bulk of a bear—or of a small beaver. It had, in fact, very little except its vague quality of shape and its distinct sea-roll motion.

For an eternity of seconds the animal kept rolling toward me. Then it stopped, suddenly alert.

The frame of the round, backlit tunnel opening gave the animal stature, almost gave it authority, and for a moment I felt sure it was at least as big as a bear. Then, as if a button had been pressed, my perceptions clicked and I saw that we stood barely three paces apart and that the animal was quite small. Was hardly bigger than a large possum.

At that moment the animal stood up on its hind legs. It still did not seem alarmed—only mildly suspicious, or perhaps simply curious. No, clearly not a possum. By this time it had assumed a rather more definite shape—a schmoo-like outline that seemed vaguely familiar. I spoke soft words, unaware of just what I said, trying only to convey reassurance. The schmoo said nothing. But it began to move its head slowly from side to side, peering directly at me. I spoke more sweet nothings. The schmoo went on peering. At last, with a better-be-on-the-safe-side air of resignation, it turned as if to retreat—and in the moment of its turning I saw for the first time the rounded back and, just discernible, the fan of trailing quills.

"Don't worry," I said. "I'm not going to hurt you."

But the porcupine went on turning. It slow-motion-hurried back down the trail for perhaps three sea-roll flubbles, then swung right into open grassland.

I eased forward, murmuring more reassurances.

The porcupine climbed onto a large stone at the edge of the grassy clearing, turned to peer back at me, then froze into immobility. It sat barely two paces off the trail, in full twilight-moonlight, but had I not seen it climb onto the stone I would have passed it by.

For a minute or two we held our tableau, the porcupine still peering, I still murmuring. Then, curious, I moved forward again. The porcupine eased down off the stone and insinuated itself under a bush. Even in the attenuated light I could see its quilled fan, half protruding. I stood for a moment, uncertain. Then I said a soft "Good night" and went on down the trail to the side creek. For it was all right, now, to camp. Although I knew that a porcupine was, after all, only a porcupine, I also knew that our meeting had moved me safely across the boundary between the two worlds.

I camped on the far side of Redwood Creek, on a gravel bar, beside another vast, dark wall of trees. It was calm and serene there, the way I had known it was for the other man when I saw him standing on his own gravel bar beside his red pack and pale flickering fire.

I lit no fire, and after dinner I sat up in my sleeping bag, listening. Moonlight flooded the broad nave of the creek bed. The place lay quiet with the sounds of night. Water sang over stones. A bullfrog gargled. An owl hooted at the universe. The rest was silence; a rich, heavy silence. I slid down into my sleeping bag; slid away into sleep.

When the noise awakened me the sun was already up. Mist still lay along the treetops, but out beyond the quarter-mile-wide sanctuary of the Worm, explosions rumbled. Nearby, a whistle punked erratically, dementedly; machines, responding to its signals, roared. Chain saws sang their background killer dirge. Then the saws fell silent for final rites and a shattering thud came shuddering down the miles.

The day's war had begun.

I cooked breakfast. My roaring stove almost blocked off the sounds of carnage. The mist began to break up. Shafts of sunlight slanted down.

A Steller's jay arrived to investigate me. It perched directly overhead on a moss-covered alder limb, sleek blue on velvet green. I began to wonder, vaguely, about the perpendicular facts of gravity. But the bird just sat there for a while, glistening and beautiful in washed sunlight, eyeing me long and steady, black and beady, then departed without unloading anything more pungent than a green, half-eaten morsel of fruit.

A pair of red-shafted flickers busily shafted their breakfasts out of the gravel at the foot of a neighboring maple. Something disturbed them. They flickered up onto a fallen trunk, back patches flashing white. They perched briefly, whickering or bickering or both, then fluttered back down to resume their breakfasts.

When I had finished mine I got up and strolled into the forest, trying to block off the sounds from the hillside.

Just below camp, the creek made a sharp bend. The flat crescent of land held in the bend's crook lay rich with centuries of sediment, and on this sediment now grew a small grove of redwood trees. Two or three huge, rotting stumps scattered through the grove testified that its biggest trees had once been logged. But that harvesting had happened before heavy machinery and clear-cutting had begun to devastate the redwoods. In those days it took two skilled axmen five days to fell a big redwood. So this grove on its crescent of flat, rich, well-watered soil had not been destroyed, only wounded—and it had already recovered. Redwoods still ruled it, tall and majestic, thrusting up from a soft green floor of ferns and decomposing, moss-covered trunks. The grove looked strong and determined; looked able to fend off all enemies except devastating flood and devastating modern man.

When I came out of the forest, back onto open creek bed, I found that the morning mist had almost cleared and that above the thin line of the Worm's protecting trees I could see a triangular strip of the hillside from which came the sounds of battle. Across this strip of steep hillside cut a newly bulldozed dirt road, ugly as a sword slash on a woman's body. At the road's end stood a blue portable latrine.

Except for this road, the hillside looked, at first glance, benignly green. But then I saw that the greenery was a mat of severed branches and mangled undergrowth. Only a few small trees still stood, and many of these leaned drunkenly, half stripped by flailing branches when their mature neighbors had crashed to earth under the chain saws' onslaught. The giants' corpses lay among the green wreckage, waiting for the final act. I could remember that part. Could remember it all too well.

Twenty years earlier I had spent two summers prospecting for a mining company in a virgin British Columbia forest that was undergoing progressive clear-cut rape, and I could still remember, vividly, the final logging act that centered on the spar trees. A spar tree was a tall tree, left standing in the center of a clear-cut area, that had been lopped to flagpole bareness. A donkey engine at the spar tree's foot operated a hawser that passed through a pulley system rigged at its peak. Once nearby felled trees had been shaved of all branches and their bare trunks sawn into convenient twenty- or thirty-foot lengths, the donkey-operated hawser, feeding through the pulley at the top of the spar tree, dragged these bare bones of once majestic life-forms to a clearing at the foot of the spar tree and loaded them on trucks for carting away to mills. The soil, especially on hillsides, was always thin, and as the dismembered corpses were dragged across it they gouged gullies—deep wounds in the earth that converged like a gross spider's web at the base of the spar tree. It was these webs that, together with the network of logging roads, completed the butchery of recently rich and virgin forest. Left it devastated, bleeding, the way men had left the fields of Flanders in 1918. Left it not only raped but crucified. Left you ashamed, I had discovered back in British Columbia, of belonging to a species that for personal gain waged war on its own planet.

That was the most vivid memory I had carried away from Canada.

As I stood on the open bed of Redwood Creek, looking up through the branches of living trees at the triangular strip of denuded but still-green hillside, there lumbered out into it, from behind one of the nearby branches, a huge yellow machine.

My knowledge of logging methods was by now twenty years out of date, but the day before, at the National Park Information Center in Orick, I had learned that spar trees had given way to huge machines called grapple yarding cranes, or "yarders." These yarders were essentially gigantic tractors bearing retractable cranes, and from their extended tips ran hawsers that dragged the dismembered logs to waiting trucks, just as the spar-tree hawsers had once dragged them. The end results would therefore be much the same. In fact, I knew they were much the same. For although I had taken care, since my years in Canada, not to stand in fresh "slash"—the desolate litter that remains after clear-cut logging—I had from time to time seen photographs. So the memory of how slash looked—close up, from in among the carnage—still stood livid in my mind. And the memory still brought my old anger seething back.

Up on the triangular strip of hillside, a whistle sounded and the yellow machine roared and clanked back out of sight behind protruding treetops. It had not, clearly, been a yarder; but it was another of the huge, blind, lumbering machines that are the symbol and epitome and backbone of our industrial civilization. Very soon, anyway, a yarder would begin to butcher that strip of deceptively green but already deflowered hillside. When the yarder and the other machines were through with their work, that particular stretch of land would be cast aside, a "useless" and bleeding wreck. Logging companies liked to talk reassuringly of reseeding programs. In Canada they referred to condemned forests as "tree farms." But the logging companies, for all their smooth propaganda, knew that no steep, bare, dusty hillside would ever recover the richness and majesty of virgin redwood forest. Not within hundreds of years, anyway. The flat, rich, well-watered grove below me had recovered relatively quickly after the selective removal of a few of its giants, but the hillside would not. Not after the huge yellow machines had savaged it. There were good, sound biological reasons why it would not. Reasons that had to do both with the nature of the yellow machines' attack and with the frail defenses of the dry and easily eroded slope. But you did not need biological knowledge to grasp that what was being done to the hillside was wrong. Was wrong in a very profound sense. If you had any feeling for the earth, you knew.

I turned at last and went back to my camp beyond the maple and sat down. I did not want to walk the final two miles up to the Tall Trees until the day's logging was over and I could stand in the Grove for the first time surrounded by a decent forest silence. So I spent most of the rest of the day in camp, rereading the report that had prompted me to drive half the length of California to Redwood Creek.

The report waxed eloquent. Redwood National Park was "in serious trouble"; was "all going to hell." The biological threat lay in its being "besieged" by clear-cut logging outside the thin protected Worm along Redwood Creek. In a normal winter, 80 to 100 inches of rain fell on the valley, and its denuded slopes were already being so eroded that the creek now carried "more sediment, per unit volume, than any other river or stream in the country." This sediment had already "raised the riverbed about five feet near Tall Trees Grove, and up to thirteen feet elsewhere." The valley's na-

ked slopes, no longer able to soak up heavy rains, meant un-
naturally severe runoffs, too, and the resultant floods were
cutting away the riverbanks and ripping out huge trees or
killing them by suffocation from cementlike gravel deposits
around their roots. The simple answer to these threats was
to enlarge the park, quickly, so that it embraced the whole
watershed.

The complete answer turned out, as always, to be far from
simple.

The report described with compassion and understanding
the threat that an enlarged park would pose to the jobs of loggers and millworkers "who take pride in the skilled and dangerous nature of their work," but concluded that "the jobs
would soon be gone, with or without the park." There was a
sad irony, too: a protective addition to the park might now
cost $600 million—in a region where, "until little more than
a century ago, every acre of land . . . belonged to the federal
government." The report also cast light on past political
power plays. It was the old, old story. The very fabric of action had been warped by politics' disabling internal conflict:
its ostensible purpose is to further the common weal; but its
currency is power—and the currency almost always over-
powers the purpose. The ultimate, though perhaps uninten-
tional, message of the report's political section seemed to be
"Put not your trust in politicians."

But the report did not restrict itself to politics. It discussed the prospects for new national parks in America in this
Age of Scarcity. At the end, it even looked beyond this question with which it was ostensibly concerned, and in doing so
quoted the book *Should Trees Have Standing?* which I had
read three years earlier, in Alaska, just before I set out for
the spruce trees. When I had finished rereading the report
that morning, sitting there in my creekside camp, trying to
block out the whistlings and engine revvings and explosions

and other battle sounds that snarled down from the hidden hillside, I found myself re-asking some of the wider questions it had raised by implication: "What should we be doing about such things, everywhere?" Or even "What should we *want* to do about them?" The report did not propose easy answers to such questions. Did not, in the end, really propose any answers at all.

About three o'clock I struck camp and walked on upriver toward the Tall Trees. I was still well short of them when, up on the hillside, the day's armistice was declared. Slowly, peace reclaimed the land. A varied thrush flashed its V sign, black on orange. There was no wind, and a hush had fallen on the forest. Once more I could hear dainty chickadees quietly chickacheering beside the trail. A little before five o'clock I arrived opposite Tall Trees Grove.

On the far side of the broad creek bed, the wall of the Grove rose green and dark, serene and impressive. But no matter how carefully I looked I could not be sure which magnificent individual in that magnificent cluster was the tallest tree in the world. Only when I had waded barefoot across the creek, then re-booted and walked into the Grove, did doubt vanish. A gray metal plaque in front of one huge double tree identified the right trunk as "the tallest known tree in the world" and gave its vital statistics:

> Height: 367.8 feet
> Age: 583 years
> Circumference: 44 feet

The trouble was, the tree did not look much different from any of the others growing nearby. When I craned my neck and peered up its red-brown, rough-barked trunk I could see barely fifty or sixty feet before my eye met an impenetrable green canopy.

Assuring myself that I was not disappointed, I walked a

few yards down a foot trail that wound through the Grove. There beneath the huge trees, dusk had now fallen, but I could still see that everything was soft, intact, untarnished. Massive red-brown trunks soaring into the green canopy. Between them, open hallways crowded with tall, richly fronded ferns. Dead, moss-covered giants rotting slowly back to rich, regenerating humus. And everything, except for the narrow trail, pristine, unmarred by man.

I came back out onto the creek bed, where dusk had not yet fallen, and sat down and looked once more at the huge green wall of the Grove. Now that the disappointment had ebbed I saw that the tallest tree did not have to stand dominant, symbolic, the way I had assumed it would. In itself, the planet's tallest tree was irrelevant—a passing accident, a mere mathematical signal of current quality. What mattered was the Grove. The Grove's integrity.

But not everyone saw it that way. Because the tallest tree had been the political lever for creating the park, pressures were now mounting to protect it at all costs. Plans included Army-Engineering out the creek bed or, alternatively, riprapping the banks along the Grove's flank. But as I sat there in the failing light it seemed to me that people who suggested doing such violence to the integrity of the Grove in order to protect—or, rather, possibly protect—what is thought to be the present tallest tree in the world would have to be mere measurers; and that such people should not be allowed to cast the dice when it came to such beautifully important things as redwood trees. I knew, though, that many conservationists supported the riprapping plan. And as I sat there in the dusk, a conservationist to my true-believing core, the message that seemed to hiss out from the dark trees was "Put not your trust in conservationists."

Night finally fell. I moved upstream in the last of the pale moonlight and camped in the only place it was legal to do so—half a mile above the Tall Trees, out on open creek bed, deep in the darkness and the silence.

Next morning, when war resumed on the stricken hillside off to my right, I was pleasantly surprised to find that the tall trees flanking the creek bed softened the sounds of battle. After breakfast I sat watching the mist burn off the deep nave of the creek. Soon, sunlight was streaming down. It fell full on another hillside, off to the left, far beyond the Grove. This hillside had clearly been logged off some years before. Already the slope had greened over. Compared with the virgin stands of redwood lining the creek it was still a tattered, ravaged place of scattered, half-grown trees, but in the morning sunlight its dense green surface gleamed. If you had never seen a virgin redwood forest you might even have called it beautiful.

I became aware of movement, upstream. Four small, dark deer were moving down the open creek bed, perhaps a hundred yards away, directly toward me. I sat very still, very quiet. The family continued to move toward me. The doe was bigger than her mate and she led the way. Two fawns followed, close. At first I thought the animals were unaware of my presence, but when one of the fawns gave a start of surprise and stood poised, peering at me, and the doe seemed to reassure her child and then the family moved forward again, I realized that the doe, at least, must know all about backpackers who camped at this particular place on the open gravel of the creek bed and sometimes sported bright orange sleeping bags and glaring white plastic sheets laid ready to ward off drizzling fog. But when the family resumed their advance, the timid fawn hung back. It eased to the right, close against the forest. The rest of the family came on, holding their line.

The doe seemed confident, unconcerned. Soon I could see with my naked eye two small black marks on the side of her mouth. I spoke quietly, reassuringly. The trio continued to hold their line of advance. At their closest, the doe and buck passed within six paces of where I sat.

The doe ignored me. The small-antlered buck, close behind her, seemed to be having trouble in screwing his courage to the sticking-place, but at no point did he break stride. The fawn just behind him paused, eyeballed me nervously, hesitated a moment longer; but then it too had tiptoed past.

Meanwhile, the timorous fawn was circling wide, inside the forest. I could see it intermittently, moving through green hallways. It looked scared stiff. When it at last came opposite me, still perhaps thirty paces away, it lost its nerve and broke into a run. It did not stop until it had rejoined the family—which by this time stood on the open creek bed, forty paces downstream, licking what looked like bare stones.

Almost at once, Mama seemed to become dissatisfied with the menu. Leaving Papa to fawn-sit, she moved off on her own, waded the creek, sauntered up along its far side until she was exactly opposite me, and began to lick, assiduously, at an apparently bare gravel bank tucked in so deeply under overhanging trees that the sun would rarely if ever strike it. The place no doubt looked, to her eyes, like a five-star lichen restaurant. Or perhaps a mineral bar.

The doe continued to lick. I got up and, reassuring her with quiet mutterings, moved slowly, camera in hand, to the edge of the creek. Soon, the doe was no more than fifteen paces away. She ignored me. Yet she kept glancing nervously in the opposite direction, into dark forest. Behind her, redwood needles and ferns and trailing creepers traced emerald patterns. Above her head, the yellow-green leaves of two moss-covered maples built delicate hanging terraces. I shot one frame, then lowered the camera and stood watching the quiet scene. With the doe standing there out on open gravel, licking the stones, it had an air of perfection about it; a sense that this was the way the world was meant to be.

Twenty minutes must have passed, with me just standing there, watching, before the doe turned, recrossed the creek and rejoined her waiting family. The whole group moved on downstream. Only then, with the spell broken, did I realize that during the twenty minutes the doe had set her perfect tableau I had not once been really aware of the distant sounds of battle still raging beyond the trees, up on the hillside.

The deer family crossed the creek, vanished into dark forest. A raven came craaking down the nave of the creek, high. It saw me, silenced itself, banked sharply into a U-turn, headed back the way it had come. I began to pack my gear.

Upstream, two backpackers appeared, walking down on the far side of the creek. As they came opposite me one of them called out, "How you doing?"

"Okay. And you?"

"Okay, I guess. Too early to tell. Only got started an hour ago. This place is too peaceful to hurry out of."

"Except for the logging."

"Yeah, but I close my ears to that. And I know they'll never get this place."

The two men continued downstream. I went on packing my gear. A pair of killdeer slanted past, elegant, black-banded. Then, up on the hillside a whistle sounded. An engine roared. Almost at once, a shattering explosion rent the air. Its aftershock rumbled away down the valley, reverberating from side to side. When it had died away, the quietness along the creek bed seemed thinner, less secure.

I spent another day and night in or near the Tall Trees Grove. As usual, I did not do very much. Nothing that can be easily written down. Just say I moseyed around, mucked about. Part of the time, though, I went on trying to formulate questions. But I still found no hint of easy answers.

In the afternoon I went down from my camp to the Grove, walking through the forest rather than along open creek bed. Mostly, I followed a faint game trail. It was the first time I had walked through a part of the park that remained totally untarnished—untrailed and uncombed even by Park Service man. It was also, I realized, the first time in twenty years that I had walked through any virgin forest while the modern world pounded at my ears.

The ancient green and brown world I moved through seemed very solid and stable and secure. The game trail meandered among ferns and creepers, across carpets of wood sorrel. It twisted past seedlings and saplings and the mature, majestically curving boles of the ruling redwoods. It circled around patches of tangled brush and dead, crisscrossed branches rotting slowly but safely back to humus.

I saw few animals. From time to time, furry caterpillars hurried by—black fore and aft, orange amidships—heading caterpillarfully for ports unknown. Once, a gray squirrel scolded me from a safe branch. A chipmunk kept a wary eye on me while it gnawed a nut held between obsequious paws.

The most startling life-forms were the fungi. Their fragile lives, lived out in the forest's shadiest, dampest places, seemed very cool, very quiet. Yet they cudgeled the eye. Flaring orange contraptions, ribbed and wrinkled. Jaunty goblin jobs sporting tilted brown hats. A red pair, old and tattered but bravely surviving, side by side. A heavily creased zeppelin pushing up through humus like a miniature rocket headed slow-motion for space.

Yet the fungi, for all their cool, quiet fragility, for all their patent temporariness, exuded an air of permanence. If they were left alone, you could not help feeling, their simple line would go on and on, essentially unchanged, down the ages. If they were left alone.

I had almost reached the Tall Trees Grove when I found myself standing beside a huge, blackened redwood stump. It had been burned many decades earlier, no doubt by a lightning strike, and from the base of the charred wreck there now grew a ring of six or seven trees. That is one of the redwoods' strengths. When a patriarch at last dies from natural causes and its realm is left relatively undisturbed, the dead loins generate offspring. In this case, the offspring had prospered. Already they rose a hundred feet, perhaps two hundred, into the forest's canopy. I stood staring up at the tight, regular circle of trees. Here too, among the forest's rulers, there was a sense of permanence. Of calm and continuity. And, once more, of inherent rightness. Provided these trees were left alone their line would also persist, essentially unchanged, down the ages.

Somewhere not far away, but out in another world, a heavy motor started up. It was just a single engine, revving —a logging truck, probably. No dynamite, this time; no chain saw; not even a whistle. But there at the foot of the close-knit redwood family the sound hit the silence like a bludgeon.

I walked on, moved in among the Tall Trees again, began to follow the half-mile trail that looped through the Grove. Now shafts of midafternoon sunlight slanted down through the forest canopy. Here, too, everything was green and brown and beautiful and, except for the trail, almost virgin. Almost. Once, at the edge of the Grove, close to the creek, an iron pipe, apparently a marker of some kind, protruded stark and ungainly and six feet tall from leaf-covered soil. Nearby, several lengths of pink and yellow plastic tape had been knotted to foliage. They bore cryptic inscriptions of the kind you learn to fear out in the developers' world because you know they announce impending bulldozers. I walked on. Before the boles of the world's third and sixth tallest trees stood two more gray plaques, and near the sixth largest tree crouched some kind of big, ugly measuring machine. No attempt had been made to tuck it out of sight, away from the trail, let alone to camouflage it in any way, and in that soft place, with a shaft of sunlight slanting down onto it, it stood out as harshly and obscenely as an oil rig in a hayfield.

I came back to the start of the trail and walked out onto open gravel and once more sat looking at the green wall of the Grove. A few feet away, a pair of slate-colored dippers, or water ouzels, dippered and dived and cheetered and bobbed and blinked, white eyelids flashing promise of Redwood Creek ouzels for centuries down the line. Distant movement caught my eye. Far downstream, a great blue heron flapped slowly away and out of sight like a big, slow-motion, flying dishcloth.

I looked back at the Grove. Now that I knew where they were, I could not help seeing the iron pipe and the pieces of pink plastic. They might be innocent enough, of course. Might be. But they existed. So did the crass measuring machine back beside the sixth tallest tree in the world. Even here, eight miles from roadhead, it had begun. The threats did not end with the possible riprapping of the Grove, or the Army-Engineering of the creek bed. There are subtler ways of tarnishing with good intentions. Put not your trust in Park Service man, either.

The sun set. I went back into the forest and sat for a spell, deep in a silence that was as absolute as a desert silence, but richer. I heard no answers, though, in the silence. I walked back to camp. Night fell. Perhaps, I decided as I cooked dinner, there were no real answers—for Redwood Creek or the rest of the planet. No simple answers, anyway. No place you could really put your trust.

Next morning I walked out. I took my time, looking and hoping, but as I walked it seemed almost as if the war being waged on the hillside that I had left behind was drawing even closer. I reached the blacktop parking lot still with no sign of an answer, no hint of a hope.

I got into the car and drove up onto a ridge that formed the eastern watershed of Redwood Creek. Soon, I left the National Park. Almost immediately I came to what had once been a little hump on the crest of the ridge. But the hump had been sliced off, flat, like the top of a boiled egg, and left bare. The place was not really a surprise: a ranger had told me it had been the site of a yarder, one of the huge machines that had replaced the spar trees I had known in Canada; but in the first moment I saw the bleak, bare flat I still suffered shock.

I turned off the road and bumped across naked subsoil. Off to the right, tatters of white toilet paper adhered to human feces. I parked near the center of the flat, got out, walked to its lip.

The ravaged hillside dropped steeply away. It was the first time in twenty years that I had actually stood on the edge of slash, and the battlefield was just as I remembered it. The bare soil gouged and churned, ribbed and rutted. Protruding from it, like diseased, sawn-off teeth in a huge dead jaw, all that remained of once magnificent redwoods: inert, flat-topped stubs, cremated by follow-up burning. Slaughtered. Finished. Between the stumps, the blackened soil supported, except for charred and shattered branches, only a few weak, straggly plants.

At my feet, the redwood stumps were filthy, chewed, defaced, obscene. Farther down the slope, distance obscured the desecration, but I knew what it would be like if I walked through the wreckage that strewed the slope for perhaps a quarter of a mile, until the slash abruptly ended and living trees began. Beyond that point, a rich green cloak reached unbroken down to Redwood Creek and up the valley's far slope. To my outer eye, the cloak seemed woven from red-wood trees, nothing else. But my mind's eye knew now that the slopes were also invested with a rich weave of fungi and lichen and wood sorrel and ferns and water ouzels and chick-adees and flickers and great blue herons and porcupines and deer and men. A rich, pulsating pageant in which every living member interlocked with the next. Well, interlocked with every member but one.

I let my outer eye run on beyond the redwoods to the blue-gray line of the Pacific—source of the summer fogs that rolled inland and kept the redwoods alive. But the huge ocean that has been called the eye of the world was almost hidden. Smoke, drifting down from a distant hillside, no doubt from a logging after-burn, hung over land and sea like a pall.

My eye began to run up the fold that was the nave of Red-wood Creek. A side fold suggested a side creek. I checked my map. The fold marked, just as I thought, the place I had paused that first evening and seen the man standing in defensive solitude beside his red pack and flickering fire, with the wall of redwoods rising dark and magnificent behind him. For the moment, at least, that place seemed secure.

I walked around to the other side of the flat and let my eye swing up beyond the fragile sanctuary of the park to the battlefield where ignorant armies slashed by day.

Even at that distance, the hillside looked mortally wounded. And now, standing on the lip of the bare flat with the charred shambles sloping away below me, I knew without the blurring of twenty years exactly how that distant, plun-dered hillside would soon look, close up.

A green pickup bounced across the flat, pulled up midway between me and my car. Two young Indian families—four adults, four children—disembarked from the cab and from the mattress-lined truck bed. Ignoring my presence, they walked to the far lip of the flat and stood looking out over the slash, beyond the folded green cloak of virgin redwoods, toward the Pacific—toward the ocean that had all but vanished, now, beneath the pall of smoke. The Indians just stood there, looking.

I did not blame them, there at that place, for disapproving of my presence, of the color of my skin. Put not your trust in white men.

Circling well clear of the Indians' pickup, I walked back toward my car. Toward the car that had made my journey up to Redwood Creek possible; my car that was cousin to the lumbering yellow machines that slashed by day, responding to the whistles blown by men on that distant hillside.

"Put not your trust in men" was more like it. In the species. In the noninterlocking species.

I reached my car, got in, closed the door, started the engine. I sat listening to it, looking at the little group of Indians standing on the lip of the flat, silhouetted against gray, smoke-filled sky.

Yes, "Put not your trust in men," that was it. That seemed to be the answer, such as it was. The only answer. Sitting in my car, at that high and special vantage point of space and time, I found that I accepted it with a stark gray certitude.

It was not a new solution, of course. It kept surfacing these days, whether I liked it or not; kept surfacing in many people's minds, not just in mine. There was only one answer for Redwood Creek, only one hope for all the other hillsides, for the planet. Only one exit. For at least a short while longer, in this little sample world, the whistles would continue to shrill and send blind yellow machines lumbering across condemned hillsides. I could only hope—all of us could only hope—that the "practical" men who controlled the whistles, or thought they did, there up Redwood Creek and clear around the world, were in fact blowing the whistle on our noninterlocking, bull-in-a-china-shop, industrial, autumnal civilization; were blowing it loud and clear, up there where they worked but would not look—up there beyond the trees, up the creek.

I slipped the car into gear, swung it around and headed for home.

Ten autumns later, I went back to Redwood Creek.

I went back from a world in which it seemed that our species had at last begun to realize what it was doing to the forests of Brazil and the Congo and the rest of the planet. A few weeks earlier I had talked to a friend—a well-traveled man, but an engineer without obvious environmental leanings—who had just returned from a visit to India, where he had been born, and who kept saying, "The jungle's almost gone! It used to be everywhere, and now it's gone!" On the broader scene, belated realization seemed in a few cases to be leading at last to action. The question was: "In enough cases?"

I also went back to Redwood Creek as a man who in ten years had moved, reluctantly but ever more firmly, toward the answer that had loomed by the end of my first visit. Then, my response had been gut reaction. Now I could focus more clearly, or thought I could. After all, what tended to happen when any species got out of control?

But I also went back with hope. You more or less have to keep on hoping, of course. Besides, you have to be careful with memories. For time edits. Edits two ways. It removes the dross, so that we can more easily recognize the stuff that has value; but it also amends, tidies up—and in doing so it may distort. This is where you have to be careful: memory is unreliable, always. So I needed an update. There was another, more pinnable thing, too: the year after my visit, Redwood National Park had been expanded to include not only the hillside we had been ravaging but also the whole lower watershed of Redwood Creek.

As soon as I arrived I found to my pleasure that the Park Service had modified its normal, purely preservationist aims. A ranger at the Information Center in Orick nodded toward a big green notice titled "Healing a Watershed" and said, "That's what this park is all about." The logged-off hillsides, the ranger advised me, were slowly healing by natural processes but in selected places they were being aided by ambitious rehabilitation schemes. For the present, these sites remained closed to the public; but all summer a small shuttle bus ferried people along the crest to a point from which a walk of little more than a mile down a foot trail brought them into Tall Trees Grove. Two weeks earlier, the bus had stopped running for the year, but the ranger was good enough to offer me a ride out to roadhead.

We had barely begun the bumpy, hour-long ride when he pulled the pickup off onto the flat, sliced-off hilltop that I had briefly shared, ten years earlier, with the Indian families. The Park Service now called the place Redwood Creek Overlook, but I had learned back in Orick that it was known locally as Devastation Point. The flat itself, I discovered, was still an expanse of naked, ugly subsoil; but the slopes below its lip had changed dramatically. They had greened over so thickly that to the casual eye they already seemed on the verge of qualifying for modern Pennsylvanian or Shropshire beauty. For a moment, my hopes buoyed. Then I began to see the impoverishment: ravaged soil, still gashed and gouged; the undergrowth's lack of richness and balance. Off to my right there protruded above the greenery a charred and splintered wreck that had once been a redwood tree. Not for the first time, it occurred to me that one life-form had no damned right to do such things to another.

An hour later we parked at roadhead and I began to walk down the trail, alone. For a hundred yards or so after I moved out of the overgrown slash into the trees, echoes of the recent war came with me: the redwoods grew tall and stately, but between them thick, tangled undergrowth, encouraged by extra air and light from the stripped land, ran rampant. Then, quite suddenly, the forest had opened up and I was walking among the familiar harmonies: silent, spacious hallways; banks of green-fronded ferns; dead, moss-covered giants rotting safely back to humus; and up from this quiet underworld, soaring, the rough, massive, red-brown trunks of that moment's mature redwoods

For half an hour I walked on down through unspoiled forest. Then, just outside the Grove, there was a small clearing, and a toilet. It was a rustic-looking, solar-operated little building, and well designed; but it was still a toilet. I walked past it, down into the Grove.

At first, everything seemed to stand unchanged. The tallest tree still soared stately and magnificent, not discernibly different from its neighbors except for the metal plaque at its foot. Then I saw that on the plaque, after the figures for height and girth, in feet, the equivalents in meters had been added, untidily, in black marking pen, by some mere measurer's hand. It was a small thing, I told myself; but it was still out of place, still unnecessary, still ugly.

I walked on, around the trail that wound through the Grove. Soon, a few feet to the left, there stood, quite unconcealed, a garish red plastic box, lined with metal sieve mesh and marked by a labeled stake. I came to the sixth tallest tree in the world. The crass measuring machine beside the tree had gone. But nearby there now stood, silhouetted stark against open creek bed, a rusty iron pipe still bearing old and now useless metal fittings. On its summit perched a wooden box bearing, upside down, a large white notice proclaiming "observation well," and announcing that it was operated by the Department of the Interior, Geological Survey, Water Resources Division, in cooperation with other agencies. I walked past this object. The creek bed now sloped up to the very edge of the forest in a long, artificial, straight-line gradient. I stood looking at the flattened expanse of pebbles and gravel, still barred by bulldozer tracks. As an attempt to fend off flood erosion, I told myself, this banking up of the gravel might be less disruptive than wholesale riprapping of the bank; but it was still sad, and it seemed unlikely to do much good for the trees. What it had really helped—what it had no doubt been designed to help—was the politics of bureaucracy. I turned and began to retrace my steps.

By the time I approached roadhead, where the ranger would be waiting with the pickup, I had begun to tell myself that I was oversensitive. The Park Service had no doubt resisted a lot of public pressure to improve access to the Grove and add amenities. So on balance they had, as usual, done a good job. Perhaps, after all, you could put a little limited trust in Park Service man. Perhaps even in man, period. After all, politicians and conservationists and the average voter had pulled together, and against heavy odds, in setting aside the large sums of money needed to acquire the land that surrounded and now protected the Worm and the Grove. You might complain that the effort had come too late; that it was a mere conscience-massaging palliative, applied when the chips were safely off the table. On the other hand, you might conclude that we had turned the corner; that we were at last learning to curb our greed.

The natural, harmonious, open forest floor gave way to crowded undergrowth. Then I had stepped back out into the green but still-impoverished world of the old slash—into a world that had been bandaged, now, but in no sense healed. The ranger started up the pickup.

As we bounced along the old logging road, the ranger told me the recent history of one of the few local logging companies that over the years had refused to clear-cut, had always operated with an eye on the future and had, by logging standards, treated the forest with respect. A few months earlier, this company—a large but privately owned outfit—had been bought out by a big-time speculator in a deal financed by junk bonds. Now, to pay off six hundred million dollars in these bonds, the owner was clear-cutting huge swaths of the remaining virgin redwoods; clear-cutting as fast and unsparingly as he could. Even loggers were protesting. The speculator had responded on national television. He operated, he said, according to the Golden Rule: "When you've got the gold, you rule."

An hour later I drove away from Redwood Creek for the second time in ten years with my questions still hanging there, as drab and insistent as ever.

8 Toward the Heights

At the bend in the road I pulled in as usual and parked tight against the rickety barbed-wire fence. Even before I got out, I saw the garbage. And when I walked around the back of the car and stood beside the fence there were three soggy beer cartons at my feet, and beyond the fence a swath of cans and bottles and Styrofoam cups. In the leaden late afternoon light the cups stood out white against the green grass, like bones.

Beyond the garbage, the familiar view spread dank and cheerless. Down at the foot of the valley, in the flatland world, where the houses and the other things lay, a scattering of lights already twinkled; but around them stretched a flat grayness. The roar of traffic wafted faintly up through the still, damp air. Somewhere behind me, a cow complained. I sought a glimpse of the distant ocean that has been called the eye of the world, but out there, too, I could see only more grayness.

There was a smell of rain in the air now, and a chill that seemed not just autumnal but almost wintry at last. That was good, really. The days had been so warm and the few Pacific storms so pacific, it was difficult to remember that the year had already eased into its final month.

I looked up the valley, toward the other, forest world. Cloud banks had begun to drift along the crests, slowly burying them, and gray-white wisps were peeling off the clouds' fringes and creeping down steep, dark green slopes. The approaching storm, I decided, might bring a much-needed downpour. I ought to camp by nightfall, and in a sheltered place. With luck, I'd make it to the leaning sycamore.

I brought my eyes back down to the present, to the familiar valley view. The light lay so heavy on the land that the plunging depths and wedges of woodland and curving grassy slopes melded into each other without drama or delight. When I checked the hanging meadow, directly opposite— checked it as usual to make certain it was still safe—I could not see clearly enough for immediate reassurance; and when I tried to verify through binoculars I thought I glimpsed something yellow and foreign and potentially threatening near its right edge. But I could not decide whether the splash of yellow, half concealed by a bush, was indeed a strip of plastic tape—that deadly harbinger of flatland developers—or a clump of the dandelion-like daisies that bloomed locally in the fall. There were, I noticed, several clumps of these daisies growing along the fence at my feet. Striving to ignore the soggy cartons that lay among them, and the possible meanings that hung over in the hanging meadow, I turned and walked back to the car.

An hour later I parked at trailhead, swung the big pack

onto my back and began to walk along the jeep track that led into the forest.

As usual, I walked at first with my mind still tethered to the outside, flatland world. I found myself ruminating, rather muddleheadedly, on a radio report I had heard that morning—an echo of the most recent scandal in the Washington administration. Now, walking away from all that toward the meadow with the little man-made pond at its center, toward the oak grove that lay on its far side and that would lead me up into the forest, I saw that the only good this latest scandal had achieved was to answer, quite unintentionally, the long-standing question of where we ought to dump our toxic wastes, our communal mercantile garbage.

The moment I reached the edge of the familiar meadow I knew something was wrong. Even in the fast-fading light I could see a blackness squatting at the meadow's center. I walked on, out over the green grass, toward the little artificial pond. I came to the place the pond had been. It no longer existed. It had been disemboweled. And the soil bulldozed from its damp bed had been spread like thick black putty along the jeep trail.

I stepped onto bare, disrupted earth that had been imprinted with an ugly, uneven grill of bulldozer tracks. My feet sank into the soft black soil. As I struggled forward, trying to ignore the dark hollow off to my right, I could almost hear, behind the silence that lay over the meadow, a big yellow machine roaring about its work. Perhaps the black earth should be dumped on the District of Columbia too, along with the toxics.

I walked on, smiling thinly at the sourness of my mood, came to the end of the black earth, stepped back onto green grass and almost at once reached the edge of the oak grove.

I think I half-expected to find that the jeeps had been stripping the grove again, roughshod, for firewood. But then

I was in among the trees and there were no new tracks, and last year's chain-saw signs had been softened by a carpet of dead leaves. I crossed the bed of a small creek. It was bone dry. In a normal year it would by now be tumbling down the grove singing sturdy songs of winter; but this year the forest's wellsprings had withered away.

In the grove, the light had almost gone. Yet as I walked past one big denuded maple, its dead leaves beneath my boots had a surprisingly rich red-brown warmth that almost glowed up out of the gloom. Then the jeep track gave way to the familiar trail—the trail that even in full daylight was faint and indecisive, small and beautiful, just right for its job—and the forest closed in around me, quiet and waiting, ready to drown out with its silence all lingering flatland reverberations.

Moonlight, filtering through low clouds, began to replace twilight. The trail was barely visible now but my feet knew the way so well that even with the fifty-pound load on my back they kept putting themselves down in the right places. The trail angled up a slope. I readjusted the pack harness, up at each collarbone. Somewhere ahead, an owl hooted: two short hoots, pause, two long. In spite of the sadness in them—sadness to a human ear—I heard the four familiar notes as a welcome. A welcoming back.

The trail spiraled around the bole of a madrone tree and climbed the rungs of the natural staircase formed by its roots—the turretlike staircase that had become my private signal that I was now ready to cross over, if I would only let it happen, from one world into another. The madrone roots were almost covered by pale, dead, indented oak leaves, and I had to step carefully because I knew the leaves would be slippery. What little I could see of the roots was very dark, almost black; but because I remembered their rich warm sheen in daylight the staircase was still a signal.

The trail leveled off. It was good to be back. Good to be walking once more up these slopes, among these trees and ferns, becoming immersed again in the harmony that interlinked them—and linked them, too, with the animals that lived here. At root, that was why I came to such places, and to this place in particular. The harmony was the key.

Somewhere in my mind, something clicked. A few days earlier I had again been labeled in print as "a naturalist." That never sat well. I didn't know enough, across the board. Besides, I distrusted and disliked labels: for all their convenience, they constrict, blur, distort, mislead. Still, we all got stuck with them, one way or another—in gossip or print, on tombstones. And all at once, walking up the steep, familiar trail, suddenly conscious of the forest's harmonies, I saw that if I really must be labeled I would like it to be as "a harmonist." That came closest. That was what kept me halfway adjusted. That was what kept drawing me back.

The trail cut across a precipitous hillside. Under my right boot, a piece of loose soil gave way. Left foot and walking staff automatically took the weight. A stone bounced down the dim, thirty-foot drop. Safe enough, of course, but better pay a little more attention, brother.

Yes, it felt good, being back—and looking forward to almost a week up high. It would be especially good up there if the forecast held and the weather cleared, a couple of days ahead. I knew the country so well that the trip would not be very exciting, of course, just comfortable. To tell the truth, few things excited me now, the way they once did. It used to be that a wild iris on the edge of a wood was enough, or a sudden throng of fireflies or a squirrel leaping, high above, branch to dangerous branch. Nowadays such things rarely seemed to trigger my blood. Call it the debit side of experience. Or age—which you could, in the right mood, classify as a synonym for experience. I had a lot to line up on the credit side of experience, though. A lifetime of walking, for example.

I came to the top of the first low ridge. The trail turned along it, level for a spell. I slackened the harness again, up at both collarbones.

Yes, looking back on my life—on the part of it that was over—there could be no doubt: walking had somehow become one of its pillars—one of its underpinnings, shorings, props, whatever you wanted to call it. In mock-macho mood I'd even said that maybe life was all "wine, women and walking." From time to time I had wondered just what I would have done without the walking. That question was stupid, though. Invalid. Without the walking, "I" would have been somebody else—would not have evolved into what was currently "me." It was as simple and as fundamental as that.

People who did not walk—did not walk, that is, in the way I meant—almost always failed to grasp what walking can do for you. Or what it does and does not cut you off from. There is no reason at all, for example, why being in synch with boots and backpacks should mean that you are in some way out of touch, over any but the shortest haul, with such reasonably important outside-world happenings as the current surge forward from electronics to fiber optics; rather the reverse, in fact. On a deeper and more positive level, your escapes to reality can help heal what have been called the three central ailments of our modern world: absence of beauty, lost connection with nature, and lack of time. You can therefore hear, fairly consistently, the thin and sinister ring of that tired equation "Time is money," and you accept, profoundly, that time must "have value and not mere use." So when you have walked enough, in the right places and the right way, you are ready to claim the hours as your own.

But I had long ago recognized that what walking had given me above all was the ability to stand back. To stand back sometimes and see the world from outside the narrow confines of my own species—insofar as such a thing is possible. Once you have walked for a quorum of years—for two or ten or twenty or forty, according to your needs—and for long spells have escaped the trappings and entrapments of the human construct and have lived so securely among the other life-forms that you sometimes feel you have melded with them, a readjustment inevitably occurs. It becomes impossible to look at the world with the man-centered gaze that most people—and most religions, too—still bring to bear on it. You accept, with more than just your intellect, that man is an animal. A very special animal, for sure, but still an animal. You therefore embrace Julian Huxley's seminal insight that man is "nothing else than evolution become conscious of itself." And then you are ready to "learn of the green world what can be thy place."

When I espoused this view back in the flatlands, people accused me of having made the green world my religion. Some even accused me of preaching. On the whole, I tended to think they were right—at least on the first count. After all, the word "religion" stems from the Latin for "binding back" —a binding back, presumably, to our roots.

The trail switchbacked up a high point on the ridge. I leaned into the pack harness.

Albert Saijo, I seemed to remember, had called backpacking "a way of honoring our beginnings."

The trail angled down off the ridge into a thicket. I could just make out its faint outline well enough to keep going without a flashlight. Only a stone's throw, now, to Leaning Sycamore Camp.

You could say, if you were in the right mood, that all religions were attempts to answer with music—that is, with poetry and pageantry—the ancient, hoary, inevitable, unanswerable question, "What is the meaning of life?" The nature of any response depended, of course, on whether the questioner was talking about his own little individual flicker or the larger human bubble or the entire anti-entropic living phenomenon or the whole knowable shebang, including the mountains and valleys and oceans and the stuff they were made of, on this planet and elsewhere. A religion, in other words, must try to answer at least two prime questions. First: "What the hell goes on around here?" or "What is the nature of reality?" Second: "Who the hell am I?" or "How do I fit into the big picture?" Or perhaps it was truer to say that, because most of us spend our religio-investigative sessions pendulating between these two conundrums, any valid religion must seek a fusion of its answers to them.

Taking the macrocosmic questions first, I found it astonishing that . . .

The trail emerged from the thicket. Almost at once, the familiar sycamore tree loomed up, leaning out over the creek, dim but definite, somehow reassuring. The small clearing at its foot did not make the greatest of campsites, but there was always water in the creek and I often stopped here when I came in late. I slipped off my pack, leaned it against the base of the sycamore, removed the polypropylene undervest and pile jacket from the pack and put them on. Almost instantly, a promise of warmth replaced the hint of chill that had touched me the moment I stopped walking. I took the lightweight candle lantern from a pack pocket and tied the free end of the lantern's nylon cord onto a branch so that it hung in what I judged to be the best place. I held a lighted match to the wick. The flame took hold—and almost at once a circle of warm yellow light created a comfortable little room, walled by madrones and undergrowth. I began to rig my clear plastic tarp: no rain had fallen yet, but in the last real daylight the clouds had seemed to be slumping even lower.

Quickly, I tied the tarp to convenient bushes and branches so that it protected the requisite rectangle of ground. The familiar task occupied only a fraction of my mind; the rest reverted to its ruminations.

. . . Taking the macrocosmic aspect first, I found it astonishing that all these years after Copernicus most of our successful religions, and especially the Middle Eastern cousins —Judaism, Christianity along with its Communist heresy, and Islam—should still cling, in the face of virtually cast-iron evidence, to dogmas that regard our roots as reaching no further back than man. If "God" was anything, it was what remained, still stretching away out there, when you had come to the limits of your mind, so it really seemed rather puerile to announce that "God made man in his own image." Fairly clearly, the opposite was true: the peacocks' god, they say, has a magnificent, iridescent tail. (Christians and their cousins, of course, claim that the peacock has no "soul." Yet some of them seem, at least at moments, to grant souls to pet dogs and even cats. Question: "Where do you draw the line?" A better question: "Why are you trying to draw a line?") One terrible result of our error about God's making man in his own image was a corollary: "Man shall have dominion." Now, such illusions had once been understandable enough, and fairly harmless. But while a religion need not—in fact, must not—be confined to current intellectual insights, it cannot fly too flagrantly in the face of them. Recently, that had happened. And the results of the old beliefs had become dangerous. They might even prove fatal to the species. What we needed—needed desperately, for sheer self-preservation— was a new religious code or framework or system that embodied a little less outright illusion. Something that came— rather more often, anyway—a good deal closer to what we currently regarded, with our intellects, as reality.

I had the tarp up now, neat and taut, and as I began to

unpack and set up camp beneath it I kept switching on the flashlight I'd hung from a cord around my neck. This was the first time in years that I had used a translucent plastic tarp (my last white one, the kind I preferred, had developed too many holes and I had been unable to find a replacement), and once I stooped in under my new roof I found that although it turned a dull, impermeable gray where the light from lantern or flashlight struck it at an angle, I could when I shone the flashlight directly upward, perpendicular to the tarp, see a veiled suggestion of bare sycamore branches and green, close-packed madrone leaves; and that if I held the flashlight lens tight against the plastic, eliminating reflection, I could see this world beyond, complete with its delicate traceries, at only one remove, no more than slightly blurred and distorted.

What we needed in our new code or system was a sense of holiness, of sacredness, unconnected with any God—if that word was taken to imply a supernatural personality. But we could not progress to that stage until we had broken free from our current myths and metaphors—especially those of the man-centered religions and their offshoots and heresies. This did not mean we must attack the religions. Persecution not only tends to produce the opposite of the desired effect (a maneuver at which we are as a species distressingly and almost comically adept), it also goes against good, deep grains. So the thing to do was to wait for the old myths to atrophy, to wither as effective global influences, the way all outdated religions eventually did. The signs of atrophy had already emerged, of course: in Christianity, burgeoning ecumenicism; in Islam, rampant fundamentalism. From the inside, these movements might look like resurgences; from the outside they looked more like natural but desperate responses to decay, to a drying up of the wellsprings.

I inflated my foam air mattress, laid it out on the black

plastic groundsheet and sat down. Then I took off my boots and socks, slid halfway into the sleeping bag and leaned back against my pack. It was all cozily familiar, there in the warm yellow room of light that the candle lantern had built. I measured a cup and a half of water into one cooking pot, lit the stove, put the pot on it, leaned back again. After a minute or two I poured myself a generous tot of Old Grand-dad, added water, sipped. The water boiled. I poured the instant rice and other pre-mixed dinner ingredients into the pot, stirred, turned the stove off. Five minutes, and dinner would be ready. I leaned back again and sat looking at the warm brown trunks of the madrones that lined my room.

If the old religions withered away, the good things about them—some of the moral values that had emerged in response to the microcosmic, personal questions—might live on. Yes, that was what we had to do: evolve beyond the old myths. "The world will be no less complicated if we proceed with a sense of the sacred in nature," I had recently read, ". . . but the way will be lit." That sounded pretty nice . . .

I must have dozed for a minute or two, then, because when I checked my watch the five minutes had already run to seven. I stirred the stew, spooned out the first cupful, began to eat. It required effort, now, to stay awake, but I tussled my way through dinner, poured a little water into the cooking pot, then leaned back once more against the pack.

The dark side of the coin was that it had begun to look as if, for the sake of the larger whole, man would have to be stopped . . .

Knowing I might drift off at any moment, I reached out and gave the candle-lantern cord a quick jerk. The candle went out. The warm yellow room vanished. I leaned back again, content in the darkness.

. . . man would have to be stopped, that is, unless *Homo sapiens*—as we arrogantly labeled ourselves—evolved from

Homo juggernauticus into *Homo stewardensis* or *Homo custodiensis . . .*

A caravan of vague thoughts meandered through my mind. It was all very frustrating, not being able to keep my eyes open. They had begun to adjust to the darkness, too: I could now distinguish the dark lines of the nearest madrone trunks, and a hint of the world beyond.

I think I became fleetingly aware that I was muddling toward the brink of the questions I had six weeks earlier carried away from Redwood Creek, essentially unanswered; then, still sitting there, leaning against my pack, I slid down and away into sleep.

Next morning, after breakfast, an odd thing happened. During the night the clouds had decanted no more than a sprinkle and then fled, and I was sitting there under the sycamore tree, watching the newly risen sun bejewel wet foliage, thinking that I didn't really feel much like going ahead just yet with my plans for the day—which were to push on up to the forest's main crest and then walk a fair distance along it—sitting there thinking of nothing else in particular except perhaps the comforting way the madrone trunks all around me curved in obscure harmonies, when something that I don't know quite what to call was up there teetering on the brink of my mind. Perhaps, replete with breakfast, I had dozed off again—and then awakened with the remnants of a dream filtering up into full consciousness. The scene that hung in my mind certainly had the unreal aura and basic bizarreness of a lingering dream. Yet in a sense it seemed more like a story I had "dreamed up" as I crossed the border into the waking world. Anyway, the scene was there for a brief interlude, up before my eyes, surprisingly vivid in its diaphanous and distant, slightly comic way.

God was floating above the Firmament in timeless silence. It was an almost amorphous, vaguely spherical presence, immanent and immensely wise, and after a while It broke the vast silence and began to voice to Its accompanying chief of staff Its unease at the way things appeared to be going on a small planet called Earth, barely visible far below.

Now, the details of my dream—or whatever you want to call it—do not matter. The point is that when the Firmament scene dissolved, as all fantasies eventually do, and I found myself undeniably sitting there under the sycamore tree, I was also, in a residual sort of way, still looking down—as from an immense height, slightly godlike and very detached—at current events on our planet.

Just before the dream scene dissolved, God had commented to Its skeptical chief of staff that a crisis of the kind Earth now faced was a routine phenomenon when events in an ecosystem reached a certain state of complexity. Once the life-stuff in it had evolved to a specific level beyond that at which it began to think in a self-conscious way, said God, it typically achieved too much knowledge and too little wisdom. In Earth's case the dominant species had—just for starters—failed to develop wit enough to control the machinery it had managed to invent.

Left alone under the leaning sycamore after the scene had faded away, I found no difficulty in going along with that assessment. (No surprise there, of course: after all, it had been my dream.) I had only to consider, from my still elevated and somewhat godlike station, the way we were stripping our sustaining foliage as if it were old wallpaper. Tropical forests were disappearing at the rate of fifty acres a minute—over 70,000 acres each day. At the turn of the century, 40 percent of Ethiopia was blanketed by tropical evergreen and deciduous forests; today, that figure has been cut to 4 percent. Yet we persisted in blaming the famines there on droughts (which no doubt could be related to the rape of the land) and on politics. The tropical forest rape was only one item, of course, on the list of what we were doing. There were all those toxic brews being buried just under the planet's skin, and the ozone hole over Antarctica, and acid rain, and the greenhouse effect, and the way we were now exterminating other species of the life-stuff at the unprecedented rate of forty per day. You could go on and on. At the root of it all lay the way we were multiplying (1,570 of us born every minute). For without our exploding numbers most pressures would ease. The astonishing thing was that the explosion had, essentially, happened in my own little life span. When I was born we totaled 2 billion. Now we were 5 billion, and racing. Racing like Gadarene swine toward a cliff. The trouble was that in our case it looked as if, unless we were stopped, we might take most of the rest of the life-stuff over the cliff with us.

High in a white oak, a squirrel flounced from branch to branch, tail gray and flowing, then paused long enough to give me a routine, tight-throated scolding for being where I was. I found myself looking past the white oak, across the creek, at the chaotic concordances of the thick, virgin forest: at the press of trees and bushes and ferns and smaller plants, all crowded in apparent disorder yet somehow sublimely balanced, one with the other, so that even a human eye, surveying the whole, found grace and elegance. Virgin forest, untouched by man.

Well, all right, man had to be stopped. The question was: "How?" More intraspecific wars looked like no kind of answer. Not the way things had been going. Our "progress" had been from Marathon, through Waterloo and Guernica and Coventry, to Hiroshima. And the next stage in the progression had become unthinkable. It could set the planet back several millennia.

Most alternatives, assuming we avoided all-out nuclear war and therefore left space for alternatives, and assuming the whole human system did not just seize up of its own accord, hardly looked inviting—to us. When a species expanded too fast, exploded, got out of hand, began to wreck the harmonies around it, nature always found a way out. One thing that often happened was that the relevant predator populations exploded too, and restored the balance. Newly prolific coyotes, for example, might take care of a rampant rodent population. Hawks could cull quail. The trouble was, we currently had no effective predators—if you accepted that Martians and UFOs and all such jazz remained fantasies, potentials that did not yet seem to have been realized.

Failing predators, the culling of rogue populations was often effected by disease: an epidemic running wild might, almost overnight, cut a species back to size. And when it came to disease, we humans looked pretty vulnerable. Plagues had hit us before, of course, but never, except among very restricted communities, with anything approaching an effective culling rate. Still, a plague of some kind had to be viewed as a possible solution. A natural solution.

Any disease that brought us back under control would have to be one that did no damage to the rest of the fabric. If you stood back a little way from our species—by sitting long enough, for example, under a sycamore tree—you could see that potential raw material for such a culling might already have evolved. It seemed to have germinated, fittingly, in what was perceived as the cradle of mankind: Central Africa. It was called Acquired Immunodeficiency Syndrome, or AIDS.

If the AIDS virus underwent some relatively simple mutation and became VEAIDS (Very Easily Acquired Immunodeficiency Syndrome), so that it spread quickly and devastatingly, then it might well solve the world's most pressing current problem, and in a nondisruptive way. That is, it might cull the disrupting species so effectively that the dangerous and growing imbalances were corrected.

From a planetary standpoint (though certainly not from our human corner), the precise nature of any plague that might cull us was irrelevant. The important criterion remained, though, that it be species-specific, or close to it, and therefore leave the rest of the fabric untouched. An effective epidemic was not, of course, a solution we should or even perhaps could set in motion, but simply something that might happen to us, just as it had happened to other species.*

If a human culling occurred, it might well follow paths quite unrelated to VEAIDS or any other disease. The very

---

* The manner in which I have discussed a natural culling of humanity practically guarantees that I'll be called "callous" or even "a monster." What I've been trying to do, though, is to stand outside our species and look at it, and its relationship with the rest of the planet, in a reasonably objective light. And I'm suggesting that the alternatives to a drastic culling are—from a planetary viewpoint, and perhaps even from a long-term human viewpoint—unacceptable and truly "monstrous." I submit that this gets me off the hook. After all, the vast majority of us see things rather differently when we use just such methods to control other "pests" by the introduction of predators or disease—a method that is certainly far less disruptive than the use of DDT and its cousins. Mostly, the pests are insects, and therefore lie outside the common boundaries of our compassion. But we don't stop at insects.

In Australia, the rabbits that white Australians introduced early in their own invasion had by the middle of this century multiplied so rampantly that they became the scourge of the country, reducing rich green natural pastures to wasteland. In 1950 the Australians imported the myxomatosis virus, which had evolved naturally in South America and which affected only rabbits. Within two years the Australian rabbit population had been cut by 90 percent. A couple more years, and wastelands turned green, with grass growing tall where for decades not a blade had been seen. For a time, the rabbit population seemed to have stabilized, at very tolerable levels. The culling remained almost 90 percent effective. But then the rabbits developed some resistance to the virus, their numbers rose—and the humans are now striving to make the virus more lethal.

complexity that has lifted us to the top of the pile could, for example, turn out to be our downfall. A recent report on the effects of irradiation on food noted that the more complex an organism, the less radiation needed to kill it. So in certain human culling scenarios—World War III, say, or ozone interference—it might well turn out that complexity is no longer an evolutionary advantage but a fatal flaw.

Any form of drastic culling would from our human corner naturally look like an utter disaster. Indeed, the prospect of it was something that many people frankly seemed unable to grasp. And as I sat there beneath my sycamore tree, deep in the silent, virgin forest, it occurred to me that this was really rather odd.

Most of us eventually came to accept, at least intellectually, the ugly, brick-wall, undetourable facts of our personal trajectories: rise, apogee, decline, death. It was curiously rare, though, for people to embrace the reality of all the similar, parallel trajectories of our larger groupings: nation, race, species. The nation part of it was obvious. It had happened often enough: Babylonia, Persia, Greece, Rome, Spain, England, others. And in due course of time the same tides would surely sweep, more or less similarly, over the U.S., the U.S.S.R., Japan and their successors. Even at this national level, though, there was a widespread blindness, or unwillingness to accept. (Perhaps I could focus at this level fairly easily because I was born and raised a Welshman and a Briton, and after that had become, seriatim, a more or less dutifully loyal resident of Kenya, Southern Rhodesia, Canada and, for thirty-odd years now, the United States. So, although I had not really thought of it before, patriotism might be for me a more plastic, less blinding concept than for most people.) To some extent, at least, the curves of racial domination, in whatever form, echoed the national ones, and at least a certain percentage of people recognized them. But the trajectory of the species, admittedly less clear to our eyes, did not seem to be something that most people could grasp in more than a very thin, intellectual way. The trajectory was there, though, for sure, tracing its presumably inevitable arc. Here again, it had happened often enough: trilobites, dinosaurs, others. So I did not see why we should shun acceptance of the fact. After all, it was wonderful to have lived through the brilliant, bizarre spasm of a dominant species.

Twenty paces beyond my feet, a chipmunk scuttered up onto a fallen tree trunk, surveyed his universe, became aware that it now included me, vanished.

From the planetary (as opposed to human) corner, the alternative to a culling of *Homo sapiens*—that is, a continuation of the present, human-dominated trends—looked likely to prove disastrous and perhaps fatal. But if some suitable form of culling took place, before things had progressed down the present road to the point of no return, then it was possible to imagine a planet restored to a decent working balance; a healthy, reinvigorated planet. It was even possible to imagine *Homo sapiens*, or perhaps a species that evolved from it, really acting as something analogous to the planet's brain. . . .

The neighborhood squirrel, somewhere up out of sight, tight-throat-scolded me again. I came back down to Earth.

Now, what I have written about what went on in my mind as I sat beneath the leaning sycamore tree that December morning is, of course, only a summary. A brief and tidied-up summary. It has to be. Because I know that, contrary to my intentions, I spent the entire morning sitting there and ruminating. Ruminating in a rambling and intermittent mode. My failure to do anything else all morning was aided, naturally, by other factors. By my habitual inertia, for one thing, fueled by prodigious powers of procrastination. Also by the weather. For the day's early sunlit promise had soon faded beneath heavy overcast and a sullen wind. So as I sat there, warm and cozy in my combined pile-jacket-and-sleeping-bag cocoon, there was no immediate and obvious encouragement to emerge from it. Besides, when I left the flatlands I had been tired in a fairly profound sense. Drained. Anyway, whatever the reasons, the fact is that I sat there, almost unmoving, until noon.

At that point I emerged long enough to take a short muscle-stretching stroll along the creek. Then I rehibernated into the cocoon, cooked and ate lunch—and slipped into my normal postprandial doze.

When I woke I had my regulation post-dozial caffeine fix of hot tea—and went on just sitting there and ruminating.

It was not easy to visualize the world as it would be after an effective culling of the human population. A lot would depend on the culling agency: internal or ecological collapse, new predator, rampant disease, none of the above; also, if disease had been the agency, on whether individual survivors remained totally unimpaired by it. There seemed to be an immense range of possibilities.

I found myself hoping, though, that when the situation stabilized, the survivors, or at least their leaders, would have learned their lesson: would understand, deeply enough in their bones, that any biological community, when it veers out of harmony with the whole, tends to be pruned to size—by agencies that at first glance may seem coincidental. I found myself hoping, I mean, that our newly aware species would have the wisdom, second time around, to impose effective internal controls—on population, consumption, pollution.

What I saw with greater confidence was the rest of the world recovering. There might be temporary enclaves of even greater destruction: human communities driven by sudden overwhelming lack of all their "civilized" amenities might ravage the local land, cutting down all trees, and worse. But with luck—either because the human survivors had learned their lesson or because they now lacked the power, at least for a spell—the planet would be spared the mechanized technological insults it was now suffering. Anaconda-like strip mining of the American West would stop. No more Russian vacuum ships would patrol off the once peaceful Seychelles, sucking giant prawns into extinction. Oil spills would end. Acid rain would abate, the ozone hole contract and eventually vanish. Buried toxics—though some would take millennia to degrade—would at least no longer be added to at a logarithmic rate. The equatorial forests might begin to reclaim their lost territories (as satellite photographs apparently show they are already doing in some Central African areas hardest hit by AIDS), and so restore weather balances. Species would resume their normal snail's pace rate of extinction. And so on and on and on, in ways I did not know enough to imagine, until the planet once more smiled.

Now, I know this brief summary does not sound like a full afternoon's ruminating. But once again, of course, I have only outlined what went on in my mind as I sat there under the sycamore tree. I also, no doubt, and as usual, spent a lot of time just sitting and doing nothing clearly definable. Anyway, the fact remains that by the time I emerged, quite suddenly, from my ruminations and redirected my mind to practical matters, the day had almost slipped away—the day during which I had planned to reach the forest's main crest and then walk a fair distance along it. For a while I toyed with the idea of spending another night at Leaning Sycamore Camp. But the overcast had now lifted somewhat and I guessed that the next weather front would not hit until morning. There was a full hour of daylight left, too, and then for a while there would be the new moon. With luck, I'd reach a certain reliable spring, up on the crest, before the moon set.

I brewed another pot of tea, struck camp, swung the pack

onto my back and followed the trail up the line of the creek. Soon heavier clouds were sliding in from the south. The light grew gray, wintry. I strode on, a little faster.

The trail unwound in front of me, curve after familiar curve, side creek after familiar side creek. My feet followed it semi-automatically. For the moment, my mind seemed almost dormant. Unbound by route-finding duty or the need to notice new sights, it refused to absorb, more than perfunctorily, those subtle changes that make walking in a familiar place so rewarding: the way a grove of young madrones, growing fast in an open space created by the death of an ancient white oak, now crowded so thick that the head-high saplings almost blocked the trail; the way two more branches of the fallen oak had rotted away from the main trunk and now lay at awkward angles on the damp earth; the way the swarm of ladybugs I had seen last time I passed were still holding their singles party on the oak's moss-covered trunk, though they had moved twenty feet along it, closer to the edge of the clearing, no doubt to catch more of the afternoon sun. I saw these things, obviously; but my mind slid over them without excitement, without joy.

It was not until the trail struck away from the creek, up the slope of a minor ridge, that my mind shifted back into gear. Then, with my body bending to the task of climbing the steep hillside, and sweating healthily in the process, I lifted without notice into one of those spells of knife-edge clarity that you almost always attain at some point in any prolonged spell of walking

At first, as I sweated on up the hill, I saw only the physical world with this new clarity. Off to the right, across a gully, two tall alders curved toward each other, building an arch of exquisite balance over an almost circular cluster of ferns. Then, close beside the trail, an ancient oak that I had passed a hundred times without really seeing it had focused, in spite of the failing light, into a hollow stump, charred long ago by a lightning strike and now an apparently lifeless skeleton—but, I suddenly saw, a skeleton that bore at its shattered summit a single living, green-leaved branch. I paused to wonder at this marvel of endurance, walked on. A few paces, and I found myself reflecting, not for the first time, that I had never been able to detect in the green world anything even remotely analogous to what was in the human world called "justice"—a commodity much extolled there, though the place hardly seemed riddled with it. A few more paces, and my mind had switched, as our minds often do—or as mine does, anyway—to a train of thought it had earlier shunted onto a side track.

Well, all right, maybe man had to be stopped . . . but that did not mean I must promptly bang or whimper my individual way out. I could still give myself up—sometimes, anyway—to enjoying the world's human joys: making love, listening to Beethoven conducted by Furtwängler, executing a perfectly disguised backhand drop shot from the baseline. This brought me, at last, to the second part of the religious agenda—to the microcosmic question: "Who the hell am I?" or "How do I fit into the big picture?"

As with the macrocosmic question, a lot depended on what you meant by "God." If I had a god, then it was something rather like a space-age Pan. *If* I had a god. The world liked to label all such beliefs "pantheism" (the apparent coincidence in syllables seemed—in this case at least—less accidental than it might appear). Current conventional wisdom tended to pooh-pooh pantheism—to say it simply didn't work. But then, conventional wisdom was still very much tied to the apron strings of the old, Middle Eastern cousins. If I had a god, had a religion . . .

I reached the top of the ridge, began to angle down through pine trees into another watershed. The light was fading fast now, and I stopped just long enough to take the flash-light out of a pack pocket and hang it around my neck by its nylon cord. Then I was walking again, not yet using the flash-light. In open stretches between the pines I could still make out, in the last daylight, new grass thrusting up green. The grass had almost buried the thin layer of discarded pine cones that covered the earth.

I found myself glancing, as I walked, at the half-hidden pine cones. It was always the same, anywhere, once I had been out long enough, had begun to quieten down: perhaps I just paused to watch a doe place herself in jeopardy to pro-tect her speckled fawn; or during one of my hourly rests I contemplated a quilt of lichen spreading green over dark granite; or I sat in camp in a clearing crisscrossed by fallen pines that were rotting century by century into long, low mounds, and then into nothingness—just sat, a happy har-monist, and stared at the mounds and the nothingness that spread in every direction beyond my two mortal feet and con-templated the seedling pines pushing up through both mounds and nothingness. Whatever the trigger, the lesson was always the same: connect, only connect. For that was an-other of the things that kept drawing me back to the green world: learning, more deeply and surely than with mere in-tellect, the bitsy finitude of individuals, the smooth conti-nuity of life.

I came to the fallen log that still marked the beginning of the bypass I had made, eliminating two creek crossings and a loop of trail. I stepped over the log, began to walk along my little cutoff. The daylight was dying now, but the moon was taking over. Even through the cloud cover, it shed a faint, diffused light.

I had yet to decide whether I'd remove the fallen log that camouflaged the entrance to the cutoff. I still relished the pri-vacy it gave me along that stretch. And maybe it would be good to know that when I died my secret stretch of trail would, too; that the forest would reclaim it, heal it over. Or was that good? Perhaps I should tell someone about it, so that the trail could be handed down. Or I might still, as originally intended, throw it open to the public—to the few people, that is, who walked this way.

I reached the end of the cutoff, rejoined the main trail.

Bitsy finitude or not, what mattered to most of us, most of the time, were, inevitably, the flickerings of our little individual lives. That was what you had to cope with day in and day out. The flicker-span got to look a bit different as you grew older, that was all. Shorter, for example. One hell of a lot shorter.

Come to think of it, there had been an autumnal nip in the air lately, all around me. Wintry, even. Nowadays there was no denying that according to the calendar I had moved into prime dying time: you only had to check the obituary pages. That was all right, up to a point. I had always said I liked to disregard statistics. And while I just might on bad days admit that perhaps I was over the hill, I certainly didn't see myself as burned out yet, not by a long candle, even if I sometimes guttered a bit.

I hesitated at the foot of a gully, momentarily uncertain in that dim light of just where the trail cut through a thimbleberry thicket. Then I saw a familiar bush beyond the thimbleberries, stepped toward it, knew I was still on the trail.

Statistics or no, I now had to grapple from time to time —all the time, really—with a knowledge of the inevitable. (Dying wasn't really the trouble, of course: what grated, and sometimes terrified, was the thought of not existing.) I had long ago decided that once you reached a certain age the only sensible response was to act as if you would live forever but know you might die before lunch. This posture took pretty good care of the superficial, intellectual, most-of-the-time stuff. Beyond that, though, questions arose. One of them was: "Can you get help?"

> "No man is an island,"
> The poet said. True.
> But it's just as true
> That after all the hazards have been made
> And almost all the other players laid
> To rest, one by one,
> And your separate little play is almost run,
> You learn that though the poet could be right
> Another dictum reads, by different light,
> "Each man is an island."

So in the end you probably had to grapple on your own.

The trail swung down to a small creek. Sticks lay along both banks but the water hardly looked deep enough for Lethe. I stepped across, began to climb the final hill. The trail angled up through dense madrones, and all at once the night was very dark. I halted, peered upward. At the few breaks in the madrones' foliage, the sky was scarcely paler than the leaves: the moon had set. I switched on the flashlight and followed its little pool of light on and up into the night.

"Do not go gentle into that good night," another poet had roared. "Rage, rage against the dying of the light." But Dylan Thomas, for all his talent and music—music with words, that is—had been a desperate and unfulfilled man. You could say, I guess, that his raging generated some damned fine poetry, and was therefore fruitful. But although he and I had some odd minor consonances (we were born only eight years and forty miles apart, for example, and Thomas's last day on earth, in New York, was my first day in that city, my first in North America), I could not really agree with him about the raging. Without individual deaths there could be no renewal, no continuity. So why kick? Once you had learned of the green world what could be thy place, perhaps you could manage to go somewhat gentle into that dark night.

There were certainly times, now, when I seemed to be moving toward a more gentle acceptance of the inevitable. (A tentative acceptance, that is: full acceptance seems to come only when the end is close and sure.) It would be easier, of course, if I could believe in the existence of human "souls"; could believe in an afterlife, in a world beyond, the way I had been programmed to believe during my Episcopalian childhood. But once I began to probe for myself I had been able to discern no basis, beyond the demands of wishful thinking, for such a belief. A nice metaphor, yes—a metaphor for the undoubted truth that the consequences of every act we perform move outward like the widening circle of ripples created when we throw a stone into a pond; move outward, willy-nilly and forever, affecting everything and everybody they touch. In that sense, sure, we lived on. That was an afterlife my "religion" would allow.

Now, one valid purpose of any religion, on its microcosmic agenda, was to sustain you in moments of crisis; and it ought not to be found wanting even in the ultimate crisis. So the question arose: Did mine pass muster? Down the years I had not only come to believe that if you kept going back to the green world, and especially if you traveled alone, you were likely to learn in the end "what shall be thy place"; I had also come to assume that this learned wisdom would amount to just such a sustaining force as any religion ought to provide. In other words, I believed it was the green world that had moved me toward my apparent and tentative acceptance of ultimate death. I had remained skeptical, though. My acceptance might be merely intellectual.

Then, about eight years ago, I faced an unexpected test.

It was the first day of the decade, and I was visiting friends to watch the Rose Bowl on TV. The friends were my doctor and his wife, who was a nurse. Soon after the game ended I began to feel faint, sat down on a convenient chair—and passed out. When I came to I was lying on the floor, members of the local fire department were administering oxygen, which felt like the breath of life, and my doctor-friend was saying calm, confident and reassuring good-doctor things; but his hands, which were examining my chest, felt by no means so confident or reassuring. I remember only vaguely being carried out to the ambulance; but as we drove away I began to emerge from the shadows—perhaps because we went downhill, and that sent blood to my head. When we turned a corner at the foot of the hill I was thinking clearly enough to know exactly where we were. Soon, though, I felt myself slipping away again, and it occurred to me that I might not make it to the hospital. With a calmness that surprised me I glanced back through descending mists to check what useful things I had achieved in my lifetime. What surfaced, just before I drifted back into new shadows, were two recent acts: leading a successful fight to foil developers who wanted to subdivide and "improve" several parcels of land near my home; and the repairing over a span of several years, with pick and shovel and chain saw and sweat, along with one other man, of a corner of wilderness that had, when threatened by a big forest fire, been devastated by bulldozers building a needless fire line. Had I been in a less stressful and foggy situation my mind would no doubt have come up with different, more logical choices. But the fact remained that, there in the ambulance, these memories were what surfaced.

I spent a day and a half in the hospital's intensive-care ward. Then the doctor's wife drove me back to their home, where my car was still parked. I felt a little weak, but reasonably okay. For a couple of hours my hostess—who was, remember, a nurse—sat and chatted with me, patently keeping an eye on my condition until her husband returned. At one point she said, "You seem very calm, considering that your heart stopped for four minutes—and you may have suffered a seizure."

"Oh, I don't pretend I like the idea. But there it is."

My hostess smiled. "Well, I'd have to say that you must have a rock to stand on, somewhere."

Now, my friends were Roman Catholics and no doubt thought in Christian terms, but it seemed clear to me that my rock—assuming I indeed had one—stood in the green world. Rightly or wrongly, and tentatively, I chose to regard the incidents of that New Year's Day as having been an unexpected opportunity to find out whether I had indeed learned from the green world to accept the prospect of death with something more than just my intellect—and I chose, with considerable satisfaction, to see myself as having passed the test.*

The trail leveled off at last onto the crest. I followed my flashlight beam along it, came to the spring I was heading for, filled my canteens, then camped in a nearby pine grove. As I cooked dinner, the rain began. By the time I fell asleep, wind was tearing through the treetops and raindrops beat an irregular tattoo on my tarp.

Some hours later I came half-awake. Both rain and wind had died away, and the night had turned chilly. Through the distorting lens of the translucent, still-wet tarp I glimpsed, before I sank back into sleep, the world beyond. It was a blurred collage of black treetops and brilliant stars.

When I woke again, the newly risen sun was flooding across a calm, ice-cold world. I eased my sleeping bag over

---

* At the time we talked, my hostess and I both understood the facts to be as she stated them. That is the important thing. But the incident turned out to have been eminently unserious. My heart had almost certainly not stopped. I suffered no seizure. And since that interesting, shadow-filled day I have flourished.

to the edge of the tarp. For as far as I could see, the pine trees stood dark and still. There was an odd brilliance about their needles, I noticed. The topmost clusters, etched against pale blue sky, sparkled like diamonds. I lay looking up at the glistening treetops, half-hearing a gust of wind come soughing up a nearby slope, half-listening to it draw closer, closer. The treetops began to quiver. Soon their dark, glittering needles were shaking, pulsating, dancing—and something had begun to move away from them. Then, as if at the touch of a wand, the whole space above me was filled with fragments of sun-spangled ice. The tiny slivers fell slowly—tumbling, sideslipping, pirouetting—and as they fell they sent pinpoints of reflected sunlight flashing outward. For a brief and perfect interval, while their dancing filled the air, the whole rain-washed, sun-washed space beneath the treetops became a separate, gleaming, shimmering world—a world that was glitteringly, joyously, miraculously alive. I held my breath. A few shards of ice pitter-pattered onto my tarp. Then the wind and the moment had passed.

I pulled on some warm clothes, walked to the edge of the trees.

Sunlight streamed down the long, grassy slopes that plunged toward the Pacific. I stood watching. The lifting sun banished, one by one, the shadows that still lurked between the ridges. Beyond, its radiance reached out across the eye of the world, vivid with the promise of the new day—of many new, still-shining days.

Colin Fletcher was born in Wales and educated in
England. After six years' World War II service in the
Royal Marines, he went to East Africa in 1947, farmed
for four years in Kenya and later surveyed and built a
road over a virgin mountain in Southern Rhodesia
(now Zimbabwe). In the 1950s he crossed the Atlantic
and prospected—among other pursuits—in northern
and western Canada. In 1956 he moved south to
California. Soon afterward he spent a summer walking
from Mexico to Oregon across California's deserts and
mountains. Later he became the first man known to
have walked the length of Grand Canyon National
Park within the Canyon's rim. Each of these feats
generated a book: *The Thousand-Mile Summer* and
The Man Who Walked Through Time. Mr. Fletcher
continues to walk—and to write books: *The Complete
Walker* (revised twice), *The Winds of Mara* and
The Man from the Cave.